Speak the Culture | France

Speak the Culture | France

F

BE FLUENT IN FRENCH LIFE AND CULTURE

HISTORY, SOCIETY AND LIFESTYLE • LITERATURE AND PHILOSOPHY

ART AND ARCHITECTURE • CINEMA, PHOTOGRAPHY AND FASHION

MUSIC AND DRAMA • FOOD AND DRINK • MEDIA AND SPORT

THOROGOOD

www.thorogoodpublishing.co.uk   www.speaktheculture.co.uk

No responsibility for loss occasioned to any person acting or refraining from action as a result of any material in this publication can be accepted by the author or publisher.

A CIP catalogue record for this book is available from the British Library.

ISBN: 1-85418-493-8 / 978-185418493-1

Thorogood Publishing Ltd
10-12 Rivington Street
London EC2A 3DU

Telephone: 020 7749 4748
Fax: 020 7729 6110
info@thorogoodpublishing.co.uk

www.thorogoodpublishing.co.uk
www.speaktheculture.co.uk

© 2008
Thorogood Publishing Ltd

Publisher/ 'Le Grand Fromage'*

Neil Thomas

Editorial Director
Angela Spall

actually 'grosse legume', Ed.

Editor in chief

Andrew Whittaker

Editorial contributors
Sam Bloomfield and
Richard Ginger

Design and illustration

Nial Harrington
Harrington Moncrieff
www.hmdesignco.com
and
Johnny Bull
plumpState www.
plumpstate.com

Printed in the UK by
Henry Ling Ltd
www.henryling.co.uk

Acknowledgements

Special thanks go to
Aurélie Guyomarc'h
(Institut Français d'Ecosse),
Marie-Camille Mainy,
Aurélien Mainy and
Catherine Delanoe
(Maison de la France)
for their insights into
French life.

Thanks to Marcus Titley
(www.seckfordwines.
co.uk) for his food and drink
expertise.

Contents

IS AN APOLITICAL LAND, THE WORLD WOULD BE LIKE IF PEOPLE COULD EACH CONTACT OTHER DIRECTLY AND SPEAK THE SAME LANGUAGE

Jean Cocteau

Publisher's Note
This series of books and this book are designed to look at the culture of a country – to give readers a real grasp of it and to help them to develop and explore the culture of that chosen country. At a time of supposed blurring of national identity, there is celebration of cultural diversity and also a quest for ancestry, roots, heritage and belonging.

There is currently much to-ing and fro-ing in travel, both for leisure and work purposes, between countries and a great deal of second-home ownership as well as more permanent changes in residence. This has heightened the interest in the cultural context in which daily life is lived. There are even citizenship courses for new residents in many countries. Inevitably all of this has brought a fascination in the cultures and lifestyles of different countries, which are the envy of some and the pride of others.

Our focus is on increasing the cultural knowledge and appreciation of a country – to enrich and nourish the minds of the readers and to give them a real cultural understanding.

This will enhance their enjoyment of a country and will certainly help their communication skills (even in their own language) with the 'locals', making it more fun all round.

I would like to thank Andrew Whittaker as Editor-in-Chief for producing this book and others in the series, and making flesh what was once only a twinkle in my eye.

It is also a book to sit alongside guidebooks and language courses – they will go together like bread, cheese and a glass of wine.

Neil Thomas
St Remy-de-Provence,
France

Introduction

Speak the Culture books

give you the keys

to a nation's culture

Discover how modern France was shaped by nature, foreign tongues and upheaval.

Meet the writers and thinkers who forged literary and intellectual life in France.

Get to know world famous artists and architects, their paintings and buildings.

Learn who's who in French music and theatre, both ancient and modern.

Become intimate with the legendary French filmmakers and their best movies.

Find out why food and wine are so important to the French way of life.

Unravel religion, sport, education and the media to learn the French mode of life.

Investigating the people, the way they live and their creative heroes, the series unlocks the passions and habits that define a country. Easily digested chunks of information, nuggets of knowledge and helpful lists decipher the complexities of a foreign culture, from composers to chefs, poets to presidents, so that you might get to know the country as one of its own citizens.

Speak the Culture: France begins with the essential milieu of the country – the lie of the land and the regions, history and language on which French culture is built. Then we immerse you in the creative side – the artists, writers and thinkers who've·lent France such an elegant swagger. Finally, we serve up an insight into how the French live – the rituals, joys and tensions that preoccupy modern life. With these three strands *Speak the Culture: France* plunges you into the French experience.

RÉPUBLIQUE FRANÇAISE
DEN FRANSKE REPUBLIK
FRANZÖSIS... ...EPUBLIK
ΓΑΛΛΙΚΗ ...ΜΟΚΡΑΤΙΑ
THE FRE... ...REPUBLIC
REPÚBLIC...
POBLACHT NA FRAINCE
REPUBBLICA FRANCESE
FRANSE REPUBLIEK
REPÚBLICA FRANCESA

1 Identity: the foundations of French culture

1.1 Geography

The rich cultural soup that is modern France has been bubbling away for hundreds of years. Landscapes, languages and people have all contributed to the traditions and modes of living that the outsider might now simply regard as 'French'. Only by understanding these different forces will you connect with the nation's culture.

An ill wind for the artists
The most notorious climatic quirk in France is the Mistral, a brutal wind that barrels down the Rhone Valley and into Provence, often lasting for days on end. Known locally as *le vent du fada* (idiot wind), the wind apparently induces a sense of dejection ahead of its arrival, symptoms which soon give way to headaches and bad temper. Some will even tell you that an old Napoleonic law pardons crimes of passion committed during a lengthy bout of the Mistral. Monet painted it blowing through Antibes, while Paul Gauguin depicted the women of Arles wrapped up against its icy breath. Gauguin's housemate, Vincent van Gogh, would anchor his easel using pegs in the ground in an effort to defy the wind. The crystalline skies also associated with the Mistral are evident in van Gogh's paintings.

Something to talk about
Discussing the weather is as popular in France as is it across the English Channel. They even have a pay TV channel, *La Chaîne Météo,* devoted to the subject.

Setting the boundaries

French school children are taught to draw their country by sketching out a hexagon. While it may only provide an approximation of shape, *l'Hexagon* does give France a neat brand that media and politicians alike seem keen to uphold. On five sides the frontiers are mapped out by natural boundaries: the English Channel, Atlantic Ocean, Mediterranean, Pyrenees and Alps. On the sixth side, the border with Belgium, Luxembourg and Germany is largely flat and low.

Lie of the land

To the north and west, France rolls with a verdant patchwork of fields and forests. Travel south and east and the land rises through the long strip of the Jura Mountains before the Alps rear up, marching all the way down to the Mediterranean. The southern heart of the country is dominated by the Massif Central and its extinct volcanic cones, while along the Spanish border the Pyrenees create a formidable wall from the Atlantic to the Med.

Climate controls

Within its broad frame, Western Europe's largest country experiences a generally temperate climate, lent variety by a dramatic breadth of topography. Moderating Atlantic currents keep much of western and northern France mild and damp. Central and eastern France enjoy the crisp winters and warm summers of their continental climate – the further into the Alps, Pyrenees and Jura that you venture, the crisper it gets – while the lands around the Med and the south-western corner enjoy hot, dry summers and mild winters. Boisterous storms mark the end of summer across the country.

Where do the French live?

Three quarters of people live in towns and cities. As recently as the 1940s the rural/urban split was equal. Today, it's the small towns and villages in the hinterlands of larger towns and cities (i.e. commuter belts) that are experiencing population growth. A trend for moving south has also begun to emerge in the last decade. Greater Paris hogs 20% of the populace, while upland areas like the Massif Central, the Southern Alps, the Pyrenees and Corsica, and even lowland swathes like Aquitaine, are often sparsely populated.

Peasant roots
Despite the modern French taste for urban living, the notion of *La France profonde* – an esoteric vision of deepest France: the rural, spiritual homeland – remains a compelling cultural concept. Indeed, Presidents Mitterrand and Chirac both invoked its spirit at various times.

Best of both worlds
A new term, *Rurbains* (a mangle of the words for rural and urban), has been coined to describe the class of people leaving urban areas to live within an hour or two of a large town or city.

Vital statistics

France covers just over 210,000 sq miles (550,000 sq km) (more than double the size of the UK)

Shares a border with Belgium, Luxembourg, Germany, Switzerland, Italy, Monaco, Spain and Andorra

Has a population of 60 million

Gets over 70 million visitors a year, more than any other country in the world

Has 36,778 towns and villages (communes)

Has an average population density of 282 per sq mile (109 per sq km)

Has life expectancy rates of 83 for women and 76 for men

Flemish stew
Much of the northern tip of France, along with parts of Belgium and the Netherlands, formed the feudal state of Flanders in the Middle Ages. Wander the streets of Lille now and it still feels more like Antwerp than Paris. Today, the Flemish culture emerges in language, a preference for beer over wine and local festivals. The Fêtes de Gayant in Douai each July parades 100 enormous Gayant effigies from local Flemish legend through the town's streets.

i. North and North-west

Encompassing the *départements* of **Nord-Pas-de-Calais** and **Picardy**, the northern tip of France shows one side to the English Channel and another to Belgium. Forest, rolling fields and large belts of declining industry characterize this thickly populated portion of old Flanders. Pockets of medieval architecture survived the trenches and blitzkrieg of respective 20th century wars: Amiens' gothic cathedral and the Flemish baroque old town of Lille are two fine examples. Agincourt, the Somme and Dunkirk all record the region's tumultuous past. The Côte d'Opale harbours windswept cliffs, dunes and beaches, while inland the Avesnois Regional Nature Park secretes walled towns amid quiet forest.

Norman cultural legacy
Norman culture remains surprisingly distinct from its Breton neighbour. Place names still reflect the Norse role in establishing the Duchy of Normandy and in a few isolated pockets the locals even maintain a Norman patois woven with bits of old English and Norse. The region's architectural legacy bears closer resemblance to that of southern Britain than to much of France.

Today **Normandy** oozes pastoral charm, but the stone and timber farmhouses, 350 miles of coastline and six million cows belie the turbulent past recorded on D-Day memorials and the Bayeux Tapestry. From the port of Le Havre, the region's modest industrial belt spreads alongside the Seine with shipping drawn in towards Paris, while nuclear power, in various manifestations, is a big employer elsewhere. The Calvados coast is home to Deauville and Trouville, elegant 19th century resorts. Further west, around the Cap de la Hague, the Atlantic coastline reveals fishing villages and the stunning Romanesque abbey at Mont St Michel. In Rouen, regional capital, you find the cathedral that captivated Monet and the square where Jeanne d'Arc burned.

Novel Norman approach
Normandy has proved a popular setting with novelists. Gustave Flaubert placed *Madame Bovary* in the village of Ry, just outside Rouen; *À la recherché du temps perdu,* Marcel Proust's semi-autobiographical epic, was charged with memories of his beloved Norman coast; and Jean-Paul Sartre set the Existentialist groundbreaker *La Nausée* in a town very similar to his own Le Havre.

8

Brittany is characterized by its coastline (rugged in Finistere, gentler further south), accounting for over a third of the French seaboard. St Malo, Brest and St Nazaire thrive on sea trade, ship building and fishing; only the regional capital, Rennes, famed for its traditional timber framed houses, lies inland. The Gulf of Morbihan is peppered with small islands bearing megalithic remnants. Forests and moorland, little altered in centuries, cover tracts of the interior. Employment still comes from the sea, although Brittany's economy remains predominantly agrarian. In recent years the region has also become the hub of the French telecoms industry.

Over half a million people speak Breton, albeit rarely as a first language.

Pardon festivals feature Breton folk music and traditional dancing. The *Fest-Noz* is a similar event held after dark.

The Festival Interceltique at Lorient in early August is Brittany's biggest celebration of Celtic music, literature and dance.

Brittany was once known as Armorica, Breton for 'land of the sea'. Today, Bretons still mentally divide their region between Armor (sea) and Argoat (forest).

The Breton 'national' anthem, *Bro Gozh ma Zadoù,* carries the same tune as the Cornish and Welsh anthems in the UK.

Five cultural icons from the North and North-west

Charles de Gaulle
Born in Lille (Nord) to a family of schoolteachers.

Claude Monet
Moved to Le Havre (Normandy), aged five, where his dad ran a grocery store.

Maximilien Robespierre
The architect of the Reign of Terror was born in Arras (Nord).

Gustave Flaubert
The author of *Madame Bovary*, son of a surgeon, grew up in Rouen (Normandy).

Christian Dior
The heir to a fortune made from selling fertilizer came from Granville (Normandy).

The Breton fight for independence
The Front de Libération de la Bretagne was founded in 1963 to promote Breton independence from France. Another group, the Armée Revolutionnaire Bretonne, has engaged in minor terrorist activity since the 1970s. In 2000 they killed a McDonald's worker in Quevert.

1. Identity: the foundations of French culture   2. Literature and philosophy   3. Art, architecture and design   4. Performing arts   5. Arbiters of style: cinema, photographic and fashion   6. Media and communications   7. Consuming culture: food and drink   8. Living culture: the state of the nation

Lip service
While Lorraine and Alsace are officially French speaking and the national tongue is widely used, both regions retain their own language. Alsatian, derivative of German, remains close to the lips of older generations in both town and country. In Lorraine, a German dialect known as Frankish clings on in a few pockets of the Moselle *département*.

Three North-east festivals to get you in with the locals

Foire Regionale des Vins d'Alsace, Colmar Celebrating Alsatian wine; mid August.

Les Fetes Johanniques, Reims Locals parade through the streets dressed as kings; early June.

Grandes Fêtes de la Mirabelle, Metz Festival honouring the succulent local plums; late August.

ii. North-east

Bordering Belgium, Luxembourg and Germany, the North-east of France has been a cultural melting pot for centuries. It shows: Lorraine gives off a subtle Germanic air while Alsace expresses itself with a hearty Teutonic twang; further north the wild Ardennes blur the lines with Belgium.

In **Champagne** you find the undisputed prima donna of world wine and, as you might expect, large portions of the gently sloping landscape are smothered in vines. The lands around Épernay, official HQ for the fizzy stuff, comprise the main growing area. The Champagne city is Reims, rebuilt after the First World War and famed for its 12th century cathedral. Further south, in Troyes, traditionally a centre for textiles, there's a glut of half-timbered medieval buildings. The Ardennes region in the north of Champagne is a land of dense forest and steep valleys popular with wild boar and, in turn, the hunting fraternity.

In **Lorraine** a gritty industrial heritage jars with unspoilt countryside. Steelworks and coal mines once made the region the centre of French heavy industry. Decline in these areas has been assuaged by the growth of high tech industry, encouraged by Lorraine's borderland location. Nancy lends the region a slice of elegance with a mix of medieval, Rococo and Art Nouveau style, while Metz, a brewing town, boasts a fine Gothic cathedral with stained glass by Marc Chagall. At Verdun, setting for one of the Great War's bloodiest battles, the atmosphere remains bleak.

Lorraine's eastern border follows the Vosges Mountains, beyond which lies **Alsace**. And beyond Alsace, across the Rhine, lies Germany. The region was annexed by Germany between 1871 and 1914, and again between 1940 and 1944. Today, prosperous Alsace, with its complex origins, still seems tugged in various directions with its mix of German, French and Alsatian culture. The European Parliament in Strasbourg embodies attempts to quell any old rivalries. The vibrant city, its old town stocked with timber houses on winding canals, is also famous for the soaring sandstone cathedral. Vineyards and bucolic villages line the route south to Colmar, itself a doyen of medieval charm.

Five cultural icons from the North-east

Émile Gallé
The champion of Art Nouveau glass established Nancy (Lorraine) as a hub for the movement.

Paul Verlaine
Life had begun normally in Metz (Lorraine) for the Symbolist poet who died in poverty, ensnared by drink and drugs.

Marcel Marceau
The king of mime was forced to flee Strasbourg (Alsace) with his Jewish family when the Nazis arrived.

François Girardon
Louis XIV entrusted sculptural work at Versailles and in Paris to the artist from Troyes (Champagne).

Edmond de Goncourt
The name of the critic and publisher from Nancy (Lorraine) lives on in the prestigious Prix Goncourt for literature.

Alsatians: are they French or German?
While the distinct culture of Alsace stems from both Latin and Teutonic roots, ask a local whether they're French or German and they'll probably tell you they're Alsatian. Under the Nazis the use of French was outlawed, and then the post-war government regulated language and media with French bias. Today, while French may be the first language in Alsace, economic forces have helped maintain the split personality: tens of thousands cross the frontier into Germany to make a living, while property and industry on the French side increasingly fall into prosperous German and Swiss hands.

Colmar is the driest city in France.

House sitting
The European Parliament, a couple of miles north-east of Strasbourg city centre, only sits for four days each month. Members of the public can observe the plenary sessions for up to an hour.

Religious tolerance in Alsace
When Calvinism found its way into France from Switzerland during the Reformation, multicultural Alsace took the new religion under its wing. Even today, one in ten Alsatians is Protestant, over five times the French average. Similarly, Jews have enjoyed Alsatian religious tolerance since antiquity – the region boasts over 200 sites of Jewish heritage.

iii. Paris and Île de France

It's hard to argue with the
Parisians' traditional self-
confidence. They're rightly
proud of all their city has
to offer and believe it,
almost universally, to
be the best city on Earth.
Such self-assurance
transposes to most
areas of life – to fashion,
politics, driving. Parisians
may initially appear
aloof and self-obsessed –
sometimes they are –
but at least they're rarely
dull. Engage them in
conversation – try not to
mangle the language –
and you find your reward.
Here, the French emphasis
on creativity and debate,
albeit without raising the
voice, attains the level of
an Olympic discipline.

At first glance **Paris** may seem like one gelatinous soup of people, food, buildings – culture. And it is, but amid the melee you also find distinct districts. The River Seine divides right bank from left in the city's oval hub, while the different *quartiers* each carry a unique character. The Marais, originally a swamp then a home to the nobility, lay unloved for 300 years: today it's a chic mix of elegance and scruff. The Latin Quarter remains the cradle of French higher education, the Sorbonne at its heart. Bohemia has famously shifted its roots about during the last 150 years, from Montmartre to St-Germain-des-Prés and Montparnasse. Today, there's no specific hang-out for off-beat culture, more a gaggle of districts that drift in and out of fashion – Ménilmontant and Belleville, both traditionally working class and migrant districts, are the latest to attract the boho crowd.

Physically unscathed by 20th century conflict, the city is a patchwork of grand designs and iconic landmarks. La Tour Eiffel, Place de la Concorde, Arc de Triomphe, Basilique du Sacré-Coeur – the city has an embarrassing wealth of globally recognized sites. *Grands Boulevards* radiate out to Baron von Haussmann's 1860s design, still providing visitors with a lasting impression of what it is to be in Paris with its wide spaces and pockets of green. However, it's in the avenues and alleyways, amid cafés, markets and bistros, that a living, intimate portrait of Paris takes shape.

Parisian bites

Paris is Europe's most densely populated capital city.

Central Paris, hemmed between the Bois de Boulogne and Bois de Vincennes, is made up of 20 *arrondissements*, spiralling out from the Louvre like a snail shell.

With 30 million tourists a year, Paris is the most visited city in the world.

A *Reader's Digest* poll to find the most polite world city placed Paris at number 15 out of 35.

1. Identity:
the foundations of
French culture

Five bohemians and their Parisian cafés

John Paul Sartre
"Man is condemned to be free", he wrote, while pondering life in the Café de Flore on the Left Bank.

Lenin
In exile in Paris in the early 20th century, Vladimir Ilyich spent much of his time in the cafés on the Avenue d'Orléans.

Ernest Hemingway
The author wrote in various Paris cafés – Le Dome in Montparnasse was a particular favourite.

Oscar Wilde
Drank in the Café de le Paix, Opéra, and died in the Hotel d'Alsace dosshouse on the Left Bank.

Pablo Picasso
Met his muse Dora Maar in Les Deux Magots in 1936. Today you're more likely to meet tourists in the Left Bank café.

Beyond metropolitan Paris, **Île de France** is composed largely of suburbs and satellite towns. Around 20% of the French populace lives here on a patch of land covering just 2% of the country. Despite this density of habitation, Île de France harbours pockets of forest – notably at Compiègne and Fontainebleau – and accounts for much of the nation's commercial flower and plant cultivation. For tourists, the big draws are the cathedral at Chartres, the Château de Versailles, Monet's garden at Giverny and Disneyland Resort Paris.

Closing time at the café?
While the image of a snug Parisian café – the espresso shots, Gauloises fug and cerebral chat – may be a popular one, in truth café culture has been declining in Paris for decades. The number of small cafés has halved since the early 1980s. Elegant establishments still enliven the *Grands Boulevards,* chairs reaching out onto the pavement to catch tourists, but the smaller back street 'zincs' – named after their metallic counters – are struggling. Other distractions, a swifter pace of life and cheap coffee from fast food outlets have all played a part. Starbucks appear unperturbed – in 2004 they opened their first Paris outlet.

A modern mayor
In 2001 Paris elected its first Socialist mayor. Betrand Delanoë was also the city's first openly gay mayor. He encouraged the arts, told Parisians to get out of their cars and created a summer beach on the Georges Pompidou Expressway alongside the Seine, none of which stopped someone trying to assassinate him in 2002.

Mixing it up
While Paris is one of the most multicultural areas of Europe – nearly 20% of the population were born outside France – no one is quite sure of the population's composition: French censuses are forbidden to enquire after ethnicity or religion.

Island life
Île de France is so named because it is hemmed in by four rivers: the Seine, Marne, Aisne and Oise.

iv. Centre and East

Many Parisian cafés
have Auvergnat roots.
Migrating from the
Massif Central in the late
19th century, so-called
Bougnats opened coal
shops in the capital,
which soon also began
selling wine and then
basic meals. People
would gather in the
cafés to eat traditional
Auvergnat dishes like
pork with stuffed cabbage
and to dance to the
sounds of the *musette*,
a small bagpipe. Many
cafés in Paris still belong
to *Bougnat* families.

Nowhere in France does the landscape do more to enunciate regional contrasts. The Massif Central, Jura and French Alps all draw their boundaries around beautiful, harsh uplands where isolation has shaped unique traditions and customs. In between, the sheltered pastures of Burgundy and the Rhône Valley nurture the finest French produce.

The Massif Central in the heart of France falls largely within the **Auvergne** region. Almost wholly rural, the area is pocked with defunct, gently weathered *puys* (volcanic cones). Two large regional parks foster the Auvergne's popularity with hikers and cyclists. Clermont-Ferrand is the big city, famous for Michelin tyres and a looming cathedral of dark Volvic stone. The spa towns of Vichy and Le Mont Dore (also a ski resort) harbour faded *belle époque* finery while the spa village of St Nectaire is renowned for its eponymous creamy cheese. Le Puy-en-Velay laughs at gravity, its medieval and Renaissance structures built on and around towering volcanic plugs.

A region apart
Despite being in the heart
of France, the Auvergne
feels atypical of the
French experience. Few
people stop here on their
way to the Med or the
Alps and to some degree
the region feels ignored.
As a consequence, the
Auvergne is among the
poorest regions of France:
property is cheaper than
anywhere else and the
population, which has
abandoned large tracts
of countryside, steadily
declines.

Funnelling south from Lyons between the Alps and the Massif Central, the **Rhône Valley** has prospered as a trade corridor for centuries. Wine has provided further wealth, not least in the Beaujolais and Côtes du Rhône vineyards. Lyons, the country's second city, throbs with culture, shops and bars. Ask a French foodie and they'll tell you that Lyons is the gastronomic capital of the country, and therefore the world. To the south-west of the Rhône, the Ardèche River has cut spectacular caves and canyons into the wild limestone scenery.

Food, wine, chateaux, forests, rivers – perhaps **Burgundy** (Bourgogne to the French) comes closest to fulfilling our romantic expectations of France. Predominantly rural, the region's north-west is veined by the Yvonne River, passing through Sens and Auxerre, each with a Gothic cathedral. Further south the Morvan region is a muted, undulating amalgam of woodland, lakes and farmland. At the northern end of the Cote d'Or *département*, an area dominated by its vineyards, Dijon enjoys its reputation for medieval architecture and, of course, *la moutarde*. Cluny, on Burgundy's southern fringe, harbours the remnant clumps of what was Middle Age Europe's biggest church.

Few foreigners venture to the **Jura**, a long finger of mountains, plateau and forests gently curling around the border with Switzerland. Part of the old Franche-Comté (free country) region, the Jura remains pastoral save for a handful of quiet towns. The biggest is Besançon, where the Lumière Brothers and Victor Hugo were born in the absorbing old town. The Jura is popular within France for its cross-country skiing network. On Mont d'Or, in the southern Jura, you can ogle the view across Lac Leman (Lake Geneva) to the Alps on the other side.

Historically, the **French Alps** have been divided into two regions. Savoy covers the northern half with Mont Blanc, Europe's highest peak, in its midst. In Annecy, medieval stone and spa town chic meet on the edge of a pristine lake, while further west famous ski resorts like Chamonix and Megève feel equally slick. Winter sports and summer sightseeing have conspired to make the wildest part of France one of the most densely populated, but away from the crowds in the cavernous Maurienne Valley you get a sense of the Alps' tough rural legacy. To really escape, head for the high walking trails of the Parc National de Vanoise. The second region, Dauphiné, harbours the Alps' major modern conurbation, Grenoble, as well as its highest town, Briançon (4334 ft).

Abbey days in Burgundy
Catholicism bequeathed Burgundy a fine architectural legacy. The Benedictine abbey in Vézelay, a stunning hilltop village, is a UNESCO World Heritage site. The site has drawn pilgrims ever since St Mary Magdalene's relics arrived in the 9th century – Richard the Lionheart and Philip II even had a pre-Crusade powwow there. Not to be outdone, the Cistercians left abbeys (or parts thereof) at Pontigny, Fontenay and Cîteaux. Founded by St Bernard himself, Cîteaux became the mothership for the order's 500 abbeys across Europe.

Le Corbusier keeps faith in the East
The architect Le Corbusier left his mark in Franche-Comté and the Rhône Valley. In both cases he created monumental ecclesiastical buildings. Described by some as the first post-modern building, the beguiling La Chapelle de Notre Dame du Haut, roof like a giant Teddy boy quiff, is in Ronchamp, northern Franche-Comté. A few miles west of Lyons, he built Sainte Marie de La Tourette, concrete home to an order of Dominican monks.

Five cultural icons of the East

Nicéphore Niépce Born in Chalon sur Saône, Burgundy, he took the world's first photograph.

Victor Hugo The author of *Les Misérables* was born in Besançon.

Gustave Courbert The Realist painter grew up in the delightful riverside village of Ornans, Jura.

Jean-Jacques Rousseau The philosopher and writer lived in Chambéry in the Savoyard Alps.

Maurice Scève Led the Lyons-based school of love poetry that emerged in the 16th century.

v. West

An hour from Paris, life
calms down a bit in the
Loire. The occasionally
abrupt nature of northern
France softens, while the
Latin temperament further
south has yet to ignite.
True, there is a certain
conservatism here,
an adherence to tradition
that emerges in all the
rural heartlands of France,
yet in the Loire you find
a people increasingly at
peace with themselves,
the world and you –
stunning scenery, fine
wine and amiable weather
no doubt help.

Say it like it is
If you want to hear cut
glass French, go to the
Loire. The residents of
the valley are traditionally
renowned for their
flawless pronunciation
virtually devoid of accent.

The Loire's other Valley
The Loire Valley you've
no doubt heard of, but
Cosmetic Valley? This hive
of beautification, located
around Orléans and
Tours, was first contrived
in 1994. A decade
later, Cosmetic Valley
gained governmental
recognition for its efforts
in broadening the perfume
and cosmetics industries.
Over 200 companies,
three universities and
dozens of research and
training organizations are
in on the act.

The **Loire Valley** is the golden child of French architecture. From Orléans the region meanders west through a greedy hoard of chateaux, cathedrals and villages hewn from local limestone. There are more than 300 chateaux (remnant of a time when the royal court decamped to the Loire), over 50 of which are open to the public. Little surprise that UNESCO proclaimed the entire valley a World Heritage site in 2000. North and south of the river, the Loire hinterland comprises forest, waterways and fertile farmland. La Sologne, close to beautiful cobbled Bourges, is a vast area of heathland, marsh and forest that continues to seduce hunters en masse. Muscadet and Sancerre come from the region's vineyards, while melons, asparagus and mushrooms (grown in Loire Valley caves) from the region are eaten nationwide.

Along the **Atlantic Coast**, between Nantes (the Loire capital which most Bretons still claim as their own) and Bordeaux in Aquitaine, France slips from the grip of northern Europe. Long sandy, and often empty, beaches stretch down the increasingly warm shoreline of Poitou-Charentes. At Dune de Pyla the sand piles up in Europe's largest dune (114m high). La Rochelle's old port is an increasingly chic holiday destination for the French, while Bordeaux too is on the up, the once grimy neo-Classical streets now shining with trams, nightlife and culture. The city also retains renown as capital of the largest wine region in the world. Inland, the grapes of Cognac draw similar scrutiny, although here they're distilled twice to make the famous brandy.

Despite an influx of property-hungry foreigners, the large regions between the Massif Central and the coastal lowlands remain sparsely populated. **Limousin**'s main city, Limoges, is renowned for its porcelain, while Aubusson has produced fine tapestries for five centuries. However, it's the melange of lush hills, lakes and idyllic villages that make the region popular with visitors. Below Limousin, the **Dordogne** (or Périgord, the old name by which most French know it) is lush, the fertility reflected in truffles, *foie gras* and Bergerac wine. Limestone villages, dark forests and secluded chateaux are inherent. *Département* capital Périgueux and the town of Sarlat-La-Canada have changed little since medieval days. Further south the dramatic limestone cliffs of the River Lot are in **Quercy** where drier weather and the local use of the Occitan language announce your arrival in southern France.

Five Western festivals to get you in with the locals

Francofolies, La Rochelle (Poitou-Charentes)
Celebrating French music and chanson with over 100 concerts; mid July.

Fête Champêtre de l'Etang de la Rochechevreux, Lignac (Loire)
Fish, hike and eat like the locals in this small town salute to country life; early July.

Festival des Nuits de Nacre, Tulle (Limousin)
The last French town with an accordion factory blows out the cobwebs with music and song; mid September.

La Jurade, Saint Emilion (Bordeaux)
The *Jurade* (a bit like high priests of wine) start the grape harvest with a parade, banquet and torchlit procession; mid September.

Fête du Chausson aux Pommes, Saint-Calais (Loire)
Celebrating the lady who gave *chausson aux pommes* (mini apple pies) to the poor in 1610; early September.

Five cultural icons from the West

Michel de Montaigne
The insightful 16th century writer served as mayor of Bordeaux (Atlantic Coast).

Pierre-Auguste Renoir
The Impressionist maestro worked in a Limoges (Limousin) porcelain factory as a boy.

François Rabelais
The earthy, inventive Renaissance writer took his first breath in Chinon (Loire).

William-Adolphe Bouguereau
The fine romanticized Realism of the La Rochelle (Atlantic Coast) artist was overshadowed by the Impressionists' success.

Jules Verne
The author of *Vingt mille lieues sous les mers* (1870) frequently sailed on the Loire near his childhood home in Nantes (Loire).

Welcome to Dordogneshire
The Dordogne has long been the epicentre of British migration to France. As many as 50,000 have made the move. Some are simply on 'bonjour' terms with their neighbour, others, not least the sizeable chunk who've registered a business, have integrated well into local life. Every settlement in the region now has at least one British family and in some instances *les Rosbifs* have virtually colonized entire villages. As property prices get higher and bargains harder to find, the migrants increasingly look around the Dordogne's fringe: north to Limousin, or south to the Lot and Quercy. But what do the locals make of the invasion? Jacques Chirac recently passed comment on his home territory of Corrèze in Limousin: he welcomed the rising property values that came with the Brits but was less enamoured with the use of English in local cafés.

Feet first
Having tasted *foie gras* and supped on cognac, the Charente département has one last luxury for the perfect evening – slippers. The famous Charentaise slipper has been made in these parts since the 19th century.

The Basque battle
The Basque (Euskadi
in the local tongue)
independence struggle
has a brutal recent history
in Spain (800 dead in
30 years), but France
(home to about one fifth
of Basques) has escaped
the worst of the violence.
However, in recent years
a crackdown on
Spanish-based terrorists
pushed ETA (Euskadi Ta
Azkatasuna) separatists
further north and French
police uncovered a large
cache of arms belonging
to ETA in Les Pays Basque
in October 2005. In 2006
the group declared a
permanent ceasefire,
but a bombing at Madrid
airport in December of the
same year looked like a
typical ETA strike.

South-west France
has a television channel
broadcasting in the
Basque language.

A leg up in Gascony
Until Napoleon III initiated
a drainage programme,
much of Gascony
degenerated into a swamp
at the first sniff
of rain. Shepherds could
only tend their flocks by
wearing tchangues – five-
foot long stilts. Today,
Gascon folklore societies
keep the stilt wearing
tradition alive.

vi. South

You can't help colliding with antiquity in southern France, but while an illustrious past still shapes the present, contemporary culture thrives, often swayed by the region's close neighbours. The Basque spirit is strong in the south-western corner, creeping along the Pyrenees before fading in Languedoc-Roussillon and Provence with their inspiring Roman heritage. On the Cote D'Azur and Corsica, Italian ancestry still pervades everyday life.

Les Pays Basque covers the western end of the Pyrenees and its green foothills. The majority of the Basque population live over the Spanish border but, on the French side, tiny hill villages and the cultural capital, Bayonne, retain the distinct Basque language and customs: bullfights and pelota are more than mere tourist fodder. Former fishing village Biarritz bucks the trend with its surf culture. Immediately north of Les Pays Basque, **Gascony** is characterized by *bastides* (medieval walled towns) and castles.

Stretching for 270 miles, the physical might of the **Pyrenees** can be divided into three segments: the Pyrenees Atlantiques are bathed in damp forest; the Hautes Pyrenees are high, wild and snow-capped; and the drier Pyrenees Orientales are characterized by patches of barren granite. Most significant Pyrenean towns shelter in the lee of the mountains. Pau's elegant streets, a Renaissance palace in their midst, offer tantalizing glimpses of the snow-capped Hautes Pyrenees, while Lourdes welcomes pilgrims praying for a glimpse of the Virgin Mary, first seen here by a peasant girl in 1858.

1. Identity: 2. Literature   3. Art, architecture   4. Performing arts   5. Attitudes, etiquette,   6. Media and   7. Consuming culture: 8. Living culture: the
the foundations of and philosophy   and design   stereotypes, photography, communications   food and drink   state of the nation
French culture   and fashion

The disparate area covered by **Languedoc-Roussillon** moves from remote, rugged mountains through forests and plains to sun drenched beaches. Today the area nurtures a quiet reputation for excellent wines and a property market that shames exorbitant Provence. However, history remains the region's trump card. Nîmes (Roman amphitheatre), Narbonne (archbishop's palace) and Carcassonne (walled medieval city) swarm with summer tourists. Toulouse, once within the region, now just to the west, is a modern day success story, home to the French aerospace industry and 100,000 students.

Provence has it all. The upper reaches catch the tail end of the Alps before softening into a rustic nirvana of stone farmhouses and rocky outcrops. Roman towns like Orange and Arles unfurl with buzzing, narrow streets, while on the Provençal coast the pretty but gritty Marseilles contrasts sharply with the wild Camargue wetlands. To the south-east of Provence the Alpes-Maritime plunge abruptly to the sea, giving the **Côte d'Azur** its craggy coastline. Between Menton on the Italian border and naval base Toulon, dramatic Riviera cliffs inlaid with fine sandy beaches shelter glitzy towns like St Tropez, Cannes, Nice and Monte Carlo, where bling, sun worshipping and gridlocked traffic are the norm. Just a few miles inland, the small villages in the leafy Massif des Maures feel like a different universe.

Multicultural mountains

The variety of peoples that call the Pyrenees home is reflected in the region's multiple names:

Catalan	Pirineus
French	Pyrénée
Spanish	Pirineos
Occitan	Pirenèus
Aragonese	Perinés
Basque	Pirinioak

Bear facts
In 2006 French and Spanish authorities abandoned the gradual reintroduction of brown bears into the Pyrenees (only about 20 of the animals remain) when lethal honey traps laced with glass were discovered. Farmers and some locals claim the bears kill livestock and scare off tourists.

French Catalonian culture
Roussillon, the southernmost portion of mainland France, is sometimes referred to as French Catalonia; the area once formed part of a Catalan state. Culture, including the famous *Sardane* folk dance, mirrors that just over the Spanish border and the Catalan language is still widely spoken. The Pic du Canigou in Roussillon has a spiritual significance for French Catalans. During the midsummer Festa Major, a flame from Perpignan is carried to the top of the mountain and used to light firewood collected from around Catalonia.

Orange in Provence is the warmest town in France.

Corsica may have been French for 200 years but it bears little resemblance to the mainland. A craving for greater autonomy gains voice in the native language and traditions. However, it's easy to see why the French cling to the island: sparsely peopled beaches, mountains and forests preserve the untamed nature often lost on the mainland. Italianate Bastia is the main town, Ajaccio the most cosmopolitan and Bonifacio – a citadel perched on high sea cliffs – the one to take your breath away. Corsica, the least densely populated region of France, has traditionally provided mainland France with a focus for derogatory jokes.

Paul Cézanne
The moody forefather of modern art was born, lived and died in Aix-en-Provence (Provence)

Maurice Ravel
The composer was born in Ciboure (Les Pays Basque) to a Basque mother and a Swiss father.

Henri de Toulouse-Lautrec
Despite the name, the diminutive genius actually came from Albi (Midi-Pyrenees), 50 miles north-east of Toulouse.

Frédéric Bazille
The talented Impressionist painter from Montpellier (Languedoc-Roussillon) was only 29 when he died in the Franco-Prussian War.

Bertrand Cantat
The former lead singer with rock band Noir Désir from Pau (Pyrenees) is currently serving eight years for the death of his lover.

How French is Corsica? For much of the last 1,000 years Corsica was ruled by Pisa and then Genoa, and the native language duly has an Italian flavour. Food is a mixture of French, Italian and native peasant fare inspired by the island's *maquis* herbs. Politically, as a *Collectivité Territoriale*, Corsica gets slightly more slack than other parts of France, yet essentially it remains a region of the larger country. Militant separatist groups have pushed for independence in recent years. In 1998 one such group assassinated the island's top government official, Claude Erignac. However, the island remains heavily dependent on France – 40% of its workers are employed by the French government – and in 2003 Corsicans voted against creating a single regional assembly with increased autonomy.

1.2 History

Who would deny the French their colourful history? The icons, from Charlemagne to Jeanne d'Arc, Napoleon to de Gaulle, came thick and fast. The gallery of heroes remains close to the Gallic psyche, often invoked today when France searches out its cultural soul.

Rock stars

The fossils of Cro-Magnon man found in a Dordogne cave in 1868 suggest that France has supported mankind for at least 35,000 years. The hunter folk blessed the nation with some of the world's earliest and best prehistoric art, as the 25 decorated Cro-Magnon caves in the Vézère valley eloquently prove. In Brittany a more cohesive, agrarian led civilization also left its legacy in stone. Aligned in long rows between 3,000 and 5,000 years ago, the Neolithic megaliths at Carnac are often thought to have some – as yet unfathomed – cosmological significance.

Classical upbringing

France, roughly as we know it, was first sketched out by the Greeks and by the Celtic tribes collectively dubbed the Gauls. Hellenic traders established ports along the southern coast in the 7th century BC, introducing the grapevine to France as they went, while a commercial centre called Lutetia, established by a Celtic tribe on the Île de la Cité circa 300BC, was the antecedent of Paris. In 51BC, after a series of bloody campaigns against the Gauls, Julius Caesar annexed the territory to Rome. A third of Gauls died in the conflicts, another third quickly became slaves, while for the remainder assimilation into Roman life brought a new language, markets and taxes.

What the Romans did for Gaul

The impact of Rome's 500-year tenure in France is easily traced today, particularly in the south of the country. Cities flourished under the Romans. More than 70 theatres and 30 amphitheatres were constructed and aqueducts bisected the landscape – Lyons, the capital of Roman Gaul, was fed by four aqueducts, the longest of which drew its water from 50 miles away.

Trade prospered while sanitation, education and architecture gave cities like Vienne and Saintes the cultural flourish they retain today. The amphitheatre at Nîmes and the Pont du Gard nearby are the surviving visual gems from a regime that yielded many of the country's modern day towns and cities. Over 30 large modern day urban centres were once Gallo-Roman cities, while 94 towns trace their ancestry back to Roman centres of local government.

A French dynasty evolves

When the Western Roman Empire finally crumbled in the late 5th century, the power vacuum sucked in the Germanic tribes that had been nibbling at Roman Gaul for more than 200 years. The Franks (originally from Pomerania on the Baltic) and their Merovingian king, Clovis, emerged successfully from the fractious mess. Edging rival tribes out of Gaul, Clovis established the territory of Francia, an initially small Roman Catholic state ruled from Paris. The famously long-haired Merovingians and later the Carolingians maintained the Franks' shaky grip on power as their kingdom splintered into feudal states over 300 years of beleaguered rule. Only with the accession of Pepin the Short and Charlemagne (Charles I) in the eighth century were power and territory resolutely secured and enlarged. Alas, Charlemagne's domain fragmented in 843 when the Treaty of Verdun split the empire between his three grandsons.

Where did the French come from?
In the 16th century the royal court cultivated the notion that French kings were direct descendents of the Gauls, supposed founders of Troy. Legend has it that after the Greeks destroyed Troy, the Gauls returned to France. While the idea of 'our ancestors, the Gauls' may have an enigmatic semblance, in truth the modern French person has their origins in a complex stew of Gaulish (Celtic), Roman and Frankish (Germanic) ancestry. And then there are the various fringe cultures that also played a part, Norman (Viking), Basque and Burgundian among them.

The Greeks in France
Marseilles (Massilia) was founded by the Ancient Greeks in c.600BC and the port's trading colonies of Nice (Nikaia) and Antibes (Antipolis) established in the following century.

1. Identity: 2. Literature 3. Art, architecture 4. Performing arts 5. Arbiters of style, 6. Media and 7. Consuming culture, 8. Living culture: the
the foundations of and philosophy and design cinema, photography communications food and drink state of the nation
French culture and fashion

The legacy of Gaul
Gaulish tribes, albeit bearing Romanized names, gave birth to many of the towns and regions that make up modern France. The Auvergne, for example, takes its name from the Averni tribe, fierce warriors who took on Julius Caesar under the leadership of Vercingétorix (now a national hero) in the Gallic Wars. Elsewhere the Lemovices (Limousin), Remi (Reims) and Namnetes (Nantes) tribes still resonate on the French map.

It began in Provence
The Roman pacification of Gaul began in 121BC with the region stretching along the Med from the eastern Pyrenees up through the Rhone Valley. The area was usually referred to simply as Provincia (the Province) – the name lives on in Provence.

Origins of Le Coq
'Gallus', the Latin word ascribed to inhabitants of Gaul by the Romans, can also mean 'cockerel'. French kings duly took the cock as their emblem in the 16th century and it later adorned the French flag during the Revolution. In 1848 it appeared on the Republic's seal and in 1899 was immortalized on the gold 20 franc coin. Today, you're most likely to see the cock used to represent France in the international sporting arena. Rugby fans even sometimes release a rooster onto the pitch.

The name France derives from the medieval Latin, Francia; in essence, the land of the Franks.

Developing a taste for glory
Charlemagne, the seven-foot son of Pepin the Short, took full advantage of his father's insistence on rule by divine right. He expanded Pepin's territories with 53 campaigns in 43 years on the throne, pushing Francia's boundaries out as far as Serbia, the Balearics, Rome and Denmark. On Christmas Day 800 he was crowned Holy Roman Emperor by Pope Leo III. Charlemagne is often labelled the Father of Europe, and

today the Charlemagne Building is central to the European Commission's premises in Brussels. In France he basks in a healthy historical glow as the expansionist medieval forerunner to Napoleon. Indeed, Napoleon's coronation as Emperor in 1804 invoked Charlemagne's own ceremony, employing 12 virgin maids with candles and adopting Charlemagne's bee as the symbol for his reign. Less gloriously, in 1944 Heinrich Himmler recruited the Charlemagne Division of the SS from French collaborators fleeing the Allies' advance.

Carolingian culture
While Charlemagne could barely write and only learned to read in adulthood, he made education for children compulsory. Indeed, his reign engendered the growth of literature, art and architecture often referred to as the Carolingian Renaissance.

Nation building

Charlemagne's empire was carved up in the Dark Ages and the emerging provinces began mapping out the country's long term composition. Aquitaine, Gascony and Toulouse all surfaced, while Norsemen invaded and settled in the north-west establishing the duchy of Normandy. The great lords presiding over the provinces elected Hugh Capet as their king in 987, deposing the Carolingians and establishing a dynasty that would survive all the way to the guillotine 800 years later. Gradually, the Capetians would piece France together. As the bonds between state and church grew between the 10th and 14th centuries, so crusades set forth, monasticism flourished and monumental Gothic cathedrals sprouted skyward. Despite such progress, France was a long way from being homogenous. Indeed, it was the Burgundians who, backing England to further their interests in France, helped initiate the Hundred Years' War in 1337.

Holding court

When the powerful duchies of Burgundy and Brittany were incorporated into the Capetian's kingdom in the late 15th century, France became an increasingly recognizable state. Cultural progression, inspired by Italy's burgeoning Renaissance, helped establish the tenets of a lavish royal court and boosted the king's influence. But war was again at hand, this time spawned by religious division.

Key dates

1214
Philippe Auguste wins Battle of Bouvines to become first king of France

1305-78
Papacy leaves Rome and takes up residence in Avignon

1337-1453
Hundred Years' War – Jeanne d'Arc ushers in French victory

1562-98
French Wars of Religion

1682
Louis XIV moves to the Palace of Versailles as absolute monarch

1789
French Revolution

1804
Napoleon Bonaparte crowned Emperor of the French

First king of France
Philippe Auguste's (Philip II) victory against an alliance of English, Flanders and German

forces at the Battle of Bouvines in 1214 was seen as the first 'national' victory. The territory secured, including

Normandy, Touraine, Poitou and Brittany, gave him a rightful claim to be King of France rather than just the Franks.

27

As the Capetian dynasty grew in strength and influence, it did so with the help of the Catholic Church. Reliant, in turn, on the monarchy for protection and revenue gathering, the papacy became increasingly allied to the state, particularly in 1305 when French Pope Clement V moved the papal see from Rome to Avignon (then within the pontifical state). Successive popes remained in Avignon until 1378, a period followed by the four decades of the Western Schism, when Rome and Avignon boasted a pope each. The sprawling Palais des Papes, today a UNESCO World Heritage site, still defines the Avignon skyline.

Reformation and the Wars of Religion

The Protestant Reformation that moved across Europe in the 1530s, attempting to reform the Catholic order, got a kick-start in France from Jean Calvin. His searing critique of Catholic worship practices gained widespread support, splitting the nation between the old Catholic guard and new Protestant devotees (also known as Huguenots – originally a derisive term). The ensuing Wars of Religion plagued France for 30 years, bringing slaughter and the destruction of property. Huguenots traditionally hailed from more skilled, literate areas of society and the exodus of 200,000 Protestants fleeing persecution in France created an early modern brain drain that affected the country for decades. Only in 1764 did Protestantism get official recognition as a religion. Today, while only 2% of French citizens are Protestant, they remain well represented in more intellectual, liberal professions.

"HIS NAME CAN NEVER BE PRONOUNCED WITHOUT RESPECT AND WITHOUT SUMMONING THE IMAGE OF AN ETERNALLY MEMORABLE AGE"
Voltaire on Louis XIV

The first heroine: Jeanne d'Arc
From 1337 to 1453 (the Hundred Years' War lasted longer than the name suggests) successive kings attempted to cull English interests in France. The average peasant trudged through a grim mire of poverty, famine and plague; however, one 17-year-old shepherd girl from Lorraine refused to accept her lot. Jeanne d'Arc persuaded the prospective Charles VII that she was an emissary from God, sent to expel the English from France. Her leadership swiftly broke the siege of Orléans and saw Charles crowned at Rouen. Unfortunately Charles did little to help when she was captured by the Burgundians, given to the English and burned as a witch in Rouen in 1431. But Jeanne had done enough, stirring the patriotism that would lead to the confinement of the English to Calais by the mid 15th century. While Jeanne is worshipped in modern France (she was canonized in 1920), she's also become something of a political pawn, used on all sides as the embodiment of French heroism. In the Second World War, Vichy propaganda cited her victory against the English, while the Resistance drew parallels with her fight against Occupation. Today, the extreme right-wing Front National uses her image in their publications.

Absolute power

Employing the guile of Cardinal Richelieu, Louis XIII built relative stability in the second half of the 17th century. The growth in trade gave birth to the new bourgeoisie and the feudal system finally perished as royal power and the nation's place at the heart of Europe were strengthened. Louis XIV pushed this influence to its apogee. Over a 72-year career the Sun King ruled by 'divine right', crushing any opposition from his nobles, gobbling territory in the Americas, Asia and Africa, and generally spending money as quickly as his brilliant finance minister Colbert could raise it through new forms of taxation.

A difficult birth for liberty

For all Louis' success, the *Ancien Régime* was on the slippery slope. His grandson, Louis XV, lost the Seven Years War and overspent gravely on the American War of Independence while his people, beset by wretched poverty, noted the revolutionary spirit across the Atlantic. The end came quickly. At Versailles in June 1789, disgruntled members of the États Généraux forged their own national assembly. The army didn't rush to Louis' side, but it would have been too late anyway – across the country mobs took to the streets demanding change. On 14th July the Bastille prison – so long a symbol of royal power – was seized while the new national assembly abolished the century-old privileges of clergy and nobility.

A constitutional monarchy was declared and *La Déclaration des droits de l'Homme et du citoyen* drafted. But the First Estate weren't finished, not quite: exiled nobles tried to fight their way back in across the Rhine.

Bad blood: French-Anglo relations

It all started going wrong between the English and the French when William, Duke of Normandy, conquered England in 1066. For the next four centuries Anglo-Norman monarchs repeatedly staked claims to different regions of France and war broke out on a regular basis. With Louis XIV's assumption of absolute power, France became the dominant European state and rivalry with England centred on colonial growth. In the Seven Years War (1756-1763) France lost much of its New World portfolio to the English. They clashed again in the American War of Independence (1775-1783), and The Napoleonic Wars (1803-1815) maintained hostility as empires were once again drawn out. Then, finally, in 1904, they agreed on something – reinforcing their respective empires and containing German expansionism. The Entente Cordiale was signed and the two nations have co-existed peacefully ever since. Today, the two nations argue sporadically – involvement in Iraq was a big issue – but maintain a kind of fragile respect for each other.

Their failed coup ushered in more radical change in Paris. A Republic was declared in September 1792 and the king was guillotined in Place de la Concorde five months later. Maximilien Robespierre, first deputy for Paris in the legislative assembly and loudest voice on the Committee for Public Safety, led the ensuing purge – traditionally labelled the Reign of Terror – of 40,000 counter-Revolutionaries, beheaded throughout France over the following year. Robespierre himself was one of the last to be executed.

"TERROR IS ONLY JUSTICE THAT IS PROMPT, SEVERE AND INFLEXIBLE. TERROR WITHOUT VIRTUE IS DISASTROUS; VIRTUE WITHOUT TERROR IS POWERLESS."

Maximilien Robespierre

Life with the Little Corporal

While the post-Revolution government by a five man *Directoire* restored a degree of calm; strong, decisive leadership evaded the fledgling republic. Enter a young Corsican general: when Napoleon Bonaparte subdued a raucous Parisian protest in 1795, the *Directoire* put him in charge of the army. After invading northern Italy and then seizing Egypt, he returned to Paris four years later, overthrew his employers and assumed power as consul of the First Empire. Napoleon I, crowned Emperor in 1804, a thousand years after Charlemagne, is remembered primarily for the wars that gave France control of much of Europe, but he also made a big impact

1. Identity:
the foundations of
French culture

2. Literature
and philosophy

3. Art, architecture
and design

4. Performing arts

5. Artefacts of daily
cinema, photography
and fashion

6. Media and
communications

7. Occupying cultural
mind and body

8. Living culture: the
state of the nation

domestically: he created the *Code Napoléon* (still the foundation of the French legal system) and established the elite *grandes écoles*. Alas, he just didn't know when to put his guns away. A disastrous campaign to capture Moscow – in which half a million Frenchmen died – ultimately saw Paris under siege in 1814 and Napoleon exiled to Elba.

Republics, Empires and kings

With Napoleon in exile, France stumbled into another fog of false dawn and confusion. The monarchy was briefly restored before Napoleon escaped his island prison and returned triumphant to Paris. Defeat against the British at Waterloo 100 days later saw him exiled again, this time to St Helena where he died in 1821. A constitutional monarchy was again restored, Louis-Philippe governing ineffectually until 1848 when a Revolution installed the Second Republic. Ten years later, Napoleon's nephew Louis led a *coup d'état* and duly proclaimed himself Emperor Napoleon III of the Second Empire. Like his uncle, Napoleon III instigated domestic change that resounds in France today. The *Grands Boulevards* of Paris are his chief legacy, drawn up by urban planner Baron Haussmann. However, he too would overindulge in foreign policy. The Crimean War in the 1850s was ruinous while the Franco-Prussian war of 1870 saw France defeated and the Emperor taken prisoner.

Empire building

In the 19th and 20th centuries the French Empire was second only to that held by Britain. By the 1920s French sovereignty covered more than 8% of the world. Today, the remnants of this Empire are found in small, dependent island groups dotted around the world's oceans. France also clings to French Guiana in South America.

Louis XIV: The Sun King
France may have been a republic for much of the last 200 years, but the collective pride still wells at the mention of Louis XIV. Widely regarded as the greatest French monarch since Charlemagne, Louis gave France an identity and culture that remain strong. The arts and learning flourished under the Sun King: Molière, Corneille, and Racine ushered in the age of great French drama, Poussin took French art to new heights and Descartes' philosophy proved seminal. Under Louis, France (the nobility at least) also got its taste for fine food. And yet his rule was often tyrannical. A liking for conflict abroad and opulence at home (Versailles has 700 rooms!) would bankrupt the nation and ultimately sow the seeds of Revolution.

Louisiane (today the state of Louisiana) in the Mississippi Basin was named after Louis XIV when explorer René Robert Cavelier claimed it for the French crown in 1682.

The wicked queen? For 200 years Marie-Antoinette was roundly vilified in France as the brazenly extravagant queen happy to count her shoes while her subjects starved. However, opinions have undergone a remarkable reshuffle in recent years. Today, some historians claim she was misunderstood, while publishers, patisseries and the Versailles estate, where the Marie-Antoinette Tour is a new venture, are happy to cash in on her name.

Revolution lives on
The French **tricolour** was adopted shortly after the Revolution, replacing the fleur-de-lys royal standard. Blue and red were symbols of Paris, and Revolutionaries wore red and white rosettes on their hats while the monarch was traditionally represented by white. By 1794 the tricolour was recognized as the national flag.

La Marseillaise was composed in one night in 1792 by Claude-Joseph Rouget de Lisle. Printed copies were given to the forces marching to Paris and it became associated with defending the Revolution although Rouget himself was a royalist. It became the national anthem by decree on 14th July 1795.

The name derives from its initial popularity with army units in Marseilles. It was banned by Napoleon, Louis XVIII and Napoleon III. Today, the spirit of 1789 retains an important place in the collective French identity. By establishing the (initially shaky) tenets of human rights and empowerment, today the nation lays claim to being the guardian of civilized society.

The scale of celebrations on the **Fête Nationale** (Bastille Day) on 14th July, hint at the gravitas still accorded to the Revolution. Military processions unfurl in front of the President on the Champs-Elysées and firework displays are held around the country. While many associate the day with the storming of the Bastille, officially the national holiday commemorates the Fête de la Fédération, a huge feast held on 14th July 1790 to celebrate the declaration of a constitutional monarchy (that didn't last).

Blood relations
In France the post of executioner was hereditary. During the Reign of Terror the incumbent family were the Sansons, led by Charles-Henri Sanson.

When the guillotine removed much of the art from his trade, Charles-Henri instead displayed prowess through speed – at the height of the Terror he beheaded 300 people in three days.

Quiet admiration:
Napoleon's reputation
Today, France bears increasingly mixed emotions about Napoleon. Traditional images of the military hero, of someone who shaped modern France, are less certain than they were. In Paris the triumphal arches remain and Napoleon's tomb continues to elicit a certain reverence, yet his legacy is under fire. In 2005, historian Claude Ribbe portrayed Napoleon as the racist dictator who paved the way for Hitler, citing in particular a reintroduction of slavery in 1802, eight years after its abolition. Meanwhile, President Jacques Chirac and Prime Minister Dominique de Villepin were conspicuously absent from ceremonies in 2005 marking the 200th anniversary of the Battle of Austerlitz.

First Empire (17th and 18th centuries)	
1608	Quebec
1624	French Guiana
1635	Guadeloupe and Martinique
1673-1739	Indian colonies established
1682	Mississippi Basin
1718	Mauritius
1756	Seychelles

Second Empire (early 19th to late 20th centuries)	
1830	Algeria
1881	Tunisia
1880s	Indochina
1895	French Federation of West Africa
1910	French Equatorial Africa
1911	Morocco
1946	French Polynesia

32

Paris revolts

The Third Republic got off to a bloody start. The socialists who established a workers' Paris Commune amid the chaos of French defeat to Prussia were brutally crushed by Versailles Troops in May 1871. Several thousand Communards died (including 20,000 by execution) in what amounted to civil war between government and city.

From prosperity to ruinous war

Despite the violent initiation, the Third Republic soon saw France – and particularly Paris – blossom in the *belle époque*. Art, architecture and science all flourished before the First World War brought an abrupt halt to anything so frivolous. For four years the trenches of north- eastern France claimed lives at a rate that dwarfed previous conflicts: in all, 1.3million Frenchmen died and two million more were wounded.

Roaring through the 20s

While industry and agriculture were left reeling by war, Paris somehow recaptured its bohemian verve in the early 1920s, spurred on by a burgeoning café culture that drew in North American writers like Hemingway and Fitzgerald. But the United States also passed France its Great Depression. Inflation and unemployment spawned polarization and in 1936 the Popular Front, a Leftist conglomerate determined to curb extreme right-wing ambitions, was elected to government.

Key dates

1871
Paris Commune that would inspire Marx and Lenin

Late 19th/early 20th century
France flourishes in the *belle époque*

1914-18
The First World War fought on French soil

1939-45
The Second World War sees France under German Occupation

1954-62
The overseas Empire dissolves amid Algerian War of Independence

1968
Government by decree sparks fierce civil unrest

2002
Six centuries of the franc end as France adopts the euro

Endangered species
When the siege of Paris during the Franco-Prussian War cut supplies to the city, the beleaguered residents resorted to eating the contents of the capital's zoo.

Neighbourly tensions: Franco-German relations

While Germanic tribes punctured French borders back in antiquity, more recent relations between Germany and France only really soured in 1870 during the Franco-Prussian War. The cession of Alsace and Lorraine to the newly unified Germany in the peace treaty generated ongoing friction. Indeed, the disputed borderland played its part, along with colonial ambitions on both sides, in the outbreak of war in 1914. At Versailles in 1919, Alsace and Lorraine were handed back to France, while Germany received a US$33billion reparations bill. France fortified its border with Germany along the costly, exhaustive Maginot Line. Alas, in 1940 Hitler simply went round the top of the border, invading France via Belgium. Overwhelmed by a desire not to repeat past mistakes, today the two nations are firmly allied. Ever since Charles de Gaulle and Konrad Adenauer signed the Elysée Treaty in 1963, the spirit of political, economic and cultural cooperation has grown. In 2003, the Franco-German alliance remained cohesive in refusing to back the United States in the Iraq War.

Cultural high

The *belle époque* refers to the 30 years before the First World War. A window of peace allowed for brisk growth: Peugeot, Citroen and Renault all began making cars and the French communications network was established. Culture prospered with the Impressionists and Art Nouveau, while the likes of cycling, newspapers and contraception all become available for mass consumption. Some screamed moral decay, but for many the era further enriched the Revolutionary ideals of liberty and free thought that remain steadfast components of French life today. In Paris, the legacy of the *belle époque* is visible in the cabarets, the Metro, buildings like the Musée d'Orsay (originally a railway station) and the Eiffel Tower, built for the International Exhibition of 1889.

The *phrase fin de siècle* can also be traced to the *belle époque*: it's used today to suggest an esoteric mix of decadence and radical change.

Divided loyalties: the Dreyfus Affair

Mild-mannered Jewish army officer Alfred Dreyfus was convicted of passing military secrets to the Germans in 1894 and imprisoned on Devil's Island. However, the evidence was fabricated and, despite acrid anti-Semitic opposition from sections of the Church and military, the case was reopened five years later and Dreyfus exonerated. Not only did the affair split popular opinion and expose simmering anti-Jewish sentiment, it also contributed to the formal separation of state and Church in 1905. Anti-Dreyfusards and their descendents would later feature prominently in the Vichy regime. Even today statues of Dreyfus suffer sporadic vandalism from right-wing extremists.

Remembrance

The physical and psychological wounds of the First World War are still felt deeply in France. From the Channel to the Vosges Mountains the landscape is peppered with war cemeteries, while farmers still regularly turn up grim mementos of the conflict. Every town or village in France has its memorial to the Great War, listing the young men who died – often bearing multiple names from the same family. Today, while the losses still weigh heavy on the collective psyche, the nature of remembrance is perhaps different to other European nations. In France, as elsewhere, they discuss the futility of those losses, yet they also recognize heroic defence; after all, the French were fighting to keep Germany off their own soil. Prolonged Occupation in the Second World War served to emphasize what those Great War soldiers died to defend.

One in six Frenchmen who served in the First World War was killed.

"THERE ARE MOMENTS IN THE LIFE OF A NATION THAT HURT THE MEMORY AND THE IDEA ONE HAS OF HIS COUNTRY...THOSE DARK HOURS TARNISH FOREVER OUR HISTORY, AND ARE AN INSULT TO OUR PAST AND OUR TRADITIONS." Jacques Chirac on French participation in the round up of Parisian Jews in the Second World War

A return to war

When Nazi Germany invaded France in May 1940, the army crumbled and surrender came in little over a month. The north and west of the country came under direct German rule; the remainder suffered puppet government led by First World War hero General Pétain from the spa town of Vichy. In November 1942 the Nazis took control of the whole country. The Occupation lasted four years, liberation by Allied troops beginning with the D-Day landings on Normandy beaches in June 1944.

Occupational hazards

The Nazis diverted 40% of all French industrial production to Germany

750,000 French men and women were sent to work as labourers in Germany

Over 75,000 Jews were deported from France, about 3% of whom ever returned

French life expectancy dropped by eight years during the Occupation

Open wounds

Wartime collaboration on all levels – individual, state, business – has nagged at post-war France. The Vichy government, particularly its police, were quick to help in rounding up French Jews, often unprompted by Nazi directives. Until the 1970s, few acknowledged what happened under the Vichy regime, but today, while it remains an intensely delicate issue, debate does occur. Immediately after the war, over 30,000 individuals were tried and imprisoned for collaboration, but it would be nearly 50 years before Vichy's contribution to the Holocaust was addressed. In 1994, after decades on the run (during which time elements of the Catholic Church allegedly colluded in his hiding), Paul Touvier was convicted of killing Jews as a leader in the Vichy militia. Four years later, Maurice Papon, deputy prefect of Bordeaux under Vichy, was tried for deporting 2,000 Jews. Rene Bousquet, accused of helping the Gestapo round up 15,000 Parisian Jews who would end up in Auschwitz, was assassinated before he could stand trial in 1993. No other French convictions have been brought. Even former French President Francois Mitterand, a friend of Bousquet, never quite explained his own dual role as Resistance leader and Vichy official. In 1995 his successor, Jacques Chirac, became the first French President to formally recognize Vichy's participation in deporting Jews during the Occupation.

Resistance activity
General Charles de Gaulle coordinated French Resistance efforts from England.

Around 1% of the population were actively involved in the Resistance. Many more read secret Resistance newspapers or listened to BBC Radio.

The Free French forces who fought under de Gaulle took the Cross of Lorraine as their symbol, as had Jeanne d'Arc in the 15th century.

Paris was liberated on 25th August 1944, Free French fighters were sent in ahead of the Americans, ensuring the capital was liberated by its own people.

The state up on trial
In June 2006, a Toulouse court ordered the French state and the national rail company SNCF to pay €62,000 compensation to the relatives of four Jews deported from France by rail during the Second World War. However, the decision was overturned by appeal in March 2007.

While the large immigrant population living in France, the majority from North Africa, provide a strong link to the country's colonial past, the nation has been accused of collective amnesia over the brutal dissolution of its Empire in the mid 20th century. In May 1945, French soldiers killed as many as 20,000 Algerians involved in pro-independence protest (a French ambassador visited the site for the first time in 2005), while the French use of concentration camps, torture and execution were features of the Algerian War of Independence (1954-62). Yet, in 2005, a new history curriculum for schoolchildren talked of recognizing "the positive role of the French presence overseas, particularly in North Africa." It was shelved in the face of outrage from French historians. A tough new immigration bill of 2006, making it harder for unskilled immigrants to settle in France, and suburban rioting in immigrant communities in the previous year, further highlighted the French struggle to accommodate its colonial legacy.

The Empire strikes back

Struggling to rebuild the devastated French economy, the short lived governments of the Fourth Republic failed to deal with growing colonial strife. Defeat in the war against Vietnam in 1954 ended French interests in Indochina, while Algeria's moves toward independence generated further bitter conflict. When international pressure finally convinced the French government to loosen the reins, the indignation of Algerian-born French citizens (so called *pieds noirs*) almost led to civil war on home soil. Only the instalment of de Gaulle as the first French President began to quell the fires. He declared a Fifth Republic in 1959 and Algeria secured independence three years later.

People power

By the late 1960s, de Gaulle's unwillingness to modernize drew students and workers out onto the streets in protest. In May 1968, students occupied the Sorbonne University and riots broke out amid heavy handed policing. Workers joined the protests and a general strike crippled the country. A rash of reform brought France back from the brink but de Gaulle was finished. He retired in 1969 and died of heart failure the following year.

Tale of two Presidents

In 1981 France voted in its first socialist President, Francois Mitterrand. He brought reform and gave France a much-needed post-war pick-me-up. In particular he instigated grand architectural projects in the capital, not least the Louvre's glass pyramid and the Grande Arche in La Défense. The legalization of homosexuality and the abolition of the death penalty also result from Mitterrand's tenure. Like Mitterrand, his successor

Jacques Chirac served two terms as President, the second stretch only secured after a head to head battle with Jean-Marie Le Pen, leader of the extreme anti-immigration Front National party. In 2002, Chirac oversaw the change of currency from franc to euro.

The latest era of French politics
Succeeding his one-time mentor, Jacques Chirac, with a healthy share of the electorate's vote in May 2007, the new President of France, Nicolas Sarkozy inherited a country with significant economic issues (unemployment was falling but remained high), simmering racial tension and social unrest. As for Chirac, viewed by many as a kind of charming rogue, his greatest success as President probably lay in his opposition to the American led invasion of Iraq. The new man, son of a Hungarian immigrant, comes from the centre right UMP party, his reputation built largely on an uncompromising approach to law and order. Economic reform, driven by his "work more to earn more" mantra, tougher action on youth crime and squeezed immigration all featured in his early statements of intent.

1.3 Language and belonging

Regional languages and dialects abound in a country that has been twisting its tongue since the Romans left. And yet, for all its different voices, France seems to carry some distinct, national pattern of identity.

1. Identity:
the foundations of
French culture

2. Literature
and philosophy

3. Art, architecture
and design

4. Performing arts

5. Arbiters of style:
cinema, photography
and fashion

6. Media and
communications

7. Consuming culture:
food and drink

8. Living culture: the
state of the nation

La Francophonie, an expression coined by French geographer Onésime Reclus in 1880, refers to the French speaking world.

Around 2.5% of the adult French population speak Arabic, largely using the Maghreb dialect of North Africa.

Conversation stopper
As recently as 1972 Georges Pompidou, then President, commented: "there is no place for the regional languages and cultures in a France that intends to make its mark on Europe."

French was the international language of diplomacy between the 16th and early 20th centuries.

Talking point
Because the Basque language has no official standing in France, its use by French citizens in a court of law is barred. Ironically, Spanish nationals are allowed to use Basque in a French court because the language has governmental patronage south of the border.

The Languedoc region takes its name from the Middle Age language of southern France, langue d'oc.

Julius Caesar brought France a language, although the modern French tongue has wriggled a long way from those Roman roots. By the Middle Ages the vernacular had diverged from formal Latin, mangled by foreign influences into a clutch of regional tongues. On a broader scale, the adapted Latin of Roman Gaul developed a north/south split: Langue d'oïl in the north and Langue d'oc in the south (the words oïl and oc both derived from a Roman version of 'yes').

Both north and south harboured distinct regional dialects, from which the northern Francien eventually emerged dominant, largely because it was spoken by the Frankish kings of the Île de France. Official confirmation came in 1539 when the Ordinance of Villers-Cotterêts supplanted Latin with French as the country's administrative and legal language. Over time oïl duly became oui. However, only when the Revolution merged the notion of liberty with nation did people begin using French in everyday life on any widespread scale. By the late 19th century, only French was taught in schools and other languages were being systematically suppressed.

Speaking out of turn

The state repression of regional languages has only ebbed since the Second World War, prior to which schoolchildren were beaten for using a provincial tongue. In 1951 the Deixonne Law permitted the teaching of Basque, Breton, Catalan and Franco-Provençal, measures extended to Corsica in 1974 and Alsace in 1982. In 2001 Education Minister Jack Lang conceded that regional languages had been systematically squashed by the government for two centuries and announced a move to recruit bilingual teachers in public schools. However, some politicians maintain that the French language has enough trouble standing up to English and that the national tongue should get any spare curricula cash. Even today, while regional languages are recognized by government, they still don't enjoy official status.

Surviving regional languages

Language	Region	Speakers (approx)
Breton	Brittany	300,000
West Flemish	Nord	20,000
Alsatian	Alsace	550,000
Moselle Frankish	Lorraine	100,000
Franco- Provençal*	Alps, Jura, Rhône Valley	15,000
Basque	Pays Basque, Pyrenees	80,000
Catalan	Roussillon	130,000
Corsican	Corsica	120,000

*not to be confused with Provençal dialects spoken in southern France

Surviving regional dialects

Langues d'oïl (north)	Langues d'oc (south)
Gallo	Gascon
Norman	Limousin
Picard	Auvergnat
Champenois	Languedocien
Lorrain	Vivaro-Alpin
Franc-Comtois	Niçois
Bourguignon	Provençal
Angevin	
Poitevin-Saintongeais	
Walloon	

Making conversation

As with many aspects of French life, social chat unfurls with flair. Debate is pursued like an art form and expressing an opinion with *élan* is everything. Meal times may linger for hours, but the conversation is often broken down into short bursts of wit designed to show off intellect. Frequent interruption is an accepted part of the discourse. Current affairs, sport, literature, film and politics are generally fair game, while the traditional minefields of religion and money are usually avoided. Expression is crucial, as reflected in the prolific use of gesturing, with vocal inflection often replaced by enthusiastic hand movements. Certain gestures have become widely ingrained: the pout of displeasure or the famous Gallic shrug accompanied by a dismissive 'don't ask me' style *'bof'*.

Académie Française – five facts

The Académie meets under the neo-Classical dome of the Institut de France on the Quai de Conti, Paris.

Over 700 *Immortels* have sat on the Académie.

The members' average age is currently 77.

Former French President Valery Giscard D'Estaing is a recent elective.

The Académie's working pace is famously torpid: in 370 years they've produced eight dictionaries – a ninth should be completed in 2015.

Correctional institution

The French language has sheltered behind the Académie Française since 1635. Established by Cardinal Richelieu no less, the learned body meets every Thursday morning, charged with preserving the purity of the mother tongue. The 40 members, known as *Les Immortels*, are elected for life by the Académie itself. In 1980 the first woman was elected; four others have since been voted on. Some *Immortels* get the elbow for misconduct – Marshal Pétain was among the most recent, removed for his involvement in Vichy France. Each year the Académie works on updating the official French dictionary (not actually on sale to the public) and also hands out the nation's most prestigious literary awards. While the Académie is the official French voice on vocab, grammar and the use thereof, the body carries no legal power. Indeed, the government can and does ignore the Académie's advice.

Increasingly, the Académie Française spends its days ruminating on the infiltration of English words into the French language, coming up with suitable alternatives to the likes of 'walkman' (*baladeur*) and 'tie-break' (*jeu décisif*). They recently chose *courriel* as a replacement for 'email'. While the choice of a word that's actually Québécois in origin angered some, the French Ministry of Culture seemed unphased – they duly banned the word email from use in any government documentation.

Jacques says *'non'* During his tenure as President, Jacques Chirac fought fiercely to protect the French language. An English speaker himself (he studied at Harvard and worked as a forklift driver in a US brewery), the President forbade his Ministers from using English on foreign trips. In 2006 he stormed out of an EU summit when a French business leader addressed delegates in English, the widely accepted language of European business. *Le Monde* mocked the President's actions in a front page cartoon. He also tried to block the appointment of Peter Mandelson as EU Commissioner for Trade on the basis that the Briton's French wasn't up to the job.

Sign language
In 1994 France passed the Toubon Law, making the use of French mandatory in all advertising, signs, product labels and government documents. Proposed by the then Minister for Culture, Jacques Toubon, the law reflected fears about the dilution of French by American English.

What do the people think?
The efforts of the Académie Française and politicians like Chirac to purify the French language rarely spark fervour among the younger generations in France. Accepting of the international trend for business and technology to communicate in English, they view the Anglo-Saxon tongue as a tool rather than a threat. Similarly, few young people in France can resist using the latest slang based on an English word.

Own worst enemy
The large number of
bestselling books and
essays on the current
French identity crisis
has led politicians to
coin a new word for their
authors – *déclinologues*.
Many politicians,
Jacques Chirac among
them, have suggested
that self-flagellation, or
declinology, is one of
the biggest obstacles to
French progress.

Town versus country
In a country as diverse
as France, many identify
more with their region
than they do with la
Francophonie. Language,
food and history are
increasingly used to
bolster these local
identities. Of course,
there's always been an
identity – some would
say personality – gulf
between Paris and the
provinces. Parisians are
traditionally viewed as
arrogant by the rest of the
country (particularly the
south) and, in return,
Paris has seen people
outside the capital as
wholly unsophisticated.

Collective spirit: The French as a nation

How the world sees France

Historically, the world has looked on France as a self-confident nation. A sumptuous artistic and intellectual heritage has given her an unrivalled cultural swagger and in foreign affairs the EU founder, former colonial giant and member of the G8 is still viewed as a world player. Even as this historic influence gradually ebbs and domestic strife plagues successive governments, perceptions of France still conjure a robust nation. The retention of a nuclear deterrent, a casual attitude to EU legislation and bold manoeuvring in the UN Security Council (not least against the USA) all point to self-assurance.

How France sees itself

Any outward displays of spirited unity tend to fizzle when France peers inwards. Today, when French debate focuses on collective identity, it usually talks of crisis and failure. It has done for decades. In the 1980s, historian Theodore Zeldin said that France has always been in crisis, but even so the current bout of theorizing on the French malaise is bleak. Immigration issues, entrenched high unemployment (particularly among the young), corruption in government and failing public services are all cited in a raft of books on the subject. Politicians, unsurprisingly, aren't as downbeat as the intellectuals, and yet none seem to offer a viable way out. Indeed, the collective gloom generated by social and economic problems is made worse by the lack of any clear solution.

"ONCE UPON A TIME THERE WAS AN OLD COUNTRY, WRAPPED UP IN HABIT AND CAUTION. WE HAVE TO TRANSFORM OUR OLD FRANCE INTO A NEW COUNTRY AND MARRY IT TO ITS TIME."
Charles de Gaulle

Single minded: the French as individuals

How the world sees the French

Opinions on the French follow certain stereotypes. Arrogant, stylish, licentious, argumentative, logical... all have some truth yet all fall short. One popular perception – pertinent in light of recent internal strife – is of a people allergic to change. Yes, the French love their fads, their innovation, but outsiders often talk of an inability to progress, with so much time being spent in debate that nothing moves forward. A reputation for intransigence duly follows, whether chatting over dinner or pursuing international affairs. It's also worth noting that the French themselves care little about how they're perceived abroad.

How the French see themselves

The French view their lives and their culture as distinctly cerebral in comparison to other nations. Intellectual credibility is hugely important, while their humour is centred on wit, clever verbal exchange and an appreciation of irony. They muster huge enthusiasm for new concepts and projects yet balance this vision with a reverence for tradition. In terms of style they view themselves (particularly in Paris), not without justification, as the arbiters of good taste. The French also revel in a reputation for hedonism (albeit within regimented time frames), bemused by the attitudes of more uptight neighbours.

"IF FRENCH IS NO LONGER THE LANGUAGE OF A POWER, IT CAN BE THE LANGUAGE OF A COUNTER POWER."
Lionel Jospin, former Prime Minister

"THE FRENCH COMPLAIN OF EVERYTHING, AND ALWAYS."
Napoleon Bonaparte

"THE FRENCHMAN, BY NATURE, IS SENSUOUS AND SENSITIVE. HE HAS INTELLIGENCE, WHICH MAKES HIM TIRED OF LIFE SOONER THAN OTHER KINDS OF MEN."
Anaïs Nin, author

Law unto themselves
The French display a healthy disregard for any law that impinges on personal or collective freedom. On an individual level, no smoking signs are frequently ignored and parking laws flouted, while as a nation France often drags its heels on – or simply snubs – EU directives that don't fit with national interests. In 2004 the European Commission pinpointed France as the worst member state for implementing new laws. In 2001 they defied laws lifting the ban on British beef imports and in 2006 were fined €57million for perpetually disobeying legislation protecting fish stocks.

Depressing statistics

The French are the biggest consumers of anti-depressants in the world.

In 2005 over 15 million French people, nearly a quarter of the population, admitted taking psychotropic drugs.

France has a high suicide rate, more than double that of the UK.

How European is France?

France pioneered the concept of a united Europe. They were led by Jean Monnet, the administrator who did so much to establish the Coal and Steel Community in 1951, an early precursor to the EU that emerged from Maastricht in 1992. They've remained fairly faithful to the concept of a united Europe ever since. In particular, alliance with Germany, and through it a limitation of German power, has often been the great motivator. In 2002 the French switched from the franc to the euro and they celebrate their European credentials annually with the *Journée de l'Europe* on 9th May. But of course for the French, as for other nations in the EU, being a part of Europe is driven by national interest. They see themselves as French first, Europeans second. And the people don't always follow the politicians' enthusiastic lead for Europe: a referendum on the Maastricht treaty saw the proposals passed on the slimmest majority while a similar vote on the proposed EU constitution in 2005 saw the *'non'* vote triumph. Recent surveys also suggest that most French think their country is worse off since the introduction of the euro.

1. Identity: the foundations of French culture

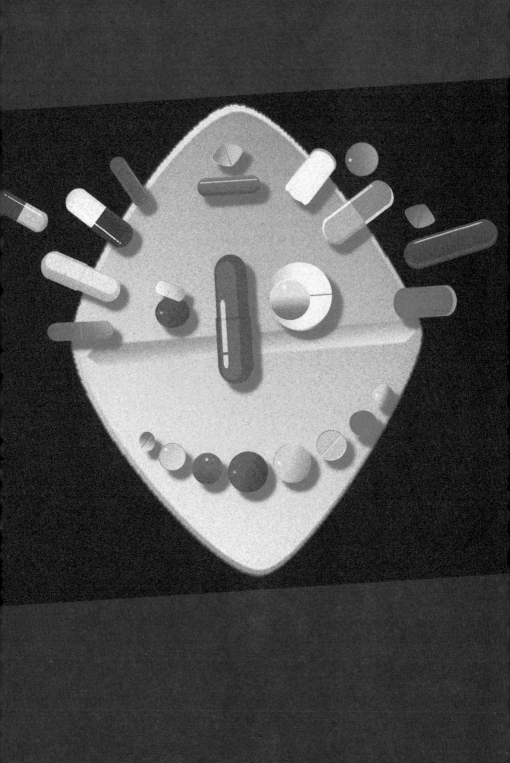

2 Literature and philosophy

2.1 Literature and poetry

Some countries get a bit sniffy about anyone with literary pretensions. Not France: a certain mystical reverence remains for the writer in a nation that, let's not forget, prides itself on intellect.

Saying the write thing

Roman à clef
a novel that uses fiction as a mask for writing about real events and people.

Roman fleuve
a series of novels with a common thread of characters or settings, but which can be read as self-contained stories.

Roman noir
originally a title given to gothic novels but applied today to thrillers.

Bandes dessinées
comic books like *Astérix* and *Tintin*, an eternally popular read for French children and adults alike.

Livres de poche
a cheap, small, popular paperback designed to fit in your poche.

Shelf life
In 1996 the new Bibliothèque Nationale de France opened in Paris, the striking building a descendant of the royal collection established in the old Louvre by Charles V in the 14th century. The four L-shaped towers of the national library represent open books. The site houses over ten million titles.

Of course, the pressure of expectation can hinder performance and, in truth, modern French literature rather pales alongside its lustrous forebears. It's got a lot to live up to – from the Pléiade poets of the Renaissance to the fabled novelists of the 19th century, France has the greatest of literary traditions.

The French still love to read, although like the rest of us they find themselves increasingly distracted, not least by television and the Internet. They draw quite clear distinctions between literary and popular fiction. The latter, from the romantic potboiler to horror, detective or sci-fi fiction, is still greedily digested. More highbrow fictional fare sells less well, yet the French still love the classics and are more likely to put a 'difficult' contemporary novel on the bestsellers list than any other country. In non-fiction areas, political, historical and current affairs books also sell more here than elsewhere. However, the novel remains king.

A helping hand: *l'exception culturelle*
Literature, like the other cultural staples, enjoys a degree of state sponsorship in France under the auspices of *l'exception culturelle* – a governmental mantra that protects the arts from the hegemony of the markets. French music, art, theatre, film and indeed literature are deemed above the dictates of commerce and are propped up and funded as such. Through the Centre National du Livre, the Ministry of Culture encourages the more cerebral end of writing with grants and loans to publishers.

If you only ever read five French books, read these

La Princesse de Clèves
by Marie-Madeleine de La Fayette. Regarded as the first great French novel.

Les Misérables
by Victor Hugo. A gritty tale of the Parisian poor by the doyen of Romanticism

Madame Bovary
by Gustave Flaubert. The searing insight into people and their emotions remains pertinent.

L'Assommoir
by Emile Zola. The apogee of Realism by the major literary figure of 19th century France.

À la recherche du temps perdu
by Marcel Proust. Okay, so you might have to retire to make time for all seven volumes, but it is regarded as the greatest French novel of the 20th century.

In the beginning was the word

French literature first flourished in the 12th century, born of the great oral storytelling tradition. Growth came in a climate of courtly artistic expression under the Capetian kings, a flowering of architecture, religion and learning subsequently dubbed the 12th Century Renaissance. Verse developed first and then prose emerged over the following two centuries. *Chansons*, poems and chronicles began retelling the heroic exploits of kings, saints and crusaders, paving the way for more romantic and mystical subject matter later on.

Chansons de Geste were the epic poems that kick-started French literature. Lengthy verse, usually arranged in lines of ten syllables, evoked the glory of Charlemagne, his buddy Guillaume of Gellone or the Crusades. Typically, a *chanson* cast would include a king, heroic knight, traitor, chunky Saracen and fair maiden. Later poems began to weave monsters, giants and fairies into the narrative. They were performed by *jongleurs* and *troubadours*, often with musical accompaniment. About one hundred *chansons de geste* survive – preserved by monastic orders – all written between the 12th and 15th centuries, many of the later ones with a recorded author.

I think this place is quite beyond criticism...

Well, I certainly couldn't put it down

The defining *chanson de geste*
The oldest surviving *chanson de geste* is often regarded as the best. Dating from the later 11th century, the *Chanson de Roland* wildly exaggerates the heroic death of Charlemagne's nephew as he battles the Saracens after an ambush at Roncevaux. Charlemagne duly pursues the Saracens and takes vengeance. Various versions survive, the earliest from the late 11th century. Most are over 4,000 lines long. The evolution and elaboration of the *Chanson de Roland* during the 12th century is typical of the genre. In truth Charlemagne didn't avenge the death of Roland, who wasn't even related to the king (or called Roland), and the initial, minor ambush was actually led by Basques not Saracens.

The first text written in vernacular French rather than Latin was the *Serment de Strasbourg* of 842, an oath of allegiance between Louis the Pious and Charles the Bald amid the 9th century fracture of Charlemagne's old empire.

The defining *roman*
The most significant surviving piece of medieval French literature is the *Roman de la Rose*. The first 4,000 lines were written by Guillaume de Lorris in around 1230. He penned a *roman* typical of the era, portraying a courtier's efforts to woo his love within the confines of a walled garden. Four decades later, Jean de Meung added another 21,000 lines, imbibing the work with a more philosophical, albeit bawdy appeal. The *Roman de la Rose* was a medieval blockbuster. The work had a strong influence on French literature up to the Renaissance and its later, embellished form survives through a number of illuminated manuscripts.

Telling stories
Texts associated with the 12th Century Renaissance appeared in the Francian language of the Île de France and in the other regional mangles of Latin that had evolved around the French lands. They were written to be read in performance – the cost of producing manuscripts, variances in language and illiteracy barred any widespread dissemination.

Love conquers all

Shortly after the *chansons de geste* emerged, romantic French literature developed. The love poems of the day were called *romans*, a term derived from their romantic content but also noting their use of Romance languages as opposed to old Latin. *Romans* first emerged in the Midi, where *troubadours* read poems about courtly love written in the *langue d'oc*. Their work then spread north, drawing in other themes and tongues. Written largely in rhyming couplets with eight syllables to a line, the verse often took Arthurian legend as subject matter (themes instigated in particular by Breton folklore). By the 13th century, prose was replacing narrative poetry, with old *romans* rewritten to fit the new style.

Three important early French authors

Geoffroi de Villehardouin
A knight turned historian who wrote about his adventures in the Fourth Crusade in the early 13th century. *La Conquête de Constantinople* was one of the first works of prose written in the French language.

Jean de Joinville
A knightly counsellor of Louis IX who travelled with the king on the Seventh Crusade, becoming one of the great medieval chroniclers. He wrote *L'Histoire de Saint Louis* (c.1309), a landmark account of the life and times of his king. He died in 1317, aged at least 93.

Chrétien de Troyes
Perhaps the greatest of the love poets, Chrétien de Troyes took Arthurian legend and created a raft of late 12th century verse. *Lancelot ou le Chevalier de la Charrette* and *Perceval ou le Conte du Graal* were commissioned by the courts of Champagne and Flanders respectively.

Popular fiction
While the royal courts and wealthy magnates enjoyed saintly chronicles and lovey-dovey verse, the masses got something less wholesome. *Fabliaux* were bawdy poems, often poking fun at the clergy or pushing a rather misogynistic angle on adultery. Moralising fables have also survived well, many featuring the character of Reynard the Fox making satirical profit from clergy and state.

New beginnings

The French Renaissance was the first great age of French literature. As plague and the Hundred Years' War finally receded, the upper strata of society squeezed in a century of high cerebral times before religious civil war brought further chaos. Throughout the 16th century, the French language began to shape and accelerate the development of home-grown literature, setting French writing on a course that would carry it through to modern times.

What was the French Renaissance?

By the early 16th century, France was soaking up the sophistication of the Italian Renaissance (partly, it must be said, by trying to invade northern Italy), the cultural revival led by a reappraisal and celebration of classical antiquity. As royal influence crept through the country, the king's increasingly ostentatious court provided a fertile arena in which to develop the arts. Over the next century, this cultural dynamism blended with the rise of Humanism (with its move toward secularization and individual expression) and embraced, in particular, the flowering of new literature. Art, architecture and music also prospered.

Renaissance poetry and the Pléiade

Renaissance poetry pushed French as the language of expression. Both Paris and Lyons became established as centres for lyric poetry in the mid 16th century. In each, writers were inspired by Greek and Roman forms of verse, and poets emerged writing sonnets and odes that took love, good living, mythology and nature as subject matter. In Paris the famous Pléiade group of poets formed. While they took their collective name from a group of 3rd century BC Alexandrian writers, the Pléiade worked to mould – rather than simply imitate – the tenets of ancient verse into a new, distinctly French form of poetry.

Reading material

The French Renaissance wasn't a purely cultural phenomenon, it also represented a period of significant economic and technological growth. Big advances were made in the field of printing; cheaper and more user friendly than manuscript, printed books encouraged the period's taste for literature. France had its first print shop by 1470 and Paris and Lyons ranked among Europe's main publishing centres by the mid 16th century

Only the educated elite
would have had access
to the work of authors
like de Montaigne and
Rabelais during the
16th century.

Printing had begun but
books were beyond the
economic means of most.
For the masses the oral
tradition remained strong
– stories were still largely
heard not read.

However, printed
broadsheets, recording
the events of the day
with sensationalist glee,
were finding a growing
audience.

Two star poets of the Pléiade

The undisputed boss of the Pléiade and a favourite of
successive kings, 16th century poet Pierre de Ronsard
was crucial to the development of the French sonnet.
He was known in his own lifetime as the Prince of
Poets. His best work was written about love.
He produced numerous short *amours* and odes to
Christine, the daughter of a Florentine banker, and also
published his *Hymnes* (1555), dedicated to Marguerite
de Savoie. Later verse reflected an unrequited love
for Hélène, a lady in waiting to Catherine de Medici.
Ronsard was also renowned for his astute observations
of nature. Meanwhile, Joachim du Bellay's *Deffence et
illustration de la langue françoyse* (1549) made the case
for establishing French as a language of expression and
debate and gave the Pléiade its unofficial manifesto.
He apparently first met Ronsard in an inn while travelling
to Poitiers in 1547. His greatest poetic work unfurled
during a stay in Rome where he wrote over 40 sonnets,
gathered together in his *Antiquités de Rome* (1558).
Du Bellay is often viewed as the most talented of the
Pléiade poets.

Renaissance prose

While the French Renaissance fuelled publishing and the
spread of literature, the oral tradition was still integral to
storytelling. Consequently, the short story ruled when it
came to prose. Marguerite de Navarre, sister of François
I, wrote the unfinished yet epochal *L'Heptameron* (1558),
a collection of 72 stories exploring love, lust and infidelity
among the nobility. Lengthier French prose fought hard to
eclipse the raft of translated Italian and Spanish adventure
novels. However, one author, François Rabelais, stood
out as a French hero.

Renaissance man: François Rabelais

No one explored the literary potential of the French language quite like François Rabelais. He was a monk, physician and scholar who wrote with wit and verve, filling his books with black humour, sexual innuendo and dirty jokes. But while the content was often bawdy, Rabelais' use of metaphor, satire and new words not only gave insight into life in 16th century France, they also forged a new way of writing. His two major novels, the satirical *Pantagruel* (1532) and *Gargantua* (1534), are still read in France today.

François Rabelais gifted more than 500 words to the French language, many derivative of ancient Greek.

Michel de Montaigne

The first essayist: Michel de Montaigne (1533-1592)

The French Renaissance shepherded another literary convention – the essay. Michel de Montaigne was the first to weave anecdotes with intellectual pondering in a series of short dissertations. A committed Humanist, he wrote about himself and his own experiences in an effort to understand mankind. His enormous *Essais* (1575 onwards), covering issues as varied as cannibalism, vanity and thumbs, are viewed as the paternal spirit behind all non-fiction writing. De Montaigne was more famous in his own lifetime for being mayor of Bordeaux.

Shakespeare kept a copy of Michel de Montaigne's *Essais* in his library.

1. Identity:
the foundations of
French culture

**2. Literature
and philosophy**

3. Art, architecture
and design

4. Performing arts

5. Arbiters of style:
cinema, photography
and fashion

6. Media and
communications

7. Consuming culture:
food and drink

8. Living culture: the
state of the nation

Fly me to the moon big nose
You've probably heard of Cyrano de Bergerac, the nasally gifted romantic of Edmond Rostand's late 19th century play. Such has been the myth's popularity that the achievements of the real Cyrano, a Parisian nobleman, have become obscured. He took the rationalism of Descartes in the mid 17th century and applied it to Baroque fantasy novels. *Historie Comique des États et Empires de la Lune* (1657) and *L'Historie Comique des États et Empires du Soleil* (1662) have been seen as early works of science fiction. Cyrano also joined the growing 17th century trend for satire, aping the strictures of life under Louis XIV in his work. He died, aged 36, in 1655 when a lump of wood fell on his head.

Controlled development

Buffeted by the Wars of Religion and then swayed by the growth of rationalism, literature learned self-control in the *grand siècle*. Poetry and prose tuned into the restrained, well-mannered Classicism transmitting from Louis XIV's court. Writing was held aloft alongside art and architecture (although it rarely soared to their heights) as evidence of how advanced French civilization had become. However, there was just time for a brief Baroque flourish before the new order took hold.

A Baroque sense of adventure

The first half of the 17th century, often termed the Baroque period, saw French culture bounce back from the turmoil of religious civil war. Remnants of Renaissance verve lingered in literature, initially in short romantic novels and later in grand adventure stories with a staple of pirates, lovelorn shepherd girls and heroic knights. These lengthy, often tangled novels developed the traditions set by the epic French poem, frequently taking fantasy as a theme. The most noteworthy Baroque French novel was *L'Astrée*, a lengthy story of shepherd love written by Honoré d'Urfe and published in portions between 1607 and 1627.

The growth of the salon
The practice of holding literary salons developed among the French nobility in the early 17th century. Essentially upper crust book clubs, the members of which often wrote their own poetry and novels, the salons provided the social elite with a chance to display their patronage of the arts and, therefore, their sophistication. Many grew up around aristocratic women, the most famous at the Hôtel de Rambouillet, Madame de Rambouillet's Parisian pad.

Reining in culture

As the power and prestige of the state grew, moulded by Richelieu and then royally cemented by Louis XIV, literature fell in line. Classicism provided the prevailing mood for culture, and its love of order, moral precision and restraint surfaced in writing. Establishing the Académie Française in 1635, Richelieu set the trend for the governmental control of literature and the French language. In truth, the Académie's restraints clung more keenly to the theatre, where creativity consistently outshone literature during the *grand siècle*. By the second half of the 17th century, the Baroque love of sprawling adventure stories had become muted.

They were replaced with shorter, less convoluted novels that often took moral dilemmas and placed them in a classical setting. Suddenly, French literature had a psychological edge.

The first writer of Classicism

Poet François de Malherbe (1555-1628) got the Classicism ball rolling. He introduced a new formality to language, emphasizing a simple, rather unemotional style that contrasted with the lyrical work of the Pléiade poets.

The first great French novel

The accolade of 'first great French novel' has traditionally been bestowed on *La Princesse de Clèves*. Written by minor noble Marie-Madeleine de La Fayette and published anonymously in 1678, the story is set in the reign of Henry II. It's a love triangle in which the silent emotions of the protagonists are explored in an environment of strict moral codes. The subtleties of behaviour had been largely unexplored by French fiction up to that point.

Heroic restraint

As the refinement of the salons spread, like royal courts in miniature with their social correctness, the concept of the *honnête homme* grew. It summarized a man who did things the right way, who followed the proper aristocratic codes of social interaction. From the 1650s onwards he began to surface in French literature, providing a restrained, classical replacement for the romantic hero of the Renaissance.

Dangerous times
The most arresting novel of the late 18th century was Pierre Choderlos de Laclos' *Les Liaisons Dangereuses* (1782), a caustic portrayal of immorality among a decadent pre-Revolution nobility.

A growing audience
As authors began writing about the different strata of French life, society responded and broadened its reading habits. Advances in printing and the use of journals, newspapers and short stories made literature widely available to the bourgeoisie and increasingly accessible to workers too. The Guizot law of 1833, establishing a primary school in every commune, helped encourage greater levels of literacy.

Thought processes

Conventional authors were overshadowed in the 18th century by *les philosophes*, a gaggle of intellectuals who forged the Enlightenment (and some have said Revolution) around reasoned thought and a distaste for the ruling elite. Some expressed their ideas through fiction: *Candide* (1759), Voltaire's acerbic satire on 18th century life, is the most famous example. Epistolary novels were popular, the philosophers making comment through a fictitious exchange of letters, but often their writing emerged simply in articles and essays. Their work is explored in greater depth in the Philosophy section of this chapter.

de Sade: the literary libertine

Donatien Alphonse François, more often referred to by his title, the Marquis de Sade, remains an infamous figure of 18th century French literature. After serving as a soldier in the Seven Years War as a young man, he roused the authorities' interest by routinely abusing lovers and prostitutes of both sexes. The younger sister of his wife was one victim. Sentenced to death for sodomy and poisoning, he escaped to Italy. Eventually de Sade was caught and his sentence revised to 27 years in prison, where he began writing novels and plays with sexually graphic content. *Les 120 journées de Sodome* (written in 1784 but not published until 1904), a tale of four rich men who inflict violent sexual abuse on various young victims, and *Les infortunes de la vertu* (1791), the raunchy story of a young peasant girl, are probably his best- known novels. Both were written in the Bastille. Released and then re-imprisoned, de Sade survived the Revolution but ended his days in an asylum.

1. Literature
the foundations of
French culture

**2. Literature
and philosophy**

3. Art, architecture
and design

4. Performing arts

5. Artisans of style:
cuisine, photography
and fashion

6. Media and
communications

7. Consuming culture:
food and drink

8. Living culture: the
state of the nation

The rise of the novel

Once the dust of Revolution had settled, France enjoyed a century of prodigious literary growth. Concurrent movements evolved, all in some way dismissive of the *Ancien Régime*'s Classicism and control of the arts. Romanticism, Realism and Naturalism all employed literature's rising star, the novel, to great effect. For the poets, Symbolism and the Parnassian school grouped important modes of writing. Writers spread their talents across the literary spectrum – many were poets, playwrights and essayists as well as novelists.

What was Romanticism?

Romanticism pulled literature from the strait jacket of Classicism. In France, the movement spread through the arts in the late 18th century and flourished in the first half of the 19th, the importance of individual thought its major inspiration in literature. Imagination was emphasized alongside subjectivity and lyricism, as inspired by philosopher Jean Jacques Rousseau: writers should be free to express themselves unbound by the state or its Académie. Many Romantic writers portrayed nature with luxurious rhetoric, while the historical novel, laced with colourful people, places and plots, became hugely popular.

Dumas: quantity and quality

Alexandre Dumas père (1802-1870) was the grandson of a French marquis and a black Haitian slave, a mixed racial heritage that brought him grief throughout his life. A novelist and playwright, Dumas père is the most read of French authors, clocking up over 1,200 pieces of work to his name. His prolific writing netted a fortune, which he squandered on an extravagant lifestyle featuring numerous mistresses. His name is often appended 'père' to distinguish from his son of the same name, also an author.

Romanticism: the big three and their books

François-René de Chateaubriand
Atala (1801) and *René* (1802). The first great works of French Romanticism were two novellas set in North America exploring personal anxiety and loss.

Victor Hugo
Les Misérables (1862). Hugo conceived of his longest novel 20 years before it was published. A discourse on the Parisian poor, the work is still widely devoured today.

Alexandre Dumas père
Les trois mousquetaires (1844). First published in serial form, Dumas' colourful story was the epitome of a Romanticist historical novel.

The *Cénacle* was a Romanticist literary salon that grew up in Paris around the writer Charles Nodier in the late 1820s. Hugo, Vigny and Larmartine were among the members. *Le Petit Cénacle*, established in homage to the original but with a more eccentric approach, included Dumas père and Gérard de Nerval.

The phrase 'Ivory Tower' was coined by critic Charles Augustin Sainte-Beuve (sometimes called the first major critic) to describe the isolation of the romantic poet Vigny.

Meaty legacy
These days, the name Chateaubriand is as familiar on a menu as a library shelf. Famously fond of his food, the Romantic author, politician and renowned egotist modestly named a cut of meat after himself, although it was actually created by his chef.

Hugo: social commentator

Victor Hugo was born in Besançon in 1802. He wrote a staggering amount in his 60-year literary career. Satire, poetry, travel writing, political speeches and plays were all penned alongside his famous novels. Hugo captured the people and life of post-Revolutionary France like no other. In *Notre Dame de Paris* (1831) he placed rich human drama in the city's medieval period; for *Les Misérables* he explored the social injustice of his own Paris. Although published 30 years apart, the novels were consecutive. Hugo was also renowned as a master of poetry – two volumes of verse from the 1840s, collectively labelled *Les Contemplations*, remain his most widely read. The death of Léopoldine, his 19-year-old daughter, in a boating accident in 1843 clouded much of his adult life. A part time politician with outspoken, critical views on Louis Napoleon Bonaparte, Hugo spent 20 years in exile – most of it on Guernsey – after Bonaparte seized power. He was re-elected to the National Assembly on his return to France. When Hugo died in 1885, two million attended the state funeral before he was laid to rest in the Panthéon.

The Romantic poets

The poetry of the bohemian Gérard de Nerval was typical of Romanticism; its dreamy vision of the world would influence 20th century Surrealists like André Breton. Other Romantic poets included Alfred de Musset, Alphonse de Lamartine and Alfred de Vigny (also a novelist), each with a talent for portraying the emotion of the individual.

The first woman of Romanticism

Aurore Dupin, Baronne Dudevant, chose to write her novels under the pseudonym George Sand. She is seen as the most significant female writer of the Romantic period. Her early work had a feminist tone, with her first novel, *Indiana* (1832), exploring the tribulations of a married woman. With *Lélia* (1833) she parted with the traditional woman's novel by exploring politics and religion alongside love. However, Sand is best remembered for her later, pastoral novels. Books like *Jeanne* (1844), based on the story of Jeanne d'Arc, combined brilliant observations on rustic life with edgy social commentary. Memories of an unhappy marriage in early adulthood were assuaged in later life by a ten-year affair with the composer Frédéric Chopin.

What was Realism?

Realism pored over the nitty-gritty. The minutiae of contemporary life, of people and their surroundings were explored and laid bare for the reader to make judgement. France was industrializing, modern science developing and social awareness growing in the mid 19th century – in the Realist novel these trends were applied to the Romantics' taste for people and places. The dissection of daily life in a novel, born of Realism, has had a huge impact on fiction ever since.

Realism: the big three and their books

Stendhal

Le Rouge et le noir (1830). The story of a young man's efforts to rise from humble beginnings was the first novel to really scrutinize the mind of its main character. Stendhal, *nom de plume* of Marie-Henri Beyle, is often lauded as the first French writer to bridge the gap between Romanticism and Realism.

Honoré de Balzac

La Comédie humaine (1842-1848). Balzac's epic series of stories (featuring over a hundred volumes) set the standard for Realism. Intense descriptions of contemporary life featured thieves, whores and politicians. The plots were less realistic; indeed many were romantic in tone.

Gustave Flaubert

Madame Bovary (1857). The showpiece of French Realism scrutinizes the life of a woman whose romantic yearnings contrast sharply with the mundanity of her daily grind.

**Naturalism:
the big two
and their books**

Émile Zola
Les Rougon-Macquart
(1871-1893). Zola's
opus is a 20-novel
series exploring life
in two families in the
Second Empire. Among
it, *L'Assommoir* (1877)
(wretched alcoholism in
a rough part of Paris) and
Germinal (1885) (life in a
mining community) are
two giants of 19th century
literature.

Guy de Maupassant
Bel-Ami (1885). A young
journalist makes it to the
top of Parisian society in
Maupassant's searing
account of *fin de siècle*
bourgeoisie society.
Bel-Ami is a rare novel
from the French doyen of
the short story.

Flaubert: devil in the detail
Although he hated literary labels, for many Gustave
Flaubert is the daddy of Realism. The son of a doctor,
he was expelled from state school and dropped out of
a law course at university. When he developed what
was probably epilepsy in his early 20s he retreated to the
sanctuary of his father's estate on the Seine to write and
rarely left for the rest of his life. He never married but
apparently had an inveterate enthusiasm for prostitutes.
The so-called Hermit of Croisset wrote his masterpieces,
Madame Bovary and *L'Éducation sentimentale* (1869),
in a style that hid the author. The narrator doesn't judge
his characters; instead their thoughts, actions and
surroundings are recorded in minute detail so that the
reader can draw his own conclusions. While today's
reader might struggle to even spot the crucial steamy
moments, Flaubert's description of Madame Bovary's
extra-curricular love got him into big trouble. He was
tried for obscenity but acquitted. Flaubert died of a brain
haemorrhage in 1880.

What was Naturalism?
Naturalism took a scientific approach to literature. In truth
it was an extension of Realism; the term was actually
invented by its undisputed heavyweight, Émile Zola,
partly to convince readers they were getting something
new. Like Balzac and Flaubert, Naturalist writers took the
tweezers to 19th century life. But the characters were
less romantic, written around the premise that people
can't change who they are. In Naturalism the characters
don't rise heroically above their origins but are shaped
and caged by their surroundings. As a consequence the
literary results aren't exactly life affirming, generating an
overriding air of gloom.

Sci-fi takes off with Jules
Jules Verne (1828-1905)
fogged the distinctions
between Romanticism and
Realism. The stockbroker

turned author wrote
human stories inspired
by the scientific and
technological advances
of the day, reconciling the

rational and the romantic.
*Voyage au centre de la
Terre (1864), Vingt mille
lieues sous les mers*
(1870) and *Le Tour du*

*monde en quatre-vingts
jours* (1873) form part of
his famous *Les Voyages
Extraordinaires* series.

Zola: mine of information

Émile Zola (1840-1902) set out to record the deeply scored society of his own time. He wrote about what he felt were the hereditary ills of abuse and drinking, often pushed along by abject poverty. He knew hardship himself – apparently he would capture and eat birds to survive before his writing began to show financial return. What he hadn't experienced he researched tirelessly, visiting coal mines and slums. In 1898, Zola accused the French government of anti-Semitism in the Dreyfus affair: the letter *J'Accuse* famously appeared on the front page of the Paris daily, *L'Aurore*. While Zola was later convicted of libel, the letter had proved instrumental in getting the Dreyfus case reopened. Zola married but had a 14-year affair with a housemaid who bore his only two children. He died from carbon monoxide poisoning caused by a blocked chimney – some cried foul play.

Who were the Parnassians?

The Parnassians were a group of poets in the mid to late 19th century. They took the writer Théophile Gautier's idea of 'art for art's sake' as a mantra, scripting impersonal, technically precise verse that reacted against the flabby emotion of Romanticism. Many chose subjects from antiquity – the name of the movement itself derives from Mount Parnassus, home to the Muses of Greek mythology. The poets published *Parnasse Contemporain*, a journal in three instalments, between 1866 and 1876.

He's not the saviour of literature; he's a very naughty boy
A lot of French writing in the 19th century was condemned as decadent. Initially a slur dispensed by critics, some writers began wearing the badge with pride and a loose Decadent movement emerged. Baudelaire, Hugo, Flaubert and Rimbaud, with their musing on violence, sex, death and morality, were all described as Decadents at some point.

Parnassian poets: the big two

Théodore de Banville
Banville began writing as a Romantic but, as per the Parnassians, became smitten with the mechanics of verse and, in particular, rhyme. *Les Odes funambulesques* (1857) is his best known collection of poetry.

Charles-Marie-René Leconte de Lisle
The epitome of a Parnassian poet, Leconte de Lisle wrote deliberate, rhythmically precise verse often based on classical tragedy. The collection *Poésies barbares* (1862) placed him as the leading Parnassian, while *Qaïn* (1869) is one of the 19th century's major poems.

Baudelaire: crossing the boundaries
Charles Baudelaire, among the greatest of the 19th century French poets, doesn't fit snugly into a particular school. He's been described variously as the last great writer of Romanticism, a Parnassian, the first Symbolist and the originator of modern literature. Baudelaire began his literary career writing outspoken art criticism, before enjoying fame as a skilled translator of Edgar Allen Poe's work. His own major collection of poetry, the darkly violent *Les Fleurs du Mal* (1857), brought censorship and a fine amid claims of immorality, yet it would prove a literary landmark. The poet's life was turbulent: a love of clothes, paintings, expensive food, opium and hashish quickly consumed his inheritance and he spent most of his adult life constrained by debt and depression. Syphilitic from early adulthood, he suffered a huge stroke in 1866 and died in the following year, aged 36.

What was Symbolism?
The last of the great 19th century French literary schools was dominated by poetry. Symbolism broke from the formality of the Parnassians and the clarity of the Realists. Avoiding pure description, Symbolist poets strove to rouse the reader's subconscious through imagery and impressions. A real scenario was used to symbolize a state of mind: so when Rimbaud wrote about a boat in a storm he hoped to conjure the turmoil of life in general. The rhythms and cadences of the verse itself were also employed to evoke moods and emotions in the reader.

1. Identity,
the institutions of
French culture

**2. Literature
and philosophy**

3. Art, architecture
and design

4. Performing arts

5. Fashion of style,
cinema, photography
and fashion

6. Media and
communications

7. Consuming culture:
food and drink

8. Living culture: the
state of the nation

Rimbaud: *Enfant terrible*

In his own time, Arthur Rimbaud was viewed variously as an enigmatic colossus of 19th century French literature and an infantile waster. The poetry of his teenage years has been cited as a driving force for Symbolism, free verse and, later, Surrealism. By the age of 16 he was a vagabond and by 19 a coffee merchant, part-time gun runner and lover to poet Paul Verlaine who first published Rimbaud's work.

Verlaine left his wife and young son to travel with Rimbaud. For a while the pair lived in Camden, London, where they would apparently have knife fights in their squalid terrace before heading out to the pub. Both liked a drink and they split after Verlaine hit Rimbaud one night with a wet fish. Reunited briefly in Brussels, Verlaine shot Rimbaud in the arm in a drunken rage. Verlaine went to prison for two years and Rimbaud gave up writing and travelled, first to Java and later to Africa. He died in Marseilles, aged 37, not long after the amputation of his cancerous right leg. The punk movement of the 1970s regularly cited the opiate loving, anarchic Rimbaud as an influence. He's also been called the godfather of the Beat poets.

Symbolism: the big three

Paul Verlaine

Verlaine set out as a Parnassian but his *Romances sans paroles* (1874) was one of the first great pieces of Symbolist poetry. An experimenter with free verse, written with little regard for metre or rhyme, Verlaine is often considered the co-founder of modern poetry with Rimbaud.

Stéphane Mallarmé

Another early Symbolist, Mallarmé would influence Dadaism and the Surrealists. He was famed for his salon and its regular Tuesday group, *Les Mardistes*. *L'après-midi d'un faune* (1876) was a particularly influential poem.

Arthur Rimbaud

When Rimbaud wrote *Le bateau ivre* (1871) at the age of 17 he set the tone for Symbolism. His most famous work, *Une saison en enfer* (1873), recalls his relationship with Paul Verlaine.

Two great 20th century French poets

Guillaume Apollinaire

is often viewed in the context of the Surrealists, rubbing shoulders as he did with the likes of Breton and Picasso in Montparnasse shortly after the turn of the century. He played with traditional form and innovative imagery in two collections of poetry, *Alcools* (1913) and *Calligrammes* (1918), the latter recounting his experiences in the First World War trenches. He also wrote a couple of erotic novels and was once erroneously arrested for stealing the Mona Lisa.

Paul Valéry

is recognized by many as the greatest French poet of the 20th century. He started out writing Symbolist poetry at the end of the 19th century but really found his form 30 years later with *La Jeune Parque* (1917), a 500 line, classically structured contemplation on life, as seen through the eyes of a young woman. It's often labelled the masterpiece of 20th century French poetry. His main collection of verse was *Charmes* (1922). Increasingly, Valéry is also recognized for his prose essays, lauded for their pioneering existential pondering.

A tough act to follow

Struggling to live up to the high standards set by its antecedents, French literature wobbled a bit in the 20th century. World war twice interrupted the literary flow and, flashes of individual brilliance aside, the ensuing pessimism quashed many of the novel's traditional qualities. Great thinkers like Breton and Sartre fuzzed the boundaries between philosophy and literature before experimentation took a stranglehold on French literature from which it still seems to be choking.

Proust: talent writ large

Marcel Proust was the giant of 20th century French literature, and his great work, *À la recherche du temps perdu* (1913-27), is big in every sense. Written over 14 years, printed in seven volumes (three after Proust's death from pneumonia) and nudging 4,000 pages, the longest novel ever published has opus written all over it. Often deemed semi-autobiographical, the story tracks the narrator's path through childhood and on into adult life as an aspiring writer. Proust's brilliance lay in capturing the sensory nature of memory (coined as 'involuntary memory'), using smell, sound and touch to regurgitate the narrator's formative years. *À la recherche du temps perdu*'s influence has been immense bearing in mind how few have actually made it through to the novel's end.

Three important French writers in the early 20th century Colette, full name Sidonie-Gabrielle Colette, was the major female author in the first half of the century. She wrote over 50 novels, often courting scandal with the risqué adventures of her heroines struggling against male domination. *Cheri* (1920) and *Gigi* (1945) are among the best remembered. In contrast, André Breton was a driving force in literature's relationship with Surrealism, bringing a Surrealist twang to his poetry and autobiographical novels like *Nadja* (1928), a work published with 44 photographs relating to the insane lady of the title. Finally, Louis-Ferdinand Céline's misanthropic novels captured lives falling apart, inspired by his own unhappy upbringing and adulthood. His first remains the most famous: *Voyage au bout de la nuit* (1932) was hugely innovative in its use of slang. Céline was declared a national disgrace after the Second World War for his aggressive anti-Semitism.

Birth of the anti-novel

If readers found the Existentialist stories of Sartre and co on the heavier side of bedtime reading, the *nouveau roman* of the late 1950s hardly brought light relief. Escapism was strictly off the menu. Novels, or 'anti-novels' as they were often called, should feature detailed description of the actual world and the objects therein ungoverned by character, plot or emotion. In this sense, the *nouveau roman* shared common ground with the contemporaneous New Wave of cinema. Alain Robbe-Grillet was head boy of the *nouveau roman* school, which lumbered on into the 1970s and still exerts an influence on contemporary French literature and its self-conscious experimentation.

Kiss and tell
Colette had little trouble sourcing ideas for her romantic novels. An affair with a stepson from her second marriage came in the wake of a riot-inducing lesbian kiss on stage at the Moulin Rouge with her marquise lover and a bunk-up with Italian maverick Gabriele D'Annunzio.

Doctoring the truth
Céline's real name was Dr Louis-Ferdinand Destouches – the author borrowed his alias from a dead grandmother. He continued to practice medicine after the publication of his novels. A surgery in northern Paris and its wretchedly poor patients found exaggerated life in his work.

The thinking man's novel
Jean-Paul Sartre was a philosopher yet his use of the novel to develop Existentialism marked him out as the leading author of the mid 20th century. *La Nausée* (1939) explored a dejected man's relationship with the world and the madness of existence while *Les chemins de la liberté* (1945-49), a monumental trilogy, reshaped these ideas in response to recent war. He refused the Nobel Prize for Literature in 1964.

Doing it by the book

While *nouveau roman* and Oulipo writers took a chainsaw to tradition, the conventional bourgeois novel they railed against survived without much trouble. Much of the mid century experimentation only found a committed audience among the literati, while the reading public never lost its nose for a good story. Indeed, the epic novel has always outsold the latest literary boundary bender by a bucket load.

What's the latest?

Contemporary French literature lacks the verve of old. Few writers appear keen to commentate on France in the vein of Balzac or Zola. The legacy of the *nouveau roman* and derision from highbrow critics apparently deters many from anything so populist. Instead, progressive lit is led by conceptual and often bleak stories. And yet when it comes to mass consumption, the French still love a good yarn. When they can't find novels by home-grown authors, increasingly they look to English and American work (France went mad for *The Da Vinci Code*) in translation. There is no current movement of the day in French literature, but there are a few significant authors producing distinctive work.

Vowel movements
Oulipo (Ouvroir de Littérature Potentielle) was founded in 1960 by an experimental clique of writers and mathematicians. They produced (and continue to produce) literature using constrained writing, applying numerical formulas to verse and prose in the hope of sparking new ideas. The S+7 method removed each noun within a text and replaced it with the noun found seven places away in whatever dictionary the writer had to hand. George Perec was a leading novelist of Oulipo. He wrote *La Disparition* (1969) without using the letter 'e', and then used 'e' as the only vowel in *Les Revenentes* (1972). A later work, *La Vie mode d'emploi* (1978), telling the story of a Parisian apartment, is more accessible.

French sci-fi

Gérard Klein has been called the most important French sci-fi writer since Jules Verne; *Le temps n'a pas d'odeur* (1963), a time travel trip, is one of his best. The author of *Le Pont de la rivière Kwaï* (1952), Pierre Boulle, also dabbled successfully in sci-fi, penning *Le Planète des singes* (1968). Bernard Werber has led the way in contemporary French science fiction. His best work, *Les Fourmis* (1991-96), is a fantasy trilogy in which humans play second fiddle to ants.

Cracking crime: the roman policier

In the 20th century, French readers developed a voracious appetite for detective fiction, the *roman policier* or *polar*. In pre- and post-war days they lapped up the work of foreign authors like Agatha Christie and the Belgian Georges Simenon with his detective par excellence, *Maigret*. After the Second World War, the publisher Gallimard brought out the darker, Gothic tinged *Série noire* collection of French and American detective fiction to an insatiable audience. On the contemporary scene, Daniel Pennac is the author of a hugely popular series of witty and wacky detective novels: *Au bonheur des ogres* (1985) was the first. He also writes children's fiction, in which dogs usually play a lead role. Didier Daeninckx has enjoyed similar success with the thriller, often threading his work with comment on social conditions in France. Daeninckx's first novel was *Meurtres pour mémoire* (1984).

Three bourgeois novels to read

Bonjour Tristesse
(1954) by Françoise Sagan. Sagan's famous bestseller, written when she was just 18, proved typical of her grasp of emotion and humanity.

Les Centurions
(1961) by Jean Lartéguy. A story of French soldiers in Vietnam and then Algeria, Lartéguy's best work sold millions.

Tolstoi
(1965) by Henri Troyat. Troyat wrote shelves of biographical novels and the French lapped them up. Many, like the Prix Goncourt-winning *Tolstoi*, featured famous Russians.

Prose prize
France hands out hundreds of literary prizes each year. The most prestigious is the Prix Goncourt, given in November to the year's most imaginative piece of French prose. The winner receives a whopping €10, while the positive effect on publisher's sales has often led to allegations of vote rigging.

Racy Read
In *La Vie sexuelle de Catherine M* (2001), respected Parisian art critic Catherine Millet lays bare her sexual history (with a particular liking for group activities) in an explicit memoir. The book sold over 400,000 copies in France.

Jean Rouaud's *Les Champs d'honneur* (1990), a novel on the impact of the First World War was a literary phenomenon. It took the Prix Goncourt but also generated popular appeal, selling over half a million copies.

Five contemporary books to read

Truismes
(1996) by Marie Darrieussecq. The witty morality tale of a prostitute who slowly turns into a pig proved an unexpected success.

Les particules élémentaires
(1998) by Michel Houellebecq. Houellebecq uses the story of two half-brothers to pass grim comment on modern life.

L'Absolue perfection du crime
(2001) by Tanguy Viel. Viel is the latest French author to pick up and run with the noir baton.

Les Ombres errantes
(2002) by Pascal Quignard. Hovering somewhere between novel and essay, Quignard's collection of memories and observations took the Prix Goncourt.

Et si c'était vrai...
(2002) by Marc Levy. This spooky love story was the debut from entrepreneur turned novelist Levy, the bestselling French author of recent years.

The misanthrope

Both loved and loathed, Michel Houellebecq is touted as a rare and original commentator on contemporary France. His first novel, *Extension du domaine de la lutte* (1994), delighted left-wingers with its contempt for consumerism; his second, *Les particules élémentaires* (1998), incited their hatred for its attack on the spirit of 1968. Famously misanthropic, the former IT worker has variously wound up Muslims (they took him to court for calling Islam stupid), Christians, women and liberalists via vocal and written polemic. Interviews with Houellebecq find the author chain-smoking and sometimes drunk – he's even been known to make a pass at female interviewers. And yet he remains a significant writer, one of the only contemporary French authors to actually address modern life.

Francophone literature

While home-grown authors navel gaze, writers from the former French colonies have produced some of the most inventive contemporary French language literature. Assia Djebar is the most famous. Her work often takes a feminist stance, with novels like *Les enfants du Nouveau Monde* (1962) portraying women coping with a changing world. In 2005 she became the first writer from the Maghreb to win a place on the Académie Française.

Jump on the *bande* wagon

You can argue among yourselves about which is more important, the text or the images, but there's no denying that the French love the comic strip, or *bande dessinée* (BD). Graphic novels are referred to as the 'ninth art' (TV is apparently the eighth, if you're wondering), hinting at their status as a serious creative force. The genre harks back to the late 19th century, with Christophe (pen name of Georges Colomb) an early pioneer, creating gentle humour in the likes of *La Famille Fenouillard* (1890). Hergés' youthful, communist-bashing *Tintin*, first published in 1929, became widely loved in the post-war years. Tintin is of course Belgian, but France and Belgium have long shared characters and ideas in a joint love of BD. The periodical *Pilote* was the main French vehicle for comic strips in the 1960s; writer René Goscinny and artist Albert Uderzo used it to launch *Astérix le Gaulois* (1961), establishing the most popular French BD series yet created. In the 1970s, *Pilote* developed a more adult content, and American artists like Robert Crumb got involved. Today, BD remains hugely popular. Pascal Rabaté is among the latest crop of authors, winning widespread acclaim for adapting a Tolstoy novel in his four-volume *Ibicus* (1999). The Festival International de la Bande Dessinée d'Angoulême, in south-west France, is probably the largest annual comic fest in the world.

The term *autofiction* has crept into French literature in recent years, used to describe novels with a strong autobiographical thread; the genre has emerged particularly through women writers.

Three francophone Goncourt winners

Tahar Ben Jelloun
La Nuit sacrée (1987). The hallucinatory story of a Moroccan woman raised as a boy whose life transforms as an adult.

Patrick Chamoiseau
Texaco (1992). An engrossing historical novel that sheds light on the author's homeland, Martinique.

Amin Maalouf
Le rocher de Tanios (1993). Maalouf scooped the Goncourt with a vivid depiction of social and cultural change in his native Lebanon in the 19th century.

The Lost Generation tag was first used by American writer Gertrude Stein. Stein's Parisian salon provided a creative arena for Hemingway, Joyce, Pound and the rest.

Feasting on Paris Ernest Hemingway best captured the Lost Generation's Parisian odyssey in print. He moved there with his first wife, Hadley, in early 1921, and duly wrote his first novels, *Torrents of Spring* and *The Sun Also Rises* (both 1926), in a garret room of the same hotel where poet Paul Verlaine had gasped his last 30 years before. Read *A Moveable Feast* (published posthumously in 1964), sprinkled with unflattering portraits of fellow ex-pat writers, for an insight into Hemingway's time in the city. The Hemingway devotee is a common sight in Paris today, nose buried in a copy of *A Moveable Feast*, doggedly searching out Papa's old haunts.

Tourist trail

France has offered both inspiration and retreat to generations of foreign writers. Charles Dickens was a Francophile who braved the Channel crossing more than once, absorbing French life and famously weaving the revolutionary spirit into *A Tale of Two Cities* (1885). American novelist Henry James, a friend of Flaubert's, was similarly smitten. Having lived briefly in France as a child he returned in adulthood and wrote *A Little Guide to France* (1884), documenting a six-week tour of provincial towns and the characters he met along the way. For Oscar Wilde, France offered a more practical experience. After release from prison in 1897, Wilde spent much of the final two years of his life in Paris, wandering the streets and surviving on the kindness of friends.

Americans in Paris

Parisian liberalism sucked in writers from around the world early in the 20th century. Many made camp in France after the First World War, where the so-called Lost Generation of American authors enjoyed the bohemian milieu and freedom from Prohibition. F. Scott Fitzgerald wrote *The Great Gatsby* (1925) in Valescure on the Côte d'Azur in 1924 and, a year later, met Ernest Hemingway in Paris. Like Hemingway, American Modernist poet Ezra Pound settled in Paris in 1921. Another poet, TS Eliot, would pop over periodically from London. Irishman James Joyce was an important part of the Lost Generation community: *Ulysses* (1922) was first published by Sylvia Beach's Shakespeare & Company bookshop on the Left Bank, where the clique of young writers would often hang out.

The Beats march in

In the 1950s and 60s, Paris attracted the American Beat writers. The big three were the poets Allen Ginsberg and Gregory Corso and the novelist William S Burroughs. They lodged in what became known as the Beat Hotel, a Left Bank dive where Burroughs and poet Brion Gysin devised the cut-up technique – chopping up a completed text and rearranging it to create new work.

Medtime stories

English writers in the 20th century found a creative playground along the Mediterranean coast. Somerset Maugham was actually born in the British Embassy in Paris in 1874 and returned to France 50 years later to spend the remainder of his adult life (bar wartime exile) in St Jean Cap Ferrat. He wrote *Cakes and Ale* (1930), a satire on London's literary scene, in his Riviera home. Graham Greene also sought exile on the Côte d'Azur in later life, living in a small apartment in the old town of Antibes, the setting for short stories like *May We Borrow Your Husband?* (1967). Anthony Burgess, author of *A Clockwork Orange* (1962), wrote *A Homage to QWERT YUIOP* (1986) about a journey from his Monaco home to visit Greene.

The immersion technique

Many contemporary authors take a more direct approach, drinking in the French experience before regurgitating it for an Anglo-Saxon readership. Peter Mayle got the *boule* rolling with *A Year in Provence* (1989), a light and warm autobiographical work on escaping to a new life in the Luberon. The floodgates opened. A raft of gently humorous *autofiction* on laying down roots in France is still emerging: look up Sarah Turnbull's *Almost French: A New Life in Paris* (2003), Stephen Clarke's *A Year in the Merde* (2004) and *Signs of the Heart: Love and Death in Languedoc* by Christopher Hope (2004). JG Ballard's *Super-Cannes* (2000), offers a less rosy vision of life in southern France.

1. Identity:
the foundations of
French culture

**2. Literature
and philosophy**

3. Art, architecture
and design

4. Performing arts

5 Arbiters of style:
cinema, photography
and fashion

6. Media and
communications

7. Consuming culture:
food and drink

8. Living culture: the
state of the nation

2.2 Philosophy

Rationale is ingrained in the French mode of thinking. They delight in reasoned debate: students sitting their high school baccalauréat still have to knuckle down to a sizeable chunk of philosophy, while nearly every stratum of society, from farm labourers to government ministers, enjoys its capacity for abstract thought. And so it follows that the French treasure their intellectuals.

2.2.1 Thinking man's game: the French and their intellectuals

Over the last 400 years, the French climate for debate has produced a wealth of internationally significant philosophers. Descartes paved the way for all that followed, from the enlightened Voltaire and Rousseau, prising the doors to Revolution, through the Existentialist superstars and on to the Deconstructionists who rewrote the book in the late 20th century.

While the UK and North America tend to find and keep their progressive thinkers in academia, France has a tradition of plucking its philosophers

I think, therefore I am...

Rubbish.

Descartes and Pascal: don't get involved, walk away, René...

from varied disciplines, from literature to science, teaching to psychology. Here the *engagés* prosper, eager to comment on contemporary life. From Voltaire to Sartre, French thinkers have thrown their *deux centimes* into social and political debate, taking a stance on everything from the *Ancien Régime* to the Occupation.

Thinking out loud
The *café philosophiques* phenomenon spread through France in the 1990s. Inspired by the Existentialists' love of gathering over a coffee to discuss current affairs or more abstract ideas, people arranged regular discussion groups. It began under the guidance of teacher Marc Sautet who held a Sunday morning forum in a Bastille café.

Who was Descartes?

René Descartes (1596-1650) has been labelled the father of modern Western philosophy. Never mind that his theories have been steadily eroded ever since publication in the 1630s, his value remains as an icon of independent thought. He granted the French – and the world – the indulgence of abstract pondering. Before Descartes, thinkers filled their time with scholasticism, basically arguing over dogmatic theories that could be traced back to Aristotle. In contrast Descartes wiped the slate clean, developing the new rational laws of science and maths, applying each to philosophy.

What was on Descartes' mind?

Descartes developed Cartesian logic. He abandoned all previous theory, reducing the world to that famous first principle of metaphysics: 'I think, therefore I am'. Having confirmed his own existence, he tried to construct the universe, not using his work to question faith but to shore it up by proving the existence of God. Descartes made distinction between mind and matter, between soul and body, a theory that became known as Cartesian Dualism. He also proposed that because we can conjure the concept of perfection (i.e. God), a God (i.e. perfection) must exist to have given us that notion of perfection. This essentially flawed piece of chicken and egg logic has been dubbed the Cartesian Circle.

Descartes' life in five key dates

1596
Born in Le Haye en Touraine. The town was subsequently renamed Descartes.

1618
Discarded his qualification in law from Poitiers University and signed up for the army for two years.

1629
Moved to Holland where he spent most of the next 20 years working in seclusion.

1633
Shelved plans to publish Le Monde, theorizing on cosmology, when Galileo was condemned by the Catholic Church for expounding similar ideas.

1649
On the invitation of Queen Christine of Sweden he visited Stockholm where he died of pneumonia the following year.

The word Cartesian derives from the Latinized form of Descartes' name, Renatus Cartesius.

Discours de la méthode
(1637). Descartes maps out Cartesian theory in French. Accompanying essays on optics, geometry and meteorology are used to illustrate his new philosophies.

Méditations de prima philosophia
(1641). This time Descartes uses Latin to expand his ideas on the existence of God and the distinction between body and mind.

Descartes was in the habit of working in bed until the afternoon.

Think tank: two of Descartes' contemporaries

Blaise Pascal, like Descartes, began as a mathematician he developed the theory of probability and even made an early calculator. But maths was abruptly ditched after a near-death experience and subsequent religious vision in 1654. From thereon, theology and philosophy took precedence for Pascal. He entered a Jansenist Christian community and scribbled two seminal works. His *Lettres provinciales* (1856), including an attack on the Jesuits, were brilliant in their use of rhetoric. *Pensées sur a religion et sur quelques autres sujets* (published posthumously in 1670) is deemed his best, analyzing the social and metaphysical problems of mankind before prescribing religious faith as the only remedy. Unlike Descartes, Pascal didn't advocate the application of science to philosophical thought, favouring a more mystical approach, and his written comments on Descartes were often dismissive.

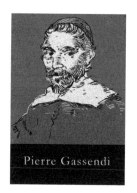

Pierre Gassendi

Pierre Gassendi, another maths wizard, penned various objections to Descartes' theories.
He rejected Cartesian Dualism and its distinction between body and mind. Gassendi reserved most scorn for the idea of rejecting all previous thought and starting from scratch.
As for Gassendi's philosophy, he gave the Epicurean ideas on atomism a Church-friendly twist, suggesting that atoms did indeed form the Earth but that God made the atoms.

2.2.3 Thought processes:

philosophy in the Enlightenment

What was the Enlightenment?

The Enlightenment (or *siècle de lumière* as the French call it)
the late 17th and 18th centuries questioned the traditions
church and state. Inspired by Descartes and Newton,
thinkers emphasized reason and individualism in all areas
life. European philosophers like Kant, Goethe, Voltaire
and Rousseau would cast the old institutions in a new light,
helping to sow the seeds of revolution.

The big brains and their big brainy book

8th century Paris provided a cerebral hub for *les philosophes*,
intellectuals who shared an interest in renovating French life.
common they advocated a reasoned, tolerant understanding
the world. Many embraced deism, rejecting predestination
and plugging man's use of logic to order a God-made world.
thers were complete atheists. The *Encyclopédie* (1751-80),
unofficial manifesto for the Enlightenment, was *les philosophes'*
bus; Voltaire, Rousseau, Diderot and Montesquieu all
contributed.

All the rage: Voltaire

François-Marie Arouet was better known by his pseudonym,
Voltaire. Revered, reviled and tirelessly controversial, he railed
against oppression and intolerance, enduring more than
he Bastille stay as a result. As a prolific poet, playwright,
novelist, historian and man of both science and letters (he
kept over 1,200 correspondents), Voltaire recorded his disgust
r religious bigotry and its suffocation of progress. Major
works included *Candide* (1759), a bruising satirical novel
med at the optimism of another philosopher, Leibniz, and
the *Dictionnaire Philosophique* (1764), hammering political and
religious institutions in alphabetical order and offering up an
ternative society governed by free thought instead. For all
at, he still ended up on the Académie Française.

"IF GOD DID NOT
EXIST, IT WOULD
BE NECESSARY
TO INVENT HIM."
Voltaire

"MAN IS BORN
FREE, AND
EVERYWHERE
HE IS IN CHAINS."
Rousseau

Even though Voltaire
apparently hated war,
he amassed a fortune by
selling supplies to the
French army.

VOLTAIRE
TIRELESS CHAMPION
OF CHANGE

Mentity
he foundations of
ench culture **2. Literature
and philosophy** *3. Art, architecture*
and design *4. Performing arts* *5. Arbiters of style:*
cinema, photography
and fashion *6. Media and*
communication *7. Consuming culture:*
food and drink *8. Living culture: the*
state of the nation

Getting back to basics: Rousseau

OK, so Jean-Jacques Rousseau was actually Swiss, but he wrote in French and spent much of his life in France. In 1749, on his way to visit chum Diderc in prison, Rousseau had a blinding vision: man was essentially good but his progress to civilization through technical and intellectual advance had crippled society. He duly denounced contemporary society and its hierarchy in *Discou sur les sciences et les arts* (1750) and then suggested an alternative in *Du Contrat social* and *Émile* (both 1762), imaginatively picturing social harmony through traditional family groupings. His frank *Confessions* (1782) marked the birth of the autobiography. The egalitarian Rousseau became a hero of the French Revolutionaries after his death. His relationship with Voltaire was less rosy – the pair hated each other.

Think tank: two more from the Enlightenment

Denis Diderot An art critic, playwright, essayist and, most significantly, the editor and prime contributor of the *Encyclopédie*, Diderot developed ideas of free will, experimenting with a wide range of beliefs from deism to materialis atheism. *Le Neveu de Rameau* (unpublished until 1804), a dialogue on moralit or the lack of it in society, is considered his finest work.

Montesquieu A liberal novelist, historian and political philosopher remembere chiefly for *De l'esprit des lois* (1748), in which he decried despotism and suggested divvying up power between the legislature, the executive and the judiciary, as later adopted by the American constitution.

Pause for thought: three post-Enlightenment thinkers

Few French thinkers of the 19th century left a lasting legacy. Enlightenment theory was digested and reappraised largely through literary fiction. However, there were exceptions:

Auguste Comte peddled Positivism, suggesting that mankind had entered the 'positive' phase, in which knowledge only came from what could be scientifically observed. Comte's conviction that society should be studied as a science saw him crowned as the father of sociology.

Hippolyte Taine developed Comte's theory of society governed by clear, immutable laws. The pessimistic conclusions – basically, you're stuck with you lot – were an important influence on writers like Zola and Maupassant.

Henri-Louis Bergson offered the main challenge to Positivism, rejecting the laws of Naturalism in favour of human spontaneity. Existentialists would later acknowledge Bergson's influence. A new take on evolution, *L'évolution créatrice* (1907), was his bestseller.

What is Existentialism?

The ideas of 19th century philosophers Kierkegaard and Nietzsche paved the way for the Existentialism that took shape under the celebrity patronage of Jean-Paul Sartre, Albert Camus and Simone de Beauvoir in Paris in the early 1940s. They asserted that people determined their existence and values through their own actions: only the behaviour of the individual could provide some kind of meaning in an otherwise random universe. It drew the interest of people uncertain about the role (if any) of God in their disenchanted, post-World War world. In the Left Bank cafés of Saint-Germain-des-Prés where the Existentialists worked, the school's cachet spawned a kind of philosophical theme park. Alas, the hangers-on somewhat cheapened the industrious efforts of Sartre and co. Despite shouting loud in a political context, Existentialism never made the leap from good idea to world changer, and it began to demise in the 1950s.

Think tank: three Existentialists

Jean-Paul Sartre Before the Second World War, Jean-Paul Sartre was a lecturer and writer. Captured during the fall of France, he was stalag bound for almost a year before holing up in smoke filled Left Bank cafés for much of the Occupation. *L'Être et le Néant* (1943) laid out the Existentialist ideas that wartime experience had clarified for Sartre: man may be defined by his own actions but the choices he makes are absurd because he operates without objective moral structure. Increasingly Sartre looked to place his theories amid the realities of life and politics. His infatuation with Marxism in the 1950s and 60s clashed with earlier notions on freedom of choice.

LOCK UP YOUR DAUGHTERS.
WONKY-EYED
BACCY-BREATH
JEAN PAUL'S IN TOWN.
(THERE MUST BE SOMETHING
IN THAT EXISTENTIALISM, THEN)

Albert Camus French Algerian journalist, novelist and playwright Albert Camus didn't like the Existentialist tag. He developed the Absurdist theory (another label he shunned), discussing man's search for meaning in an incomprehensible and, more often than not, bleak world. His foremost novel, *L'Étranger* (1942), dealt with the absurdity of being alive. An inveterate leftie, Camus nevertheless questioned the brutality of radical Marxism and split with comrade Sartre as a result. Like Sartre, he didn't hesitate to take sides on

No ordinary love
Simone de Beauvoir
and Jean-Paul Sartre
were partners from
their student days
until Sartre's death,
aged 75, but they had
an open relationship,
or what Sartre
called 'an essential
love'. Skirting the
conventions of
marriage or family,
they lived separately
and pursued other
love interests, de
Beauvoir with both
men and women.

Anthropologist
Claude Lévi-
Strauss used
Structuralism to
study kinship in
primitive societies.

matters in the wider world, in particular calling for moderat■
in the Algerian crisis. He died in a car crash two years befo■
Algeria gained independence.

Simone de Beauvoir Simone de Beauvoir has been called
the most influential female intellect of the 20th century.
Existentialist as much by association as want, she always
claimed herself a writer rather than a philosopher. Howeve■
her work explored the moral angles of existence she
discussed with Sartre. *L'Invitée* (1943) was her first novel
and *Les Mandarins* (1954) the one that scooped her a Prix
Goncourt, but she's best remembered for *Le Deuxième Se*
(1949), a ground-breaking study on the oppression of wome
throughout history.

What is Structuralism?
The Existentialists had lost their drive by the late 1950s,
increasingly preoccupied with debating communism. In
stepped the Structuralists, rejecting Existentialist notions of
individual choice and asserting that people lived according t■
certain, underlying structures. They maintained that speech,
writing and general behaviour are governed by common
codes: cultures may vary but are essentially based on the
same primary rituals and habits. As much a method as a
mode of thought, Structuralism was applied to a wide range
of disciplines, employed in anthropology, linguistics, literary
criticism and mathematics. Nearly all the disparate figures
connected with Structuralism denied the association.

Barthes reads the signs
Roland Barthes has been called the high priest of
Structuralism even though his work as a writer and literary
critic (he wasn't a pure philosopher) covered a much wider
spectrum. Barthes applied a structure to the study of mass
culture in his *Mythologies* (1957). Modern culture was full
of signs, like adverts or magazine covers, which had to be
deciphered. For instance, he suggested that a washing
powder advert crammed with housewives perpetuated the
myths about a woman's role in society. He died after being
hit by a laundry truck on his way home from a lunch party
hosted by François Mitterrand.

84

2. Literature
and philosophy

What is post-Structuralism?

Structuralism quickly succumbed to revision in the late 1960s as thinkers – some of whom, like Barthes and Foucault, had previously applied Structuralism to their work – developed a fresh outlook. Some have argued that post-Structuralism wasn't a fully formed movement but simply 'what came next': it both questioned and furthered Structuralism. There were no universal theories but themes did emerge, such as Barthes' notion that individuals interpret what they read, hear or see according to their background or own modes of thought. Thus, the reader or listener becomes more important than the author or speaker.

Think tank: two philosophers from the late 20th century

Michel Foucault's ideas developed radically over time, passing through both Structuralist and post-Structuralist spheres. He addressed the history of power and how it controls general attitudes towards sexuality, insanity and criminality. *Les mots et les choses* (1966) was a bestseller, despite predicting the rapid demise of mankind. He died of an AIDS-related illness.

Jacques Derrida was frequently accused of difficult writing and obfuscation. Staff at Cambridge University challenged plans to grant Derrida an honorary degree in 1992, branding his work 'absurd' – they were outvoted.

Jacques Derrida waded in against Structuralism in the late 1960s, developing the art of Deconstruction to reassess existing works of literature. He questioned everything that had gone before, scrutinizing old texts and philosophical doctrines in an effort to reveal new meaning.

Mindset: the current intellectual climate

Today, France finds itself without a brilliant mind in the mould of Camus, Foucault or Derrida. The *nouveaux philosophes* of the 1970s, reacting against Marxism, aspired to such heights and were duly accused of courting publicity. Their main man, Bernard-Henri Levy (1948-), remains the highest profile thinker in France today. His second book, *La Barbarie à visage humain* (1978), made him an overnight star. Married to actress Arielle Dombasle, the media savvy BHL (as he's known) is a regular on talk shows and magazine covers. Television became important to the ongoing popular interest in philosophy in the 1980s: Bernard Pivot's *Apostrophes* provided a weekly diet of topical intellectualizing. The success of *Apostrophes* and the continued popularity of literary debate on TV confirm that the French public retains its taste for intellectual musing, even though most progressive thought has stepped from the limelight into the shadows of academia.

Art, architecture and design

3 Art, architecture and design

3.1 Art

Few nations can rival the visual arts heritage of the French. They began slowly, following the Italians' lead for a long time, but then burst into life in the 19th century. For a hundred years, France played host to one of the most colourful phases of painting and sculpture the world has ever seen. Realism, Impressionism and Cubism all emerged within its borders; even non-French artists recognized the need to live and work in France.

A helping hand

The stars of French painting, from Courbet to Monet, Cézanne to Matisse, began as pariahs, initially ignored by the establishment, and yet France has a long history of state patronage in the visual arts – it can just take the powers-that-be a while to catch on to the latest thing. French kings began commissioning artists to glorify the state in paint in the 16th century and artists have been subject to government intervention ever since. Cynical observers have claimed that even today the Fifth Republic's *exception culturelle* simply works to re-establish French cultural prestige overseas, but with funding extended to teaching art, new exhibition spaces and grand public commissions, the judgement seems harsh. Debate also rumbles on over whether state funding helps breathe new life into art or whether such parental guidance stifles new development.

French art: ten key dates

1640
Nicolas Poussin, early giant of French art, became court painter to Louis XIV, establishing the Classicism that prevailed through the 17th century.

1648
The creation of an Académie Royale de Peinture et de Sculpture formalized governmental participation in the visual arts.

1737
The Salon, an exhibition of paintings selected by an Académie jury, secured an annual date in the Louvre.

1824
Eugène Delacroix painted *Scènes des massacres de Scio*, a work that became iconic to the emerging Romantic movement.

1864
Edouard Manet ushered in the Impressionist age with *Le Déjeuner sur l'herbe*.

1874
The Impressionists held the first of their eight exhibitions in Paris.

Late 1870s
Cézanne developed the solid style so influential to Cubist and abstract art.

1886
The king of French sculpture, Auguste Rodin, fashioned *Le Baiser*.

1907
Georges Braque and Pablo Picasso begin the Parisian collaboration that led to Cubism.

1917
Marcel Duchamp kick started conceptual art by exhibiting everyday objects, in this case a urinal, as art.

Late developer

You could argue that the Dordogne cavemen were the first French artists, painting bison portraits in their bijou riverside condos. Thousands of years later came the illuminated manuscripts of the Merovingians, followed from the 11th century by painting and sculpture of the Romanesque and Gothic periods, all of it devised as religious decoration. However, only when France awoke belatedly to the Renaissance did the significant artists begin to emerge.

Poussin: the first French master

In the 17th century Italian painters finally had some competition. However, Rome was still *the* destination for any self-respecting master, and so it proved for Nicolas Poussin, the first great French painter. Poussin was the prolific maestro of Classicism, painting orderly, powerful landscapes and scenes inspired by the myths of the ancients. Louis XIII appointed him first painter to the king, a post he endured for two years before scuttling back to Rome, despondent at the intrigues of courtly life. Poussin's tireless pursuit of structure in his work would directly influence the likes of Cézanne. The Louvre houses a sizeable collection of his paintings and drawings.

Painting the Baroque way

Poussin's Baroque contemporaries included Claude Lorrain, similarly smitten with Rome but more concerned with a poetic interpretation of land and seascapes. Georges de la Tour was more interested in people, painting religious subjects in the manner of Caravaggio. Charles le Brun was Louis XIV's artist of choice, selected by the Sun King to direct the Académie where he built on the classical, structured approach of his former tutor Poussin and painted grandiose, heroic scenes suitable for an absolute monarch.

Artistic control

The Académie Royale de Peinture et de Sculpture was founded by Cardinal Mazarin in 1648. It centralized French art under royal control but also provided a place where artists could learn, exhibit in the annual Salon and seek out wealthy patronage. Louis XIV controlled the Académie to promote royal power, even establishing a hierarchy of genres that gave priority to the historical epic. The Académie lives on today as part of the École des Beaux-Arts.

Rococo painting developed the *fête galantes* genre, in which people (usually aristocrats) were portrayed enjoying a dreamy al fresco moment.

The word 'rococo' derives from the French words for cockleshell *(coquille)* and small stones *(rocaille):* both motifs were commonly used in the decorative arts of the period.

Today, the name of 18th century sculptor Pigalle is more often associated with the red light district of Paris, clustered around the square that bears his name.

The French Revolution opened up the Louvre's art treasures for public viewing.

Rococo turns on the light

Rococo brought a lighter touch to French art in the early 18th century. The sturdy heroics of Baroque were shed for natural, dreamy visions of aristocratic opulence. Jean-Antoine Watteau led the charge with pastoral revelry and fantasy that, despite its lightness, often carried a melancholy absent in most Rococo painting: *Gilles* (1719), featuring a glum Pierrot, is a fine example. Watteau's Rococo disciples rarely matched his depth. Jean Honoré Fragonard painted luminous, ethereal scenes of the rich relaxing amid nature, while his teacher, François Boucher, created decorative portraits and voluptuous nudes that earned accusations of licentiousness.

The master of still life

Jean-Baptiste-Siméon Chardin initiated modern still life painting in the mid 18th century: his work would directly inspire Delacroix, Manet and Cézanne. He ignored the ostentation of his era – while others painted rosy flesh and a lush natural world, Chardin chose buckets, crockery and dead ducks. He also painted the everyday folk of 18th century Paris.

Back to the Classics

The airy-fairy fun of Rococo was trampled by a Jacobin boot in the late 18th century when neo-Classicism fell in line with the formality of republican life. Jacques-Louis David was the leading light. Chummy with Robespierre, David portrayed the Romans and Greeks celebrating republicanism. He became a propagandist for the Revolution, his most famous work recording *The Death of Marat* (1793), a Revolutionary friend. Interned after Robespierre's execution, David later became court painter to Napoleon, chosen by the Emperor to depict his Coronation in 1804. Jean-Auguste Dominique Ingres (1780-1867) followed in David's footsteps with even greater formality, flouting the growing Romantic trend with technically exact portraits, although his nudes proved more sensuous.

Romanticism reignites the passions

The rigidity of neo-Classicism inevitably brought reaction, and in the early to mid 19th century Romanticism spread through the arts. Eugène Delacroix was the paragon. He had a talent for drama, splashing an inflated vision of life, with its passion and suffering, across the canvas. He famously placed Marianne atop the barricades in *La Liberté guidant le peuple* (1830). Delacroix's expressive brush strokes would later inform the Impressionists. Théodore Géricault was another whose work wowed with colour and tense energy. A Romantic with a Realist touch, his short career became defined by two subjects – horses and the insane.

Rodin: the master of French sculpture

Rodin was a one-off: a Romantic sculptor who came to portray nature through Realism, an artist who broke from Classicism yet often placed his figures in a classical pose. He remains the colossus of French sculpture. Figures like *Le Penseur* (1880) and *Le Baiser* (1886) aren't simply stunning for their realistic form, they also expertly convey a rich emotion. Such was the natural realism of his work that early in his career some accused Rodin of using a cast (cheating) to create *L'age d'airain* (1875-76). In 1880, Rodin was commissioned to produce *La Porte de l'Enfer* for a museum of decorative arts that never materialized. The work remained unfinished on his death, 37 years later, although figures taken from the plans did inform some of his most famous singular pieces. He married his partner of 53 years (not all of them faithful), Rose Beuret, in 1917. Both died later that year.

Disappearing art
Jacques-Louis David was chosen by the Jacobins to commemorate the Tennis Court Oath (in which the Revolutionaries pledged unity) with a painting. The work was never finished, partly because certain characters required to sit for the painting began disappearing during the Reign of Terror.

Manet died, aged 51, from a paralyzing disease of the nervous system, a symptom of untreated syphilis.

Courbet paints it like he sees it

French art finally took off the rose tinted specs in the 1850s and began looking forward. The formality of Classicism and flounce of Romanticism were eclipsed by a new Realist approach. Jean-François Millet painted the rural poor, while Gustave Courbet earned the critics' disapproval with oils like *Un enterrement à Ornans* (1859), using actual funeral mourners as models. Painting both landscapes and people, Courbet captured the irregularities of nature and society. His later work became increasingly erotic, and paintings like *L'Origine du monde* (1866) were banned from public view.

The Barbizon village people

Jean-Baptiste Camille Corot, Théodore Rousseau and Jean-François Millet shaped the mid 19th century Barbizon school, named after the village in the forest of Fontainbleau where they worked. They rejected classical landscapes for direct studies of nature that would influence the Impressionists. Images of the rural poor toiling the land also pushed the school into Realist territory. Millet harnessed the piety of poor peasants as social commentary in the endlessly reproduced *L'Angélus* (1857). Salvador Dali made frequent reference to the painting in his own work.

Manet, ruefully contemplating the cheap fun that illustrators might have with *Déjeuner Sur L'Herbe*

Manet: A foot in both camps

Edouard Manet smoothed the transition from Realism to Impressionism. Like Courbet he took inspiration from the everyday – Parisian beggars and drunks haunted the canvas. Other subjects were more bourgeois, drawn from the social sphere to which Manet himself belonged. He challenged both establishment and viewer. In *Le Déjeuner sur l'herbe* and *l'Olympia* (both painted in 1863), unapologetic nudes stared directly out from the canvas. Both aroused public outcry and were rejected from the Salon as obscene, yet both excited the gaggle of young artists who would shape Impressionism, not least Claude Monet. They were intrigued by Manet's technical innovation: his use of harsh lighting, eliminating so-called mid tones (starkly contrasting light with dark), and the unwillingness to hide brush strokes.

What was Impressionism?

The young artists who gathered around Manet in the late 1860s imitated his direct appraisal of everyday life. They placed great emphasis on colour. Applied in short, broken strokes to capture a moment of light and movement, the paints were often used unmixed, urging the eye to form its own impressions of colour. Unlike their predecessors, the Impressionists often painted outside (*en plein air*), working feverishly to capture a certain light or time of day. They would meet, Manet their reluctant mentor, at the Café Guerbois in the Batignolles quarter of Paris. Discussions at the Café Guerbois often became heated. One shouting match between Manet and art critic Louis Edmond Duranty ended in a duel. Duranty was honourably wounded and their friendship duly restored. In light of their popularity today, it's hard to comprehend the scandal the Impressionists' work caused at the time. One critic suggested they had "declared war on beauty."

What's in a name?
Poet and painter Louis Leroy was the first to coin the term 'Impressionist' while reviewing Monet's *Impression: soleil levant* in 1872. The harbour painting took Monet just 40 minutes to complete.

Subverting the Salon
In the 1860s, the only path to critical acclaim lay in having a painting accepted to the annual Salon de Paris run by the Académie des Beaux-Arts. Unfortunately, the establishment weren't overly receptive to innovation. And so the Impressionists set up their own exhibition space. In 1874 Monet, Degas, Renoir, Pissarro and others set up an Impressionists' show in a photographic studio. Another seven exhibitions followed over the next 12 years. Although he fervently supported the enterprise, Manet never exhibited, determined to find success through the official channels.

Monet, Renoir, Morisot, Bazille (a promising Impressionist painter killed in the Franco-Prussian war) and Sisley first met at art class in the Parisian studio of Charles Gleyre.

First lady of Impressionism Impressionism wasn't a total washout for female painters. Berthe Morisot (1841-95) was a prominent Impressionist from the start. After studying under Corot of the Barbizon school, she introduced Manet to working outside and exhibited in all but one of the Impressionists' exhibitions. Painting with luminosity, she typically depicted women, often showing them engaged in everyday domestic life, as in *Le Berceau* (1872) showing a woman and her baby.

In later life Monet's eyesight failed. Cataracts impaired his perception of colour and he resorted to applying paint simply by reading the paint tube label.

Impressionism: the big five

Claude Monet The figurehead of Impressionism sold caricatures at school and was soon painting outside on the beaches of Normandy. Living in the village of Argentueil in the 1870s he produced the test cards of Impressionism, snapshots of colour and light like *Les Coquelicots à Argenteuil* (1873). He would line up easels, painting canvases simultaneously as the light varied. Haystacks, rivers, cathedrals, even the Houses of Parliament, were rendered in brilliant dappled light by Monet's short brush strokes. He refused to use black paint, instead producing shadow by mixing other shades. Monet moved to Giverny in 1883, where he was fascinated by the hues and shades of his garden, brilliantly exampled in *Le bassin aux Nympheas* (1899), until his death. Derided early in his career, he died rich and famous.

Pierre-Auguste Renoir Renoir was another devotee of light. Untamed brush strokes and soft colours were used to give a quivering air of immediacy. The Impressionist most concerned with people, his figures blended with their surrounds. He painted the famous *Bal au Moulin de la Galette, Montmartre* (1876), crammed with people dancing outside, in situ. A trip to Italy in the early 1880s pushed his style back towards Classicism with its clear lines, which he used particularly to paint nudes, before he refound his original hazy style a decade later.

Camille Pissarro The elder statesman of Impressionism painted rural and urban scenes, depicting life on the agricultural lands around Paris or in the city itself, as in the bird's eye view of *Boulevard Montmartre, effet de nuit* (1897). He was a great technician, inventively manipulating the paint; his experimentation helped direct the post-Impressionists. Using the dappled blur of Impressionism and later the staccato of Pointillism, Pissarro evoked the spirit of Millet with scenes of rural labour.

"EVERYTHING IS BEAUTIFUL, THE WHOLE THING IS KNOWING HOW TO INTERPRET."
Camille Pissarro

Alfred Sisley Born in France of English parents, Sisley was the undisguised landscapist among the Impressionists. He had a particular talent for depicting a snowy scene. His work is often regarded as a more formal version of Monet's: *Le Pont de Villeneuve-la-Garenne* (1872) crystallizes the approach. Sisley didn't comment as directly on his age as the other Impressionists and his work progressed less – for a long time his paintings were neglected as a result. He died in poverty.

Edgar Degas Degas hovered around the Impressionists from the off, colluding in their development of colour and observations of reality. Yet he always stood slightly apart, an eye on the past as well as the future. He caught the fleeting images of life, from the twist of a dancer (*Le class de dance* (1874)) to a woman washing (*Femme au tub* (1885)). He was also an accomplished sculptor and draughtsman, while an interest in photography often inspired the composition of his paintings. Unlike his contemporaries, Degas always worked in the studio.

"NO ART WAS EVER LESS SPONTANEOUS THAN MINE,"
said Degas, renowned for capturing a snapshot of movement

What's in a name?
English art critic Roger
Fry coined the term
post-Impressionism in
1910, searching for a
convenient umbrella
under which to shelter
the varied French
artists who emerged
immediately after
Impressionism.

A fresh palette
Advances in the
chemical industry
and the discovery
of chromium vastly
improved the colour
palette available to
artists from the 1870s.
Suddenly, vibrant
yellows and oranges
were available
to blend with darker,
traditional earth
colours.

What was post-Impressionism?

Impressionism shone for a decade but was already old
hat by the early 1880s, the Impressionists themselves
responsible for many of the new ideas emerging. What
came next had no defining principles à la Impressionism
– the post-Impressionist tag didn't cover a particular
style, rather a disparate collection of artists bored of
painting simply what the eye could see. Instead, they
experimented with line, colour and structure, exploring
their subjective, emotional response to the world. They
were, however, indebted to the Impressionists' use
of colour, realist subject matter and radical brushwork.
Indeed, many of the big post-Impressionism names,
again dominated by the French, began by painting in
the Impressionist style.

Post-Impressionism: the big five

Paul Cézanne Cézanne, often called the father of modern
art, resonated through 20th century art. Encouraged by
Pissarro he flirted with the tenets of Impressionism, but
soon turned away from the light, developing instead an
interest in solidity and structure. The stroke of a brush
shouldn't simply mimic nature, it should convey the
fundamental substance of the apple, mountain, woman
etc. He wanted to harness every aspect of an object,
person or landscape and to concentrate it in paint. Such
elusive quarry made the irascible Cézanne obsessive. His
later years were spent painting the same scenes over
and over, most notably images of bathers and of Mont
St Victoire near his Provençal home. Eventually he tried
reducing everything to three shapes – cylinders, cones
and spheres – a progression that would emerge in Cubist
and abstract art.

1. Identity:
the foundations of
French culture

2. Literature
and philosophy

**3. Art, architecture
and design**

4. Performing arts

5. Arbiters of style:
fashion, photography
and cuisine

6. Media and
communications

7. Governing culture:
food and drink

8. Using culture: the
state in the home

Georges Seurat Like Cézanne, Seurat exhibited in the Impressionists' Parisian shows, adopting his hosts' interest in light and everyday subjects. However, in contrast to the spontaneity of Monet and co he painted using scientific colour theory, relying on the viewer's eye to blend tiny dots of paint into discernible forms. Most called the technique pointillism, some preferred divisionism. Seurat painted scenes of Parisian leisure, from the musicians of *Parade de Cirque* (1887-88) to the dancers of *Le Chahut* (1888-89). However, his most famous work was an early one: *Un dimanche après-midi à l'Ile de la Grande Jatte* (1884-86) with its statuesque figures on the banks of the Seine. Seurat died of diphtheria aged just 31.

Vincent van Gogh Well spotted, he was indeed Dutch. In fact, van Gogh only spent the last four years of his life in France, but such was the physical and spiritual impact of that period on his work that he can be considered in the context of French post-Impressionism. After viewing the Impressionists in Paris, van Gogh shed his rather sombre style in favour of vibrant colour. In particular he admired Seurat, as betrayed in his use of dots. As his style diverged from Impressionism, van Gogh was influenced by the strong, flat colours of traditional Japanese woodprints. Relocating to Arles, Provence, in 1888, his brushwork became increasingly expressive, with paint applied in thick dabs (impasto) to create the writhing energy so apparent in *Sunflowers* (1888) and *Starry Night* (1889), the latter painted during a stay at a Saint-Rémy asylum.

Paul Gauguin Like van Gogh, Gauguin's early work was informed by the Impressionists. However, he soon chose a more radical path, led away by the art of so-called 'primitive' cultures. A stockbroker by trade, Gauguin abandoned his wife and five children in 1886, moving to an artists' colony in Brittany where he painted life through flat shapes of vivid colour enclosed by black lines. Four years later he moved to Tahiti and further developed his primitive style, portraying island life in the likes of *Femme de Tahiti ou sur la plage* (1891). He died in obscurity aged 54, alone in his hut on the Marquesas Islands, and yet within a few years his painting revolutionized European art. His use of colour and the shaping of primitivism would guide Picasso's work.

1. Identity: 2 Literature   3. Art, architecture   4. Performing arts   5 Arbiters of style: 6. Media and   7. Consuming culture: 8 Living culture, the
the foundations of   and philosophy   and design   cinema, photography   communications   food and drink   state of the nation
French culture   and fashion

Anyone for coffee?
Toulouse-Lautrec only
grew to a height of
4ft 11in. Some have
suggested that years
of inbreeding by his
aristocratic heirs (his
parents were cousins)
caused the genetic
disease that stunted
his growth. He seemed
unperturbed, often
commenting: "I may only
be a small coffee pot,
but I have a big spout".

Vinnie suffers for his art
Van Gogh famously sliced
off part of his left ear,
later offering it wrapped
in newspaper to some
lucky lady of the night,
after a row with his
Yellow House-mate, Paul
Gauguin. By the time the
artist shot himself fatally
in the chest two years
later, he'd only actually
sold one painting. Yet
he produced hundreds
of startlingly vivid
compositions during
frenzied periods of work,
churning out 70 alone in
the final two months of
life. His work was roundly
eulogized within mere
months of his death.

Cézanne apparently broke
ties with his childhood
friend Emile Zola when
the author gave an
unflattering account of a
failed artist in his novel
L'Oeuvre.

Henri de Toulouse-Lautrec Unlike his contemporaries, Toulouse-Lautrec enjoyed some mortal success. His thick lines and flat bold colours – inspired by Japanese woodcuts – made fine bedfellows for new lithographic technology, and his reputation as one of the first great poster artists flourished. His oil paintings employed the same lines, coupled with masterly brushwork to convey the seedy sparkle of his subjects. Living in Montmartre, Toulouse-Lautrec sketched the bohemian life that surrounded him: cabaret dancers, prostitutes and inebriates all featured. The artist had broken both legs as a teenager and a congenital disorder stopped the bones from healing properly. Thus his legs stopped growing while his torso developed to normal proportions. Toulouse-Lautrec drank to excess in response to this physical deformity and was also an inveterate skirt chaser – passions that drew an alcoholic, syphilitic death aged just 36.

What was Pointillism?
George Seurat and the artists he inspired, in particular Paul Signac and Henri-Edmond Cross, devised Pointillism around the theory of scientist Eugène Chevreul.
He deduced that a colour could be radically altered depending on what other colours were placed next to it. 'Complementary' colours brought the most intense reaction from each other. The Pointillists painted tiny colour dots on the canvas and let the viewer's mind make the leap to composition.

Like watching paint dry
In contrast to
the spontaneous
Impressionists, Cézanne's
working methods
were meticulous and
painstaking. His friend

and art dealer Ambroise
Vollard sat 115 times
for a portrait that was
eventually abandoned.
Sitters were regularly
reprimanded for fidgeting
by the testy artist, while

the fruit he used in still
life paintings like *Nature morte: Les grosses pommes* (c.1890) would
sometimes shrivel before
the work was finished.

3.1.5 Seeing the world afresh: from prophets and wild beasts to Cubists

A new outlook

The French post-Impressionists shaped 20th century art. Schools and movements may have grouped amid the frenzy of themes and styles that emerged after Cézanne et al, but all, however radical, were the children of those late 19th century pioneers. In common they realized that art didn't have to directly represent the world, overturning centuries of creative convention.

Who were the Nabis?

The fleeting Nabis (Hebrew for 'prophets') movement actually emerged in the late 1880s, a direct and rapid descendant of post-Impressionism. Inspired by Gauguin, the Paris-centric members dispatched traditional perspective, preparing the ground for later abstract art. They favoured vivid colour, reflected not only in paintings but also in stained glass, ceramics and book illustration. Maurice Denis was the founder, but the main Nabis were Edouard Vuilllard and Pierre Bonnard. During his short-lived Nabis period, Bonnard drew inspiration from the simple form and bold colour of Japanese woodprints. However, his later work painted delicate domestic dramas, recording life with his lover Marthe, who often appeared on canvas mid-ablution or lounging on the bed.

What was Art Nouveau?

The turn of the 20th century saw Art Nouveau flourish across Europe and North America. It wasn't high art as such, led instead by the decorative arts, design and architecture. Flowing lineal design and elegant curves reflected the style's natural, organic influences, while shells and flowers exhumed the spectre of Rococo. In France, Art Nouveau found elegant form in the decorative glass of Émile Gallé and the jewellery of René Lalique.

An alternative Salon
Henri Matisse and André Derain helped to organize the first Salon d'Automne in 1903. It was an exhibition pitched against the conservatism of the official Salon de Paris. Renoir, Rodin, Cézanne, Picasso, Chagall and Braque all exhibited at what became a showcase for artistic innovation. The Salon d'Automne is still held each October.

The naïve customs official
Henri Rousseau carved a niche of his own with so-called 'naïve' painting. His best known paintings, *La charmeuse de serpents* (1907) among them, portray figures in the jungle although Rousseau never actually left France. Widely ridiculed, except by a few fellow artists like Picasso and Paul Signac, Rousseau was also known as *Le Douanier* on account of his career in customs.

The Fauvist Maurice de Vlaminck was a professional cyclist until typhoid cut his career short in 1896 and he turned instead to painting.

Name calling game
Fauve, which translates as wild beast, was a term first blurted in jest by art critic Louis Vauxcelles at the 1905 Salon d'Automne. Loud mouth Louis was also responsible for coining the term Cubism three years later after mentioning 'little cubes' whilst viewing a Georges Braque painting.

Too cool for school
The term *École de Paris* refers not to a specific school but to the collection of young foreign artists, Picasso, Modigliani and Brancusi among them, who flocked to the city in the early 20th century. Most stayed in Montparnasse.

Who were the Fauvists?

The Fauvists didn't have a doctrine, more a simple interest in outlandish colour that favoured pure expressionism over reality. Often unconcerned with perspective, Fauvist painting looked to the work of Gauguin and Cézanne, borrowing their thick lines. It was a short-lived affair beginning in 1905, spawning a trio of Parisian exhibitions and reaching its end within three years. Fauvism's leading light was Henri Matisse. He raided the piggy bank to buy Cézanne's *Trois Baigneuses* (c.1879-82) as a young man and studied the painting for inspiration each morning. He loved flat, colourful shapes bearing more expression than detail, as witnessed in *Le bonheur de vivre* (1905-06). André Derain and his studio-mate Maurice de Vlaminck were also important to the Fauve clique. The unrealistic colour and composition of Derain's paintings of London embody the Fauvist spirit.

Matisse: colourful character

Henri Matisse is regularly labelled the most significant French painter of the 20th century. As Fauvism and its main artists foundered, he continued to flourish, pursuing expression through colour right into the 1950s. Matisse moved from Paris to the Côte d'Azur in 1917 and remained there for much of his adult life. He painted the Mediterranean coast in bold shades, but became better known for capturing interiors, still life and women in various media. Unlike his friend and rival Picasso, Matisse never injected his work with political or social comment. Four decades after Fauvism, Matisse was still producing iconic work, as seen in the *Nu bleu* paper cut-out series of the early 1950s.

Who were the Cubists?

Cubism took a sledgehammer to traditional ways of seeing: art shouldn't be construed from a single angle, but rather its subject simultaneously viewed from various perspectives, allowing the viewer to move around inside the painting. The Cubists chopped the world into simple geometric shapes, as pioneered by Cézanne, and rebuilt it on the canvas. However, by mingling background and subject, Cubist paintings created a flat feel, intentionally emphasizing the two-dimensional nature of the canvas. Primitivism and non-western art, particularly African, influenced the shapes and emblems used in Cubist painting and sculpture. Think of Cubism and one name dominates, Pablo Picasso. Spanish he may have been, but his work unfurled largely in France. In Frenchman Georges Braque, Picasso had a close collaborator. They met in Montmartre in 1907 and developed Cubism in the years before the First World War. Picasso's *Les Demoiselles d'Avignon* (1907) is usually held up as the first Cubist painting but Braque's work was also crucial, developing the Cubist mode with paintings like *L'homme à la guitare* (1911). Juan Gris was another Spaniard whose work evolved in France, borrowing loud colour from his friend Matisse and applying it to Cubism. Robert Delaunay's brief relationship with the genre rendered *La Ville de Paris* (1912) in Cubist form, while Fernand Léger made an impact with colours and cylindrical shapes before renouncing Cubism during the First World War.

Picasso
The all-seeing I

Picasso painted his masterful statement on Spain's civil war, *Guernica,* for the Spanish Pavilion at the Paris International Exposition of 1937.

Cube of two halves
Early Cubism can be divided into two phases. The first, analytical Cubism, encompassed the early work of Picasso and Braque, in which an object was broken into different parts. From 1912 synthetic Cubism evolved, gathering different objects to construct new forms. Synthetic Cubism saw Picasso produce the first collage with *Nature morte à la chaise cannée* (1912).

Dada and the Surrealists

In 1917, former Cubist Marcel Duchamp presented the art world with a signed porcelain urinal. It was 'ready-made' art he enthused. He embraced the anti-art of Dada, a movement that looked to smash the order and rigidity it felt had been responsible for the First World War. Two years later, Duchamp drew a moustache on a print of the *Mona Lisa* and called it *LHOOQ* (1919). Surrealism emerged from the Dada movement in the early 1920s. Young artists and writers in Paris began exploring the unconscious mind, inspired in part by the writings of Sigmund Freud. The main protagonists weren't from France although they spent much of their time within its borders. Belgium's René Magritte, the Spaniard Salvador Dali and Germany's Max Ernst moved among the Surrealist community of Montparnasse.

Chagall's colourful imagination

Marc Chagall joined the many foreign artists moving to Paris in the early years of the 20th century. Born a Belarusian Jew, he spent much of his long life in France. He painted dreamy, folkish scenes inspired by childhood memories, a furtive imagination and the techniques of Cubism. Angels, cows and magic cockerels were all fair game. Living in Provence after the Second World War, he incorporated sculpture, stained glass and ceramics into work that was always imbued with vivid colour.

Post-war wind down

French art lost momentum after the Second World War. Paris, king of the art world for nearly a century, ran out of puff and New York took its crown. Foreign artists continued to trickle into the city but the emerging movements lacked any real significance outside their own narrow margins. Indeed, individual motifs – in which an artist's work was instantly recognizable – took increasing precedence. Even so, it's not easy to pick out the significant artists – there was no Monet, Rodin or Cézanne.

Abstract art in France

French artists embraced Abstract Expressionism in the 1940s and 50s, led by developments in North America. Labels like *l'art informel*, *tachisme* (derived from the French for 'stain') and *abstraction lyrique* helped to Frenchify the experience. They covered a wide range of styles and artists, most of who used dabs, splodges and drips of paint alongside more conventional methods. The rigid shapes of Geometric Abstraction, as pioneered by Belgian Piet Mondrian (who moved from Paris to New York in 1938), found fewer French devotees.

Scratching a living: Jean Dubuffet

Although he was influenced by the Surrealists and worked in the spirit of *l'art informel*, Jean Dubuffet personified the individualism in post-war French art. He amassed a collection of what he termed Art Brut: artwork he deemed truly expressive, ungoverned by intellectual theory – paintings by children, mental patients and prisoners. His own work reflected this interest with naïve, childish paintings. He scratched, textured and thickened (with tar, cement, leaves etc) the paint to make graffiti-like images of animals and people, best seen in the crude portrait, *Dhôtel nuancé d'abricot* (1947). He later turned to sculpture, carving rudimentary figures in polystyrene and large works in concrete.

Two French abstract artists

Georges Mathieu created impulsive, calligraphic explosions of paint on a huge scale. He painted one of his most famous, the six-metre long *Les Capétiens partout* (1954), in an hour and 20 minutes.

Pierre Soulanges worked largely in black on a white background, using thick impasto strokes and scoring the surface to reflect light. In the 1950s he added strong colours to the mix.

From the early 1960s, French artists worked increasingly in mixed media. Painters embraced sculpture and installation art, blurring the boundaries between disciplines.

The new Realists

The *nouveau réalisme* of the early 1960s is often viewed as a French answer to Pop Art. But the movement was less painterly, often expressed in collage or sculpture, with everyday rubbish a popular material. Arman famously created *Bluebeard's Wife* (1969), sculpting the female form by entombing old shaving brushes in polyester resin. His friend (they met through a shared love of judo) and fellow Nice boy was Yves Klein. Klein's 1958 exhibition *Le Vide* involved an empty gallery with bare white walls. However, his most famous work was *Anthropométrie de l'epoque bleue* (1960), in which naked women covered in blue paint rolled around on a white canvas to the appreciation of an audience in evening dress. Perhaps the excitement was too much – Klein died of a heart attack aged 34.

The Supports/Surfaces movement

As *nouveau réalisme* slipped from the avant-garde, the Supports/Surfaces movement honed into view in the early 1970s. Based largely in southern France, they weren't defined by a particular style as such, more an interest in taking apart the conventions of painting. They turned the components – the canvas, frame and other materials – into the actual artwork, painting on whatever objects or surfaces they chose. The movement also had a political edge, and some artists tried to weave the Maoist spirit of May 68 into the project. It was a short-lived affair; they held four exhibitions between 1969 and 1974. Claude Viallat, known for his flat knot motif, was among the most successful.

The conceptual artists

Conceptual art also flourished in the 1960s and 70s. It placed the artist's ideas above the finished artwork, generating challenging results. The French variant had its source in Marcel Duchamp's urinal and trickled down through the work of Yves Klein. Daniel Buren is one of the best known, famed for his use of the humble stripe in public spaces. He began by fly-posting stripy posters on the Paris Metro but soon became part of the established order, as seen with *Les Deux Plateaux* (1986), a 3,000 metre square arrangement of columns (stripy, of course) commissioned by Mitterrand's government for the courtyard of the Palais Royal.

Five contemporary French artists

Christian Boltanski A leading artist since the 1960s, Boltanski paints, sculpts, installs and photographs on themes preoccupied with memory. Using everything from anonymous passport photos to biscuit tins he arranges altar-like compositions tackling themes like the Holocaust.

Sophie Calle The leading French conceptual artist Calle once followed a man to Venice, taking surreptitious photographs later exhibited as *Suite Venitienne* (1979). For *Room with a View* (2003) she spent a night in bed at the top of the Eiffel Tower.

Orlan A much-hyped performance artist who examines perceptions of the body. Since 1990 she has been working on *The Reincarnation of Saint Orlan*, undergoing regular plastic surgery for a new look that blends Mona Lisa, Venus and Europa.

Annette Messager An installation artist who often clumps fragments, such as photographs, together to make new work. *Mes Voeux* (1988-91) featured dozens of photos of body parts hung in the gallery in clusters.

Philippe Parreno A French-Algerian artist who often works collaboratively in video or film. *Zidane, un portrait du 21e siècle* (2006) used 17 synchronized cameras to film the former French football captain through the length of a whole game.

Read all about it

In 1983 artist Sophie Calle found an address book on a Parisian pavement. She sent it back to the male owner but not before photocopying its contents. Calle then called some of the contacts in the address book to talk about the man. Her findings were serialized on the front page of Libération newspaper every day for a month. The book's owner, a film-maker, was outraged and demanded settlement. That settlement came when Libération published a front page photo of Calle, nude, as demanded by the man and agreed to by the artist.

A lot to live up to

In light of its noble ancestry you can see how contemporary French art might suffer from a little performance anxiety. How do you follow Cézanne or Matisse? Individual artists continue to create challenging new work, often in collaboration, but little of global import has emerged over the last two decades. When it does, it will no doubt be shown first in Paris at the famous Centre Georges Pompidou or the Palais de Tokyo, a radical museum where you can get interactive with the avant-garde.

3.1.7 Form and function: French design

The Duralex Picardie Glass
You know the one – the unpretentious beaker on every restaurant table in France, perfect for slurping wine. Mass-produced since 1927, the multi-sided glass is still being made near Orleans.

The Citroën DS
The shark-nosed icon of French motoring was actually designed by an Italian, Flamino Bertoni. It sold 12,000 on its first day in 1955, while philosopher Roland Barthes pondered whether it had "fallen from the sky". *Fashion Fades, but Style Remains* read the prophetic advert.

The Juicy Salif
Philippe Starck designed the tripod lemon squeezer for Alessi in 1990 and it soon found its way into numerous homes, not to mention the MOMA in New York. Just don't ask whether it actually works…

Form and function: French design

French society has harboured an urbane, design-conscious layer ever since it first kicked back in a Louis XV chair. In the last century or so, the appreciative clique has broadened and embraced Art Nouveau, Art Deco and Modernism, guided by the likes of Gallé and Le Corbusier in their choice of buildings, furniture and gadgets. Today, the style-loyal masses expand alongside disposable incomes and the irrepressible French love of new fads – being *de rigueur* still counts for an awful lot. Instinctively the French seem to give aesthetics equal billing to function, and many of the icons of modern French style, from the Metro sign to the Citroën 2CV, are drawn from the working world. Philippe Starck is the best-known contemporary French designer. Prolific and ingenious he brings an offbeat twist to everyday objects that consumers love, as seen in the Dr Kiss Toothbrush and the Gun Lamp. Starck has also designed interiors around the world, from Mitterrand's Elysée Palace apartment to the St Martins Lane Hotel, London. Many of the most successful French designers of recent years have found an outlet in the transport industry, not least Paul Bracq who came up with the Mercedes-Benz 600 before helping to concoct the TGV. In graphic design, the M/M duo in Paris has drawn international attention through projects with Björk, Calvin Klein and Stella McCartney. If you want to see what the latest French design crop are up to, seek out the bi-lingual *Intramuros* magazine.

Roland Barthes about to be very impressed

3.2 Architecture

Classical tenants stamped their own tastes on the buildings of Roman Gaul before the French themselves led the charge in a wave of more recent architectural schools. The result is a structural smorgasbord of different styles.

3.2.1 Classical remains: Gallo-Roman architecture

Location is everything
The Romans built throughout France. However, surviving architecture from the Gallo-Roman period is best seen in the Auvergne and, in greatest abundance, Provence. The reason? These areas suffered less at the hands of invaders and haven't been reshaped by development to the same extent as more populous areas to the north.

To the Victor the spoils
In the Latin Quarter of Paris lie the remains of a Gallo-Roman amphitheatre. The Arènes de Lutèce was built to seat 15,000 people in the 1st century AD. It was rediscovered in the 19th century during excavations to build a new tram depot. Author Victor Hugo led the successful campaign for its preservation.

Built to last
The Romans gave France its first sup of civic pride. Their arrival in Gaul brought a flourish of public buildings, town planning and civil engineering projects to a region previously free of architectural swagger. A thousand years on, their talents resurfaced in the guise of grand Romanesque cathedrals and, later still, Napoleon III recalled the classical pomp of Rome as he rebuilt central Paris.

What did the Romans build in France?
Between the first and the fourth centuries, the Romans and their Gaulish lackeys built theatres, arenas, public baths, temples and aqueducts throughout France, some of which remain almost wholly intact. Granted, they pilfered their best architectural motifs from the Greeks (columns) and the Etruscans (arches), but indigenous French architecture was nevertheless humbled in the face of Roman grandeur. They could rightfully claim concrete as their own, usually hiding it beneath brick, stone or marble to bring a cheap and brilliant solidity to their buildings. Domestic dwellings were less grandiose, apart from the large villas that used the sculpture, mosaics and frescos hitherto unseen in France.

Super structures: five sublime pieces of Gallo-Roman architecture in France

Nîmes Amphitheatre
An elliptical two-storey survivor from the 1st century AD, Les Arènes once held 25,000 people. Today the crowds still flock to watch bullfighting.

Théâtre Antique d'Orange
The restored Roman theatre in Orange is still used for concerts, plays and an annual summer opera festival.

Vaison-la-Romaine
The largest archaeological site in France, located in Provence, was a Roman city for five centuries. It's the nearest thing you'll find to Pompeii on this side of the Med.

Temple d'Auguste et Livie
Chief among the varied Roman remains of Vienne in the Rhône Valley, the 10BC temple sports the kind of grand Corinthian columns that came to epitomize classical architecture.

Pont du Gard
The highest aqueduct ever built by the Romans, crossing the River Gard north of Nîmes in three arch-lavished tiers, remains a startling sight nearly 2,000 years after its inception.

Roam around France today and before too long the pinnacle of some monumental church pierces the horizon. We've got the God loving architects of the Middle Ages to thank: between the 10th and 15th centuries they set their adoration in stone, clarifying the clergy's growing clout and creating some of the country's most inspiring buildings. The period of building, encouraged by an era of relative political stability, can be viewed in two phases – Romanesque and Gothic.

Romanesque architecture and how to recognize it

The Romanesque building spurt began circa 950 and continued for two centuries. Crumbling Roman structures and Byzantine style inspired western European builders who, amid the climate of fervent monasticism, erected churches with round arches, barrelled vaults and chunky piers. They tended to be quite dark, the only light often coming through small, high 'clerestory' windows. Carved stone decoration appeared for the first time since the decline of the Roman Empire. Regional styles rapidly emerged. Burgundy was a hot bed of Romanesque architecture and Cluny harboured its monastic big boy, a gargantuan limestone abbey eventually undone by the Revolution. In Provence the style took an elegant, simpler shape, the closer proximity to Rome reflected in the use of domes. In western France, stone carving made the buildings more ornate, while twin towers became a feature of northern Romanesque churches.

Five of the best Romanesque buildings in France

Abbaye de Sénanque
Gordes. The simple Provençal Romanesque abbey still houses a monastic community.

Basilique Madeleine
Vézélay. Burgundy's finest Romanesque church also features Gothic embellishment.

Basilique de St-Sernin
Toulouse. The largest Romanesque basilica in Europe boasts a tiered octagonal belfry.

Abbaye de Sainte-Foy
Conques. A fine Romanesque abbey church in the Lot valley.

Église St-Etienne
Caen. Typical of the austere, undecorated Norman approach to Romanesque architecture.

What's in a name?
The Romanesque and Gothic labels were coined centuries after the periods they describe. The term Gothic appeared in the Reformation, perhaps used derogatorily to describe a style some saw as barbaric. At the time of construction, Gothic churches were referred to as being in the 'French Style'.

Vicious circles
Many of the Gothic cathedrals were built with pavement labyrinths made up of 11 concentric circles, around which the faithful would shuffle on their knees as a form of penance. Chartres and Amiens cathedrals retain their floor patterns.

Gothic reaches for the heavens

When architects in the Île de France began to innovate in the 13th century they really outdid themselves. Gothic was born: ceilings and spires got higher, windows larger and stonework more ornate. The development of the flying buttress provided exterior support for the nave, which was raised to astounding new heights. Arches became more pointed and supported greater weights, while tracery (carving) gave walls and windows a brittle icing of decoration. Thin, soaring columns allowed more light in and stained glass came to the fore. Gargoyles and statues completed the look. The great cathedrals of the High Gothic period clustered in northern France, offering structural confirmation of the region's sophistication. Towns like Chartres, Amiens and Reims did battle for the most spectacular church; Beauvais took it too far and their overambitious 46-metre high nave crashed to the ground. Style overtook scale in Gothic's 15th century denouement with the so-called Flamboyant period of ornate carving. Gothic architecture enjoyed something of a revival in the mid 19th century. The resurgence was most pronounced in England, while in France the restoration of the fortified city of Carcassonne in Languedoc-Roussillon was spectacularly realized in the Gothic style.

Old new towns

The 13th century *bastide* towns of southern France represent a more practical facet of medieval French architecture. Like the great abbeys and cathedrals, they emerged in a rare period of European stability, built in sparsely populated areas to encourage new growth. Residents were tempted by the promise of their own land on the edge of town. Typically perched on a hilltop for security, *bastides* were built to a grid pattern arranged around an arcaded central marketplace. They became key strategic targets during The Hundred Years' War. Hundreds of *bastide* towns, Najac, Domme and Montauban among them, survive between the Dordogne and the Pyrenees.

Following the clergy's lead, the post-medieval aristocracy began to splash cash on their buildings. The new-found solidity of royal power in the Île de France allowed kings and nobles alike the luxury of investing in what they called hunting lodges. The chateaux and palaces that emerged between the 16th and 18th centuries had one overriding theme, Classicism.

Riverside living: the Renaissance chateaux

Grand architecture in northern France was still Gothic-led in the early 16th century when François I returned from the Italian Wars with Renaissance ideas, architects and craftsmen in tow. Their timing was perfect: chateaux had previously been designed with defence in mind but now, as the threat of feudal violence receded, they were built or adapted with showy elegance. The transition from Gothic to Renaissance unravelled alongside the Loire where nobles set up shop within earshot of the king. The decoration and symmetry of the Renaissance with its classical base met with the elaborate pointy majesty of Gothic and produced a very French style. Chambord, the Loire's biggest chateau, embodied the new mode, its Gothic structure cloaked in cupolas, domes and other Italianate ornamentation. Some have suggested Leonardo da Vinci, a guest of the French king, worked on the designs. The double helix staircase certainly carries his ingenuity.

Baroque growth spurt

The building frenzy on the banks of the Loire continued over the next century, depositing dozens of chateaux with their distinctive conical slate towers. But, as the king's power settled around Paris, so the grand structures moved closer to the capital. The Baroque

Dome improvement
The dome was an important feature of Baroque architecture, and for France the most famous Baroque dome of all adorns the classical 17th century church of Les Hôtel des Invalides, Paris. Louis XIV commissioned the cupola-topped golden dome in 1676 from Jules Hardouin-Mansart, whose great uncle Mansart had done so much to instigate classical design in France.

period moved French architecture from the decorative Renaissance style to the plainer form of Classicism. Columns, in the shape of ornamental pilasters, were back. Architect François Mansart did much of the legwork, hammering away at symmetry. He was responsible for the iconic mansard roof with its four steeply pitched sides. Louis Le Vau left an even greater legacy. He designed the geometrically immaculate Vaux le Vicomte chateau in the 1650s, before beefing up his efforts for Louis XIV's palace at Versailles a decade later. Le Vau worked in tandem with landscape gardener André Le Nôtre to create the classical order that reflected the state's unbending authority.

Creative differences: Rococo and neo-Classical
A rather flaky backlash to the *grand siècle's* formality came with the Rococo design of Louis XV's reign in the early 18th century. While Rococo originated in France, it rarely infiltrated architecture here as it did elsewhere in Europe. The highlights were largely limited to rambling decorative and interior design features incorporating shells, leafs and other natural shapes. In the mid 18th century, Classicism kicked back and remained the dominant architectural style right through the regime changes of the following century. Strict symmetry, porticoes, triangular pediments and small *oeil de bouef* windows were all features of the reinvigorated style. The Panthéon in Paris, completed in 1790, shows how neo-Classicism took the earlier reverence for antique models to new levels. The Revolution and Empire did little to halt its progress, as seen in Napoleon III's so-called Second Empire-style Paris.

Lost civilizations

Lutetia, as the settlers of Roman Paris called their city, left little architectural trace, its gridiron pattern erased. Alas, little remains of medieval Paris either, a time when the city, like many in Europe, found its feet. The Gothic churches, Notre-Dame particularly, we can still see, but the labyrinthine tangle of narrow streets overhung by timber-framed housing has disappeared apart from the odd Marais pocket. The original Louvre, then a fortified palace, was built into the city walls in 1190. La Conciergerie on the Île de la Cité, for centuries a fearsome prison, dates back to the 11th century in parts.

Where the other half lived

When wealthier Parisians began building in stone at the end of the medieval period they created the *hôtel*, essentially an aristocratic residence. Early versions had coned turrets projecting out over street corners. The Hôtel de Sens, built at the end of the 15th century, is a rare survival story. While successive kings lavished their money elsewhere, the *hôtels* were left to develop Classicism in the capital, conforming to symmetrical modesty in building, courtyard and garden.

Space age

The spaghetti of medieval Parisian streets survived the *grand siècle* largely intact. State expenditure went on war and palaces rather than large scale urban planning, and most grand public buildings remained hemmed in by a mesh of aged housing. Things began to change under Louis XV. The 20-acre Place de la Concorde (initially called Place Louis XV) replaced a swamp in 1775 under Louis XV's guidance, kick-starting a move towards large public spaces. Jacques-Ange Gabriel was the architect of choice, patronizing Classicism with the straight lines and facades of the big piazza. Ironically, it wouldn't be long before Louis XV's kind were being executed in the same square.

Street crime

Henry IV was assassinated in 1610 in the Rue de la Ferronnerie when a traffic jam in the narrow street provided his assailant with a perfect chance to draw his knife. The street was duly widened under Louis XIV.

Louis does Paris

The most spectacular public building in Paris left from the Sun King's reign is the Collège des Quatre-Nations, built on the Right Bank by Versailles architect, Le Vau. In the 1670s, Le Vau also initiated the capital's penchant for a classical triumphal arch: the Porte Saint-Denis, designed by François Blondel, is a suitably grand example of what followed.

The triumphs to which Paris' most famous arch refers were Napoleon's, under whose rule it was conceived in 1806. Work on the 51-metre-tall neo-Classical titan stalled under the restored monarchy and took 30 years to finish. Urban planner Baron Haussmann later used the Arc as the axis for Place de l'Étoile in the 1860s, radiating 12 grand avenues from its hub.

Exhibition piece
La Tour Eiffel was built in 1889 as a temporary showpiece at the Universal Exhibition. A timely comment on engineering prowess as much as architectural design, the 1,063ft tall tower got a critical battering when it first went up.

Baron's Paris

Modern Paris was forged in the 19th century, developing its neo-Classical character under Napoleon III. In 1853 the Emperor commissioned Baron Haussmann, Prefect of the Seine, to level the medieval mesh and replace it with wide, elegant boulevards. The move was partly inspired by the 1848 Revolution: Napoleon astutely figured barricades would be easier to remove in wider streets.
He created an extensive sewerage system, made new parks, including the Bois de Boulogne and Parc Monceau, and reduced other green spaces to accommodate new, tree-lined streets. Uniformity was crucial – building height was regulated by road width. Some say he destroyed medieval Paris, others that he replaced squalor with modernity. The Second Empire-style that developed amid Haussmann's new plan is best seen in the lavish neo-Baroque of the Opéra Garnier (the Opéra de Paris, renamed after its architect in 1989), commissioned in 1861.

Ego building: five *grands projets*

Paris remains a city of grand architectural gestures. There's always some big, state commissioned project on the go, attempting to radicalize the Paris landscape or simply immortalize a leader's legacy in stone. Here are five *grands projets* guaranteed to raise heated debate:

Centres Georges Pompidou
Finished in 1977, the famously inside out home of French modern art was designed by a Brit and an Italian.

Pyramid du Louvre
Built for the Revolution bicentenary in 1989 to Mitterrand's commission, the Louvre's glass pyramid has always been controversial.

Grande Arche de la Défense
Another of Mitterrand's *grands projets,* an arch celebrating humanity inaugurated in 1989, bookends the Axe Historique like a 100-metre high croquet hoop.

Fondation Cartier
A rare French design among Mitterrand's architectural legacy, Jean Nouvel's 1994 home for contemporary art is a translucent mix of glass and steel.

Musée du Quai Branly
Chirac's *grand projet*, a museum dedicated to world art, gained a mixed response on opening in 2006 despite being another Nouvel design.

Architecture in the belle époque

The cultural and social freedom of the *belle époque* appeared in Parisian architecture at the end of the 19th century. Art Nouveau was the main movement and Hector Guimard its chief of staff. New materials, particularly iron, were woven decoratively among glass and brick in radical, flowing curves. The 1901 exterior design of Jules Lavirotte at 29 Avenue Rapp, all plants, animals and naked ladies, shows off Art Nouveau at its decorative peak. The style also lives on in the Metro station designs of Hector Guimard, most spectacularly at the twisting entrance to Porte Dauphine. The Grand Palais, Galeries Lafayette department store and Musée d'Orsay (formerly a railway station) all capture the elegant Art Nouveau preoccupation with iron and glasswork in the early 20th century.

Communication
breakdown
While Le Corbusier's most original buildings lie within France, his visions for a new mode of urban living found equal success outside the country, as seen in the new city of Chandigarh in India or the Brazilian Ministry of Health and Education building in Rio. The French state picked up Le Corbusier's grand plans rather late in the day; when it did eventually adopt his ideas for mass housing and urban planning, the grim, slabbed interpretations lacked Le Corbusier's eye for style or social interaction. The uninspiring medium-rise *banlieues* attached to the fringes of large French cities are the product of this communication breakdown.

Art Nouveau's architectural ambitions died a swift death in the early 20th century and little of significance filled its immediate wake. When architects did get the chance to work afresh, much of what they produced drew on the neo-Classicism of the 19th century. The reflective mood continued during the interwar years, albeit pepped up with Art Deco and the growing taste for Modernism. However, with little spare cash available for grand architectural projects, the era's rather flaccid spirit left little to celebrate in the way of grand erections.

What was Art Deco?

The term Art Deco originated with the Exposition des Arts Décoratifs in Paris in 1925. In architecture, as in design, it was characterized by precise, functional lines and shapes, enlivened with strong colours and the sensuousness of Art Nouveau and Expressionism. The spectacular old swimming pool in Roubaix, in the Nord region, recently converted into a museum, is a rare and brilliant example of French Art Deco architecture.

What was Modernism?

Modernism in architecture, also referred to as the International Style, took its lead from the wonder material of the interwar years, reinforced concrete. Straight lines provided a new take on the symmetry of Classical design. Belgian-born concrete lover Auguste Perret was an earlier pioneer: he built the first reinforced concrete church in Le Raincy, an eastern suburb of Paris,

Corb finding inspiration when before there was nun

with his brother Gustave in the early 1920s. After World War II, Auguste played an important role in rebuilding Le Havre in concrete. However, the undisputed maestro of Modernism in French architecture was Le Corbusier.

Designs for life: Le Corbusier

Charles-Édouard Jeanneret, born in the Swiss Jura in 1887, was a giant of 20th century architecture. Better known to all as Le Corbusier (adopted from his grandfather's name), a French citizen from 1930, he pioneered functionalism – a building, street or entire city should be designed as a "machine for living". Villa Savoye, built in Poissy near Paris in 1929, used concrete to create a house with thin pillars, strips of windows, an open plan interior and a flat roof terrace – it proved seminal. In the 1940s he created his first *Unité d'Habitation* with the Cité Radieuse in Marseilles. A large apartment block incorporating shops, a school and a hotel, the building crystallized his utopian vision of urban living. Later on, still working largely in concrete, Le Corbusier began using softer lines. The curvy Notre-Dame-du-Haut Chapel in Ronchamp, Jura, built 1950-55, remains remarkably original.

Returning to form: contemporary architecture

Architects on the *grands projets* (Pyramid du Louvre, the derided Bibliothèque Nationale de France etc) of Paris were largely sourced through competition, and most came from overseas. The home-grown post-modern architecture that surfaced in the final decades of the 20th century came in the shape of individual idiosyncratic builds often made with traditional materials. They took their cue from Le Corbusier's Ronchamp chapel. In the 1990s, glass and steel came to the fore, with public buildings making correlation between internal and external space. Jean Nouvel has emerged as the contemporary French architect de rigueur. In Lyons, he placed an arched metal and glass vault atop the neo-Classical opera house in 1993. The engaging glass and granite Musée d'Art Moderne et Contemporain in Strasbourg was completed in 1998 by another leading French architect, Adrien Fainsilber. The most exciting public project of the new millennium is the Centre Pompidou, Metz; a €35million offspring of the famous 1970s Parisian parent featuring a vast 'thrown over' lattice glass roof.

Troubling developments
A number of grand new builds in France have been dogged by problems. After the towering buildings of the new Bibliothèque Nationale were constructed largely in glass, the sunlight that poured in was found to damage the books. Elsewhere in Paris, parts of the Grande Arche de la Défense began falling off early in its life. Paul Andreu, one of the architects who worked on the arch, also drew up the plans for Terminal 2E at Charles de Gaulle airport, a section of which collapsed in 2004 killing four people.

Over half of French homes have been built since the end of the Second World War.

As with all things French, domestic architecture is subject to marked regional variation. Traditional house styles have been shaped by available materials, farming practices and weather patterns. In the cities the established urban French living space, the apartment, remains dominant. Yet new towns were created in the 1960s and elsewhere suburbia creeps out, allowing more and more people to own their own house. The less financially blessed find themselves in high-rise housing projects.

Life with the animals

French farmhouses have always been designed by function. Traditionally, animals and people shared one roof. The so-called *maison bloc* was common: the *chalet* of the Alps and Jura incorporated a cattle shed, house and large hayloft, while the *longère* of Brittany and Normandy placed animals and people side by side in one long building. Courtyard homesteads, as found in the cereal growing regions of northern France, were slightly less intimate, their buildings sheltering activity in the farmyard. The wine regions produced farmhouses built over or around a large cellar.

Rising to the occasion

As the post-war population drained from the land, a building programme of new apartment blocks began. The HLMs (*habitations à loyer modéré*) were built around French towns and cities in *grands ensembles*, replacing the shanty-like settlements that had grown up amid a chronic housing shortage. Today, around one in five people live in the repetitive rectangular blocks, and they account for almost half of all rented accommodation in France.

Vernacular architecture around the regions

Normandy
Charming half-timbered facades inland and in the north, and sturdy granite houses further south and on the coast.

Brittany
A humble mix of granite (both pink and grey) walls and slate roofs. Also harbours half-timbered medieval buildings.

Nord and Picardy
A rare brick enclave, the northern tip of France features largely post-war housing.

Alsace
Half-timbered houses with steeply pitched roofs, becoming more chalet-like in the Vosges Mountains.

Auvergne
The dark, slate buildings of the Auvergne uplands reflect the area's traditionally harsh living conditions.

Provence
Chunky limestone walls bound by an earthy mortar and small windows defy both summer heat and the Mistral. Terracotta tiles lie on the softly pitched roofs.

Alps and Jura
Alpine chalets, a mix of stone and local timber, dominate the uplands.

Les Pays Basque
Large whitewashed farmhouses and brightly coloured timbered properties.

Filling in the gaps
A mix of cow dung, clay and twigs was traditionally placed between the studs of half-timbered houses found as far apart as Alsace, les Pays Basque and Normandy. Wealthier residents sometimes used brick. Other areas built in stone, although when the raw material proved unavailable or too expensive builders used *pisé*, blocks of compressed clay – the word translates as 'pounded'.

The phrase *Maison Bourgeoise* typically refers to a large stone house, traditionally built for a wealthy businessman. Grand windows and roomy interiors are the norm.

Performing arts

4 Performing arts

4.1 Music

Think of French music and the warbling of Piaf might come to ear. Maybe you catch a relaxing fragment of Satie or perhaps your feet move to the industrial beats of Daft Punk. Either way, you're tapping into a remarkably diverse aural legacy.

"TOUT FINIT PAR
DES CHANSONS"
(EVERYTHING ENDS
WITH SONGS) –

French proverbial phrase

National anthems

On the international music stage, one indigenous musical form remains closely associated with France – the *chanson*. Aligned to French national identity, the *chanson* has undergone many transformations in its long history and remains elusive to encapsulate, yet it forms a musical link from the Middle Ages to modern day. Popularist, rallying, melodramatic and introspective, this multifaceted and ambiguous genre still manages to tug at France's heartstrings, encompassing everything from the 13th century writings of Adam de la Halle to the anarchic slices of life produced by punk poet Renaud.

Where did the *chanson* come from?

The *chanson*'s tradition of setting poetry to music has its roots in the *troubadours*, or *trouveres*, who were invariably attached to the princely courts of the Middle Ages, with some actually being of royal blood. Guilhem IX, Duke of Aquitaine and Count of Poitiers (1071-1129) is one such royal Prince whose poems have survived. Others drew their livelihood directly from their art – the height of the *troubadour* culture in the second half of the 12th century spawned three big names: Giraut de Bornelh, Arnaut Daniel and Bernart de Ventadorn. They created songs that were performed by musicians called *joglars* in Provence or *jongleurs* in northern France. During the 16th century, *chansons* gained wider popularity when France's first music publisher, the prolific Pierre Attaignant, produced some 50 collections in Paris.

Keeping the *chanson* tradition alive

In the modern age the *chanson*'s popularity has waxed and waned, and in the early 20th century found itself rapidly ousted by the crowd-pleasing talents of music hall and burlesque. During the 1930s, however, the *chanson* was revived by the likes of Edith Piaf and Charles Trenet. The tradition continued to evolve during the 1960s with Left Bank cabaret singers, or *chansonniers*, such as Serge Gainsbourg, Georges Brassens and Jacques Brel, a Belgian who spent much of his life in Paris. Today, as popular French music increasingly derives global inspiration, the *chanson* is slowly becoming a niche musical form. While contemporary artists such as Patricia Kaas keep the tradition alive at home, the genre still fails to sell significantly abroad despite the translation of many celebrated songs into English.

Birdsong: Edith Piaf

The fragile, diminutive frame of France's legendary 'Singing Sparrow', Edith Piaf, belied her powerful vibrato. Piaf brought the *chanson* to international renown with the instantly recognizable *Non, je ne regrette rien* (1960), a torch song for the lowlife survivor. Her early life is shrouded in mystery but it's believed she was raised in a Normandy brothel by her grandmother. This gritty upbringing may have given her later songs their authentic realism. Active in the French Resistance during the war, a car accident in 1951 left Piaf addicted to morphine. She died on the French Riviera in 1963: 40,000 fans jammed the cemetery at her Parisian burial.

The five modern *chansons* you need to hear

La mer
Charles Trenet (1946). He wrote nearly a thousand songs, but none more famous than this, covered a staggering 4,000 times.

Les amoureux des bancs publics
Georges Brassens (1953). An anthem to young love from a singer who has been called the French Bob Dylan.

Non, je ne regrette rien
Edith Piaf (1960). Piaf dedicated the most famous of *chansons* to the French Foreign Legion.

Ne me quitte pas
Jacques Brel (1972). A story of romantic disillusionment from an album of the same name.

La mer opale
Coralie Clément (2002). Softly sung proof that the *chanson* is alive and well on home turf.

Edith Piaf was born Edith Giovanna Gassion. The name Piaf, Parisian slang for sparrow, was adopted for the stage.

Centre of excellence

During the late Middle Ages, France was recognized as being at the centre o~ European music and the leading influence in all styles. The earliest forms of polyphony (music with a number of parts), known as organum, are discovered in manuscripts from 10th century French cities such as Tours, Chartres and Montpellier. Limoges was home to a group of musicians in the Abbey of St Martial who were particularly important to musical development throughout the 10th and 11th centuries. Of similar stature are the composers who were associated with the cathedral of Notre Dame in Paris during the 12th century. Perhaps the most notable of these were Leonin and Perotin who produced some of the earliest motets, providing a rhythmic section distinct from the longer chant-like organum, as well as various theoretical treatises on music.

The secular voice

While the monks and co made sweet early music in their abbeys, the medieval period also gave rise to secular music in France, celebrated in the works of the itinerant *troubadours* and *trouveres*. The *troubadours* performed songs in the vernacular style and created musical forms such as the *lai* and *ballade*, which repeated a refrain at the end of each stanza. Perhaps the most famous *trouvere* is the aristocratic Adam de la Halle who moved from writing liturgical poetry to the secular form. His most memorable work is *Jeu de Robin et Marion* (late 13th century), cited as the earliest French play to include secular music.

To Burgundy and back: mixed Renaissance fortunes

The Renaissance era saw music's centre of gravity shift from Paris to Burgundy, a separate state at that time. Burgundy played host to the leading musicians in Europe who came to the area in the 15th century to study with the state's leading composers, men like Guillame Dufay and Gilles Binchois. However, as the 15th century drew to a close, a distinctive style of music emerged in the royal court and ecclesiastical centres back in France, turning away from the Franco-Flemish variant and seeking out a lighter, more approachable sound, most recognizable in the secular *chanson*.

Songs of the Reformation

The Calvinism of the 16th century Reformation convinced Protestant musicians to produce music of a much simpler form. Moreover, in areas where Calvinism was strictly adhered to, the only music permitted took the form of songs sung in unison of French translations of the Psalms. Works indicative of the era were produced by Claude Goudimel and Claude Le Jeune. Goudimel was killed in the St Bartholomew's Day Massacre, like much of Lyons' Huguenot population.

Baroque stars

By the 17th Century, opera was flourishing and French composers such as Jean-Baptiste Lully, court composer to Louis XIV, and, in the 18th century, Jean-Philippe Rameau were writing operas that were particularly French in style. French harpsichord music was also highly respected in the Baroque era. Composers such as François Couperin and Jacques Champion de Chambonnieres introduced new styles of fingering and keyboard technique.

A Romantic affair with Berlioz

The early 19th century found France still reeling from the unrest and turmoil of the Revolution and the Napoleonic wars – both doing little to further musical progression – yet also gave birth to one of the Romantic period's greatest composers, Hector Berlioz. Credited with pushing forward the development of the modern symphony orchestra, Berlioz's most famous work is the semi-autobiographical *Symphonie Fantastique* (1830), which explored the composer's obsession with the Irish actress Harriet Smithson. Typical of the Romantic period in its depth of emotion, Berlioz's mastery of the orchestra at times bewildered 19th century audiences but his extravagant style is now widely recognized as being ahead of its time.

A pole apart
Frédéric Chopin, the great Romantic composer for piano, was actually a Pole who spent his short adult life in Paris. He wrote and played expressive, small-scale pieces like the *Waltz in D flat major* (better known as the *Minute Waltz*)(1846) and *Étude in C minor* (or *The Revolutionary Étude*)(c.1831).

Five greats of French classical music

In the late 19th and early 20th century, French classical music enjoyed its most successful period. Berlioz had laid the foundations with his Romantic style, and a number of globally significant composers subsequently kept France near the top of the musical tree. Bizet brought flamboyance and colour to the opera (see the Theatre section for more information), while elsewhere five great composers emerged:

Camille Saint-Saëns Child prodigy Saint-Saëns (he composed his first piece aged three!) grew into a moody adult, spending much of his time sniping at his musical peers. However, he still pulled off the 14 light movements of *Le carnaval des animaux* (1886) with deft virtuosity. He duly forbade the performance of nearly all its content during his lifetime. Refusing to immerse himself in Romanticism, Saint-Saëns wrote conservative (some said unemotional), elegant and immaculately structured music. He also wrote plays, philosophy and poetry.

Gabriel Fauré Saint-Saëns' pupil and close friend developed the Berlioz tradition but invested it with a cleaner, more polished edge. In particular Fauré is remembered for his mastery of the French song, or *mélodie*, many setting the music to poems by literary giants like Hugo, Baudelaire and Verlaine. He arranged a cycle of Verlaine's poems in *La Bonne Chanson* (1892-94), one of his finest works. However, Fauré is best remembered for his poignant *Requiem* (1877-90).

1. Identity:
the foundations of
French culture
2. Language
and philosophy
3. Art, architecture
and design
4. Performing arts
5. Pleasures of a grand
cuisine, photography
and fashion
6. Media and
newspaper news
7. Laws and political
force, the state
8. Living culture: the
street of the nation

Claude Debussy Usually referred to as the Impressionist composer, a label that infuriated him, Debussy brought new, radical harmonies to Western music. He tried out new chords and employed progressive rhythms, reacting against the formality of composers like Saint-Saëns, and duly influencing everyone from Olivier Messiaen to Duke Ellington. Like Fauré, he composed songs to the words of contemporary poets, not least Baudelaire, Verlaine and Mallarmé, the latter of whom inspired Debussy's famous *Prélude à l'après-midi d'un faune* (1894).

Maurice Ravel Tutored at the Paris Conservatoire by Fauré, Ravel was perhaps less radical than Debussy, keeping more to the classical form in composition, albeit with new harmonies. Like Debussy, he is often termed an Impressionist composer, influenced by new harmonies from East and West. Of course, he's known best for *Boléro*, a work for which Ravel himself showed little enthusiasm and which, with its overly dramatic style, isn't particularly indicative of his oeuvre. Much of his work had a Spanish edge, not least *Rhapsodie espagnole* (1907), enhanced no doubt by his mother's Basque origins.

Naughty Eric: "I liked the bit about quarter to eleven. (on Debussy's "Dawn to Noon on the Sea")"

Eric Satie The charmingly whacky Satie beguiled audiences with his three *Gymnopédies* (1888), gentle yet intricate works for piano. They were typical of his approach: avant-garde at the time but recalling aged, subtle melodies. His influence on composition was felt throughout the 20th century.

Six of the best
Les Six was the name bestowed upon a group of Montparnasse composers in the early 1920s. Inspired by contact with Satie and Cocteau, they created pared down modern music at odds with Wagnerian Romanticism and the imprecision of Impressionism. Francis Poulenc would become the most famous of *Les Six*, composing witty, highly eclectic music. He turned to opera later in his career.

Situated on La Villette
Park in Paris, once home
to the city's central
slaughterhouse and
livestock market, is the
cutting-edge cultural area,
the Cité de la Musique.
Designed by the architect
Christian de Portzamparc
and inaugurated in 1995,
the enterprise aims
to make world culture
and the creative arts
accessible to everyone.
The site boasts a concert
hall, educational facilities
and a museum housing
the French national
collection of musical
instruments. It also hosts
a truly eclectic mix of
musical performances in
a year-round programme.
Audiences can enjoy
musical forms from
the Middle Ages to the
present day, comprising
everything from world
music, rock and jazz to
chanson, Breton bagpipes
and the avant-garde.

Satie: music and madness

One of the most interesting of the 19th century
composers is Eric Satie, both for his approach to music
and eccentricity of character. Satie failed to shine as
a piano student during two lacklustre periods at the
Paris Conservatoire in 1879 and 1885, yet his artistic
ambitions were encouraged by his father who ran
a music publishing business. During his teenage
years, Satie revelled in the bohemian atmosphere of
Montmartre. Socializing
with the area's artists
and intellectuals,
the budding composer
developed unusual
personality traits.
He never went out
without his overcoat
and umbrella come
rain or shine. The
meaningless titles of
his compositions were
similarly irregular: a
couple translate roughly
as *Things Viewed from
the Right and the Left
(Without Spectacles)*

The Cité de la Musique

(1914) and *Dried up Embryos* (1913). Moreover,
directions given to musicians for playing the
pieces raised quizzical eyebrows and included
'*In the morning, on an empty stomach*' and '*Crabbed
and Cantankerous*'. A heavy drinker, Satie died from
cirrhosis of the liver in 1925, aged 59. The room in
which he worked, and which no one else had entered
for 27 years, was found clogged with umbrellas,
snippets of composition and seven velvet suits.

Classical music in modern France

Contemporary classical music has been defined by the likes of Olivier Messiaen, who drew on his staunch Roman Catholicism, love of birdsong and global travel to create such complex pieces as *Vingt regards sur l'enfant-Jésus* (1944) and *Éclairs sur l'au-delà* (1987-91). His pupil, Pierre Boulez, continues this atonal musical abstraction and experimentation, for example in the use of modern electronics, and is considered a leader in modern and

post-modern music. Pierre Schaeffer gave the world *la musique concrete*, the first genre to make use of recorded sounds; an early piece, *Étude aux chemins de fer* (1948) used train sounds.

An appreciative audience

Classical music in all its forms is flourishing in France, with more than a million students studying at conservatoires across the country, nourished by such venues as L'Opéra de la Bastille in Paris. Home to L'Opéra National de France, this stunning, modern opera house symbolizes the country's desire to keep classical music relevant while encouraging wider appreciation. L'Opéra's first gala performance, conducted by Georges Prêtre, was staged in 1989 on the 200th anniversary of the storming of the Bastille.

Five French classical works to get you started

Grande messe des morts (1837)
by Hector Berlioz.

Le carnaval des animaux (1886)
by Camille Saint-Saëns.

Prélude à l'après-midi d'un faune (1894)
by Claude Debussy.

Gymnopédies (1888)
by Eric Satie.

Catalogue des oiseaux (1956-58)
by Olivier Messiaen.

Hot spot
Le Quintette du Hot Club de France grew out of informal jam sessions held at the Hotel Claridge in Paris between Django Reinhardt, Stephane and Joseph Grappelli, Roger Chaput and Louis Vola in 1933. The all-string quintet were quickly spotted by Pierre Nourry and Charles Delaunay of the city's Hot Club and invited to perform there. The pair also arranged recordings to be made of the new band who were soon in huge demand both at home and abroad.

Born in the USA

As an imported musical form, France greeted the arrival of jazz during the First World War with a certain suspicion. The author Georges Duhamel described it as music "that shrieks through its nose, weeps, grinds it teeth and caterwauls throughout the world." The reluctance amongst French musicians to embrace the genre was further exacerbated by the knowledge that their American counterparts earned much more lucrative salaries playing in the Parisian clubs. Jazz, however, was winning converts helped by the arrival of dancer and singer Josephine Baker and, in the 1930s, Le Hot Club de France, honouring the 'hot jazz' played by the likes of Louis Armstrong. Soon French musicians were taking on the Americans to create a distinctive French style of jazz. The likes of violinist Stephane Grappelli and three-fingered gypsy guitarist Django Reinhardt began playing at the Parisian Hot Club with their all-string band, Le Quintette du Hot Club de France. By the 1950s, it was Claude Luter and his Dixieland Band who were winning rave reviews, and many American jazz musicians travelled across the Atlantic to bask in France's continuing love of their music.

Split personality: Josephine Baker

Born in 1906 in St Louis, Missouri, singer, dancer and actress Josephine Baker adopted France as her homeland in 1925, drawn by the country's greater acceptance of black performers. Her fame grew with performances of her sensuous 'banana dance' alongside her pet leopard, Chiquita, in the Folies Bergère, inspiring plaudits from the likes of Ernest Hemingway and Pablo Picasso. During the war years, Baker became an active member of the French Resistance, using her fame and charm to work as an intelligence agent. In 1961 Charles de Gaulle rewarded her war efforts with the Legion d'Honneur. A life-long advocate for equality, Baker adopted 12 children of different races, calling them her 'rainbow tribe', and never played at venues that refused an integrated audience. She died in 1975, a week after a tribute performance at Club Bobino in Paris.

Legendary left hand

Gypsy guitarist Django Reinhardt is a legendary figure in jazz circles. His remarkable playing becomes all the more impressive when you learn that two of the fingers on his left hand were semi-paralyzed after a fire. Determined to continue playing, Reinhardt developed a unique style built around his left hand's two good fingers, using the semi-paralyzed fingers to play only the bottom two strings. Solos were performed with just his index and middle finger. With the advent of the Second World War, the Hot Club quintet disbanded and Django remained in Paris under Nazi Occupation while violinist Stephane Grappelli sought safe haven in England. The Nazis regarded jazz as a decadent music and Reinhardt's own Romany roots make it surprising that he avoided the Nazi concentration camps. Fortunately there were some in the Nazi ranks who were closet jazz fans and one of their number, Dietrich Schulz-Koehn or 'Doktor Jazz', admired Reinhardt's work and offered him protection from persecution. After the Liberation, the original members of Le Quintette du Hot Club de France were able to resume their careers. Reinhardt died of a brain hemorrhage near Paris, in 1953, aged 43.

Jazz still jumping

Today jazz remains hugely popular in France, witnessed by the number of clubs and festivals scattered across the country – over 250 festivals take place, mainly during the summer months. Along with the larger international festivals held at Nancy, Nice and La Villette in Paris, smaller events in Junas and Mulhouse feature everything from Dixieland and avant-garde to neobop and gospel. Young people in France are also embracing the musical form with enthusiasm and there are numerous jazz courses at schools such as the École de Jazz et Musiques Afro-Américaines in Paris. In line with the policy of *l'exception culturelle*, the government even funds the country's Orchestre National de Jazz whose revolving director is chosen by the Minister of Culture. Despite the music being a largely masculine domain, most recently it is women who have been making their voices heard in the French jazz scene with Mina Agossi, Elisabeth Kontomanou and Anne Ducros all snapped up by jazz labels. Others in the crop of current stars include Erik Truffaz, St Germain and Michel Legrand, all of whom are signed to the legendary Blue Note label, which also hosts its own annual festival.

Swinging Sisters

Typical of the new breed of French female jazz singers, Elisabeth Kontomanou recently won the prestigious Best Jazz Vocal Artist of the Year gong at the Victoires de Jazz awards following the success of her fifth album *Waitin' for Spring* (2005). Born in France to a Greek mother and Guinean father, Elisabeth cites Charlie Mingus and Ella Fitzgerald as her influences.

A helping hand from the state
Musicians in France creating "works of the mind" are granted with the special status, *intermittents du spectacle*. This entitles them to full social security, holiday and unemployment benefits based on the number of hours worked and taxes paid as indicated on their payslips.

Yé-yé baby

During the 1960s French pop music, or *variété*, closely imitated the ubiquitous American style while attempting to invest it with the French sensibilities of *chanson*. The *yé-yé* genre, taking inspiration from US teen idols and girl groups, gave rise to singers such as Johnny Hallyday, Françoise Hardy and Sylvie Vartan who all became phenomenally successful. Blending a mix of French-language covers of American songs and those by French writers, songs typical of the era include Hardy's *Tous les garcons et les filles* (1962) and Vartan's *La plus belle pour aller danser* (1964). The bubblegum pop of the *yé-yé* genre was, however, also assaulted by the provocative output of Serge Gainsbourg, who marked his early career with songs such as *Soixante Neuf Année Erotique* (1969).

Gainsbourg pushes the boundaries

Serge Gainsbourg's inflammatory, nihilistic take on pop music made him adored and reviled in equal measure. *Aux Armes Etcetera*, a 1979 reggae version of the *Marseillaise* knocking French republicanism, drew large-scale protests from war veterans at his live shows. Other songs explored incest, sexual diseases and phallic symbols with Gainsbourg's characteristic dark humour. In 1968 he released his most successful hit, the erotically charged and nihilistic *Je t'aime...moi non plus* (I love you... neither do I) sung with his lover Jane Birkin. Banned by the BBC and condemned by the Pope, the song secured Gainsbourg's place in the modern *chanson* tradition. As the 1980s' bad boy spokesman of the *bof* ('so what') generation, Gainsbourg cultivated and exploited this facade throughout his career. During one TV chat show he breathily asked fellow guest Whitney Houston whether she'd "like to fuck with me." He died in 1991 at the age of 62 and remains a cultish influence on artists outside the mainstream.

Age of rock

By the 1970s rock had arrived in France. The main exponents of the style, ranging from the progressive to the operatic, were artists like Triode, who shone brightly for just one album, *On N'a Pas Fini D'avoir Tout Vu* (1971), the 'French Pink Floyd', Pulsar, and Vangelis, the Greek prog rocker the French found so endearing that they awarded him the Chevalier des Arts et des Lettres medal. As the decade progressed, French artists explored the possibilities of electronic music and enjoyed some international recognition, with Jean Michel Jarre's *Oxygene* (1976) one of the most successful albums of the era. The punk and new wave movements brought artists such as Les Thugs and Oberkampf to national notice in the early 1980s. The latter caused outrage when they burned the French flag on stage.

Living Legend

Monolith of French rock, Johnny Hallyday, was born Jean-Philippe Smet in 1943. Since arriving on the national stage as the Gallic Elvis in the early 1960s with his first album, *Hello, Johnny!* (1960), the star's position in French hearts has remained virtually unassailable. With a career spanning five decades, 80 million discs sold and 900 songs, Hallyday has displayed all the attributes of the true showbiz survivor and his music has adapted to changing fashions, encompassing everything from rock 'n' roll to soul, and blues to psychedelia. Standards like *L'idole des jeunes* (1962) and *Quelque chose de Tennessee* (1985) are universally renowned in France. The overblown spectacle of his stage sets and vitality of his live performances are similarly celebrated. Yet, alongside these career highs, there have been the lows of divorce (three so far), a suicide attempt and a car crash. At the end of 2006, Hallyday moved to Switzerland to avoid paying as much as 60% tax on his income back in France. His move sparked a furious row in government about the pros and cons of France's notoriously fierce wealth tax.

The contemporary scene

Contemporary music is thriving in France. The inherent protectionism of *l'exception culturelle* may help to push home-grown talent forward, but many of the new acts that emerge, often from the margins of society, do so through popular support. Three genres have found particular success in recent years:

Dance, techno, electronica, house – call it what you will, the music of French clubland surged in the late 1990s and continues to flourish today. Daft Punk set the tone with the industrial beats of *Homework* (1997), before Air, another duo, slipped lithely onto the scene with *Moon Safari* (1998). Air infused their dreamy electronica with *chanson*-like vocals, bending worldwide ears in the process. A third duo, Cassius, introduced their house sound with the album *1999*. All the above are still making significant music enjoyed well beyond the bounds of France.

Rap and hip hop are huge in France. Both represent the sound of *les banlieues*, signifying a rare art form in which immigrant communities have found a voice. Dakar-born rapper MC Solaar led the charge in the early 1990s: his first album *Qui sème le vent récolte le tempo* (1991) sold 400,000 copies in France. Suprême NTM are more hardcore (the NTM acronym makes an inappropriate suggestion about your mother) yet equally popular, offering an aggressive take on racism and inequality in France. Their eponymous album of 1998 was a huge success. IAM (Invasion Arrivant de Mars) originated in the housing projects of Marseilles but took Paris by storm with politicized lyrics and North African undertones on ...*de la planète Mars* (1991).

World music also reflects the ethnic diversity of modern France, indeed it has informed much of the rap and hip hop emanating from *les banlieues*. Much of it has a North African origin. Algerian and Tunisian immigrants fuse Berber folk with western rock, rap and techno to create raï music. Algerian Cheb Khaled has been its big star in the last two decades – the album *Khaled* (1992) cemented his reputation in France and overseas. The Senegalese artist Youssou N'Dour and West Indian female trio Zouk Machine also command a large French fanbase. The French Latin folk singer Manu Chao plumbs his Spanish roots and myriad other influences to huge acclaim on albums like *Próxima Estación: Esperanza* (2000).

Market movers and shakers
Singles sales in France are largely driven by Francophone pop. Within the last ten years, French exports – once limited to French-speaking countries – have steadily grown to reach the one million units mark for many acts, including Daft Punk and St Germain. The French are ranked seventh in the world according to their record buying habits. France's music market is dominated by the supermarkets' distribution. In France, music categories are broad because people are used to hearing various fusions of styles and cultural influences.

The ten albums you need to understand modern French music

Jane Birkin/Serge Gainsbourg (1969) Serge Gainsbourg.
An album of duets with Jane Birkin finds Gainsbourg's '60s liberalism at its height.

Est-ce que tu le sais? (2005) Sylvie Vartan.
A great 'best of' sampler for Hallyday's gap-toothed *yé-yé* ex.

Que je t'aime (1969) Johnny Hallyday.
This live album is as good a place as any to acquaint yourself with the joys of Johnny.

Halloween (1977) Pulsar.
Symphonic French rock reaches its conceptual peak.

Oxygen (1976) Jean Michel Jarre.
A slice of early electronica lauded the world over.

Prose Combat (1994) MC Solaar.
The rapper's best selling second album brought international recognition.

Baida (1997) Faudel.
The debut album from *le Petit Prince du Rai* draws brilliantly on his Algerian roots.

Moon Safari (1998) Air.
Ambient, eloquent and unmistakably French electronica.

Rose Kennedy (2001) Benjamin Biolay.
The debut album from a popular young singer/songwriter in the Gainsbourg mould.

Musique, Vol.1: 1993-2005 (2006) Daft Punk.
An excellent 'best of' infused with new work.

Protective policy takes the rap
Indigenous French music is ring-fenced by the government's policy of *l'exception culturelle*, obliging radio stations to play at least 40% home-grown music. During the summer riots of 2005, rappers who provided the disaffected voice of the riotous youth in *les banlieues* found themselves in a somewhat ironic position. While the government's cultural policy ensured them wide exposure, at the same time politicians were calling for legal action against their aggressive and inflammatory lyrics.

Return of the native: French folk music
Like the UK and the USA, the French dipped their toes in the folk revival of the late '60s, tuning in to the likes of Joan Baez and Bob Dylan and feeding in a few of their own ideas, al somehow wrapped up in the spirit of May 1968. Malicorne were probably the biggest French band; *Almanach* (1976) was their most acclaimed album. However, the resurgence also breathed new life into *musique traditionnelle*, the age-old musical heritage of the regions. These local variants remain, played in halls and bars – usually getting louder the further from Paris you venture.

Around the regions

The south remains in robust musical health, with the bagpipe and hurdy gurdy (part violin, part accordion) cranked up particularly loud in Provence. Often the songs come in Occitan: the band Massilia Sound famously blend the local tongue with reggae. As in Provence, the native music of Brittany (here with a Celtic base) traces its roots back to the wandering minstrels of the Middle Ages. Any Breton band worth its salt will have a *bombard*, a bit like a stubby oboe, and a *biniou*, the local variation on bagpipes. Alain Stivell, an expert on the ancient Breton harp, the *telenn*, has done most to keep the region's music alive over the last few decades. The remote Auvergne also retains a sturdy folk tradition, again with the bagpipe (their variation is called a *cabrette*) and the hurdy gurdy at its heart. Music halls in Les Pays Basque resonate to the sound of the *trikitixa*, an accordion like instrument; Peio Serbielle was the region's big singer-songwriter until arrested in 2004 for possible links to ETA. Over in Corsica they specialize in polyphonic singing, usually performed by male trios.

Five French music fests

Jazz and blues
Banlieues Bleues – performances throughout February to April near Paris.

Pop and rock
Printemps de Bourges – annual April festival covering rock to techno.

Classical music:
Festival de Saint-Denis – a leading classical music festival taking place each summer in north Paris.

Folk and world
Festival Interceltique – huge annual festival celebrating Celtic music and culture.

General
La Fête de la Musique – this one covers the whole country. Every summer solstice, France celebrates music with a raft of free outdoor concerts.

4.2 Theatre

Perhaps French drama shot itself in the foot by being so blindingly good in the 17th century under Corneille, Racine and Molière. It's been trying to live up to those dizzying heights ever since, achieving varying degrees of success.

The *Jeu d'Adam* is the oldest surviving French play. Dating from the mid 12th century it was written in the vernacular but with Latin stage directions.

Opening act: French medieval theatre

The roots of French theatre lie in a medieval cocktail of moral fortitude and downright naughtiness. A wealth of surviving texts dating from the mid 11th century suggest that medieval theatre was hugely popular, instructing and entertaining across the divides of literacy. In particular, five forms of play emerged before the 16th century:

Miracle plays took centre stage in the 14th century, inspired by the miracles of the Virgin Mary and the saints. Stories, rarely longer than 3,000 lines, were often placed in an everyday context.

Mystery plays gave a biblical twist to the miracle plays, often featuring scenes from the life of Christ. The name derives from *mysterium*, a Latin word relating to the handicraft of the guilds that performed mystery plays. Most were about 10,000 lines long but some reached 60,000, a scale that turned theatre into a big event staged in the main town square. Variety and nuance in the stories kept the paying crowds agog.

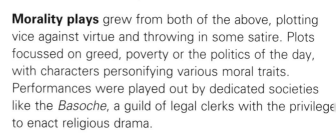

Morality plays grew from both of the above, plotting vice against virtue and throwing in some satire. Plots focussed on greed, poverty or the politics of the day, with characters personifying various moral traits. Performances were played out by dedicated societies like the *Basoche*, a guild of legal clerks with the privilege to enact religious drama.

Farce may have begun as a light interlude in the midst of a morality play, or perhaps its origins lie in the *fabliaux*, short medieval fables with a frequently pornographic lilt. They were almost universally popular. Lecherous priests, unfaithful wives and halfwit husbands all featured large in work that laughed at people's failings but also drew on wordplay and rhyme.

Soties offered more intellectual humour. They were short comic plays featuring numerous foolish characters, the sots. Each sot, usually bedecked in a pair of donkey ears, represented a different point of view. There was no denouement, simply a series of conversations or opinions that mocked some social or political target.

Turning to the classics: Renaissance theatre

Secular material steadily encroached on French religious drama during the 16th century. The Classicism of the Italian Renaissance filtered into French cultural life, and theatre gradually absorbed its principles. Playwrights either looked to the Humanism of the Greek classics or continued to entertain the masses with farce. The likes of Sophocles and Seneca were translated and adapted, and biblical tragedies and contemporary events were given a classical makeover. Etienne Jodelle wrote the first Classical French tragedy, *Cléopatre captive* (1553), applying the Pleiade poets' love of classical structure to the stage, notably in the use of five acts.

The golden age of French theatre

Under Louis XIV French drama found the limelight. Tragedy and comedy emerged dominant from Classicism, the latter gently swayed by the traditions of farce. The work of three playwrights stood out: Pierre Corneille and Jean Racine, best remembered for tragedy, and Molière, a master of comedy. They worked with the laws of classical theatre as dictated by Aristotle's three unities – a play should focus on one storyline set in one location over the course of a single day. Characters were also supposed to keep to certain moral codes. The laws weren't always followed to the letter, particularly if they interfered with dramatic tension.

The Comédie-Française
Paris got its first permanent theatre in 1548. The Théâtre de l'Hôtel de Bourgogne was built on the Right Bank by a brotherhood called the Confrérie de la Passion, who had the exclusive rights to stage mystery plays in the city. The theatre was long and narrow with a deep stage, built on the second floor of the Duke of Burgundy's former town house. In 1680 Louis XIV merged the Hôtel de Bourgogne with its traditional rival, the Hôtel Guénégaud, to form the Comédie-Française. The new theatre and its company of actors got sole rights to perform plays in French in the capital. Revolution purged this monopoly yet the Comédie-Française survived, still survives in fact, supported by the state to preserve, perform and advance the nation's theatrical heritage. HQ has been the Salle Richelieu since 1799.

17th century audiences
loved *pièce à machines*.
Employing the services
of Italian designers
and technicians, these
'machine plays' were
über-theatrical. Actors
ascended to heaven
suspended on wires and
fountains gushed real
water, all backed up by
vigorous music and dance.

Dramatis personae: the big three French playwrights

Pierre Corneille's career began with comedies and
tragicomedies but the Rouen dramatist is best known
for his brilliant grasp of tragedy. Of nearly 40 plays,
Le Cid (1637), based on the Spanish legend of *El Cid*, is
considered his finest. The public loved it but Richelieu's
new Académie Française decided it flouted the three
unities, contained morally dubious characters and was
thus defective. Corneille's subsequent tragedies (the
best – *Horace* (1640), *Cinna* (1641) and *Polyeucte* (1642)
– came in quick succession) were duly more classical in
construct.

Jean Racine usurped Corneille as the tragi-king in the
1670s and built a searing early reputation. He wrote
in the Classical style, deeply indebted to the Greek
tragedies and usually in deference to the three unities.
Racine riddled his protagonists with human flaws,
using expert and varied language to draw out the drama
and passion of oft-doomed characters. *Phèdre* (1677),
a reworking of Euripides' *Hippolytus*, was among his
finest efforts. Racine also played out a role as royal
historiographer to Louis XIV, whose support helped keep
both critics and bailiffs at bay.

1 Identity:
the foundations of
French culture

2 Literature
and philosophy

3 Art, architecture
and design

4. Performing arts

5 Actueurs of signt:
cinema, photography
and fashion

6 Media and
communications

7 Consuming culture:
food and drink

8 Living culture, the
armor of the nation

Molière, born Jean-Baptiste Poquelin, was the Woody Allen of 17th century France, acting, directing and writing his way to stardom. Medieval farce, comedy of manners and the improvised *commedia dell'arte* all informed his work. Molière poked fun at contemporary society; *Le Misanthrope* (1666) mocked the behaviour in an aristocratic salon, *Le Médecin malgré lui* (1666) satirized the medical profession and *Le Bourgeois Gentilhomme* (1670) was a veiled attack on Louis XIV's chief minister, Colbert. His work often scandalized – *Le Tartuffe* (1664) outraged courtly folk with its tale of religious hypocrisy but went on to be his biggest money spinner. Fortuitously, the king loved him. His marriage to the daughter or sister (no one's quite sure which she was) of his lover raised a few eyebrows.

A night at the theatre

Early theatre differed from other French cultural pursuits in the diversity of its clientele. Society retained its oral tradition and, as such, drama was something that could be enjoyed by all. Granted, plays were written by the bookish and casts often comprised the well-to-do folk capable of commissioning new work, but pretty much everyone could watch the end product. All the world was literally a stage; at court in front of the king, in private bourgeois residences, in converted tennis courts, in barns, streets and market squares. Travelling companies and troupes roamed the provinces while in Paris the medieval stage was dominated by guilds, some attached to trades, others to the Church. In contrast to England, women in early modern France were never banned from appearing on stage, although few did – acting was considered a pretty degenerate activity. Actors weren't even allowed burial on consecrated ground until the Revolution.

A hard act to follow

The high times of Molière and friends weren't recaptured in the 18th century. More and more writers scribed for the stage but few could match their predecessors' verve. Playwrights worked increasingly in prose rather than verse and the borders of tragedy and comedy began to blur. A more general *drame* emerged, which, while it took various forms, often portrayed contemporary life. The public thirst for theatre showed little sign of drying up. Two state sponsored companies, the Comédie-Française and the Opéra, found rivals in the shape of the Comédie-Italienne company and the fairground-based farce of the *théâtres de la foire*. The latter eventually evolved into the *théâtres de boulevard*, a generic term given out to the privately run theatres of Paris that would flourish in the 19th century and remain important today.

The important French playwrights of the 18th century

Voltaire, he of the fiery intellect, found fame as a playwright in the early 18th century. He began aged just 19 with *Oedipe* (1718) and continued to write tragedy for the stage over the next 50 years. He was usually a stickler for form, upholding the three unities and remaining unimpressed by Shakespeare's efforts to mix tragedy and comedy. Alas, Voltaire's tragedies never quite hit the heights of Racine or Corneille, in part because he got carried away pushing Enlightenment theory on stage.

The biggest name in 18th century theatre was **Pierre de Marivaux**. He wrote over 30 comedies for the stage, most of a romantic bent but some exploring class friction. His best romcom was *Le Jeu de l'amour et du hazard* (1730). Marivaux's work pulsated with clever banter; indeed, the word *marivaudage* was coined to describe his particular brand of flirtatious chitchat. His plays fe from favour even in his own lifetime, but a healthy reputation was restored i the 20th century when directors like Jean Vilar readdressed his work.

Pierre Beaumarchais, inventor, entrepreneur and rogue, is another whose comedies remain on stage. *Le Barbier de Séville* (1773), *Le Mariage de Figar* (1778) (both of which later became operas) and *La Mére Coupable* (1792) offer an insight into the turbulence of pre- and post-Revolutionary France, often taking a daring pop at the nobility.

Having a laugh: the rise of vaudeville

It might not have been top of the bill at the Comédie-Française, but vaudeville was French theatre's star performer throughout the 19th century. The theatrical form that began in the 15th century with satirical rhyming couplets had developed into short, prose-led comedy. Often based on a comedy of manners, vaudeville could feature farce, singing, dance and general cheekiness. The name comes from Vau de Vire, the valley in Normandy where the first vaudevillian songs emerged. Playwright Eugène Scribe was the big name in 19th century vaudeville. His comedies took inspiration from bourgeois lives, although he's best known as the creator of the *pièce bien faite* – the 'well-made play' of tight, twisting plot and well-defined denouement – that became an enduring dramatic structure.

Romanticism makes it to the stage

Parisian theatres enjoyed a sudden growth spurt after the Revolution as restrictions on the staging of drama were lifted. But the freedom was short lived: Napoleon reintroduced strict controls and censorship, measures that remained in place during the monarchy's brief resurrection and also later under Napoleon III. In the boulevard theatres, the Revolutionary era saw *drame* further erode the comedy/tragedy double act. In particular *drame* spawned *mélodrame*, the leading French writer of which was Guilbert de Pixérécourt, who expertly harnessed the genre's taste for heroes, villains, gothic sets, special effects and killer dialogue. Melodrama's outlandish antics helped set the scene for Romanticism. William Shakespeare and German playwright Frederich Schiller also influenced the brief Romantic flourish that entered 'serious' French theatre at the Comédie Française in 1830 with Victor Hugo's *Hermani*. Fighting between dyed-in-the-wool Classicists and Hugo supporters

Dog star
Le Chien de Montargis (1814) was one of the best plays by Guilbert de Pixerécourt, doyen of melodrama. The lead role was played by a dog.

Acting changed over the course of the 19th century, the declamatory posturing gradually replaced by something more naturalistic. And, as commercial theatre found its feet and Parisian actors began touring, the best in their trade became stars.

Frédérick Lemaître

The gifted, emotive stage presence of French Romantic theatre starred in Dumas père's *Kean ou Désordre et genie* (1836).

Rachel

Real name Elisa Félix, Rachel was the greatest French tragedienne. She found fame aged 17 after playing Camille in Corneille's *Horace* with the Comédie-Française and went on to dominate the company. But her career was short – she died of TB aged just 37.

Sarah Bernhardt

Often adjudged the greatest of all French actresses, Bernhardt's fame was worldwide in the late 19th century. Lithe, versatile and of golden voice, she did the lot – Racine, Hugo, Dumas fils. Even the acquisition of a wooden leg in 1915 couldn't keep her off the stage.

made opening night one to remember. *Ruy Blas* (183█) a commoner-pulls-queen tale set in 17th century Spai█ was considered Hugo's finest hour on stage. The other literary giant of Romanticism, Alexandre Duma█ père, also wrote for the theatre. *Antony* (1832), a moody take on his own machinations with a mistress, was a big hit. However, despite these successes, dramatic Romanticism failed to gather th█ momentum it did in print and shone only briefly.

Theatre comes to life

French theatre in the second half of the 19th century was a varied affair. Boulevard theatre continued to prosper with vaudeville and variations of *drame*, and the trend for portraying contemporary life on stage gathered momentum. Alexandre Dumas fils reigned over Second Empire theatre as the king of social drama, best seen in plays like *La Dame aux camellia█* (1852), in which a courtesan and well-to-do gentlema█ share an ill-fated affair; Verdi picked up the story in *La Traviata*. While Dumas fils perfected the tragic female character (as an illegitimate child, he was often directed by memories of his own mother's tribulations), Émile Augier cast his social net wider, bucking Romantic extravagance with artfully constructed plays on adultery, poverty and shady politics. For light relief he wrote the odd comedy.

Naturalism on the stage

Naturalism, drifting over from Zola and friends in literary circles, added to theatre's interest in the real world. André Antoine did much of the legwork, establishing the small Théâtre Libre in 1887 and showing plays with unpoetic language and detailed sets. By only admitting his audience through subscription, Antoine avoided censorship. His success eventually led to a job offer from the state, which he took up at the Odéon in 1906. The weightiest playwright to emerge from Naturalism was Henry Becque, ahead of his time with work like *Les Corbeaux* (1882). He ignored the happy endings of Romanticism in favour of ruthless, brilliantly realized pragmatism.

Symbolism goes to the theatre

The other significant late 19th century trend couldn't have been more different. Symbolism used drama to consider less earthly ideas. Language and sets became elaborately poetic and mystical. Director Aurélien Lugné-Poe opened the Théâtre de l'Oeuvre in 1893, staging innovative work from the likes of Alfred Jarry. His deeply irreverent *Ubu Roi* (1896), with surreal set and opening proclamation of 'merde', lasted one night but helped set the tone for Symbolism and pre-empt the Theatre of the Absurd in the 20th century. However, the big name in Symbolist theatre became Paul Claudel. A career diplomat, the young Claudel wrote huge poetic plays (one lasted 11 hours) using free verse. Exotic locations harboured richly spiritual characters and ideas on love and absolution, inspired by Claudel's deep-seated Catholic faith. Claudel remains a controversial figure in France. To some he's a giant of 20th century drama, to others a rather misogynistic figure who wrote an overly nice poem about Marshall Petain at the moment of French surrender in 1940 (although he later condemned Nazism).

Bums on seats

The late 19th century saw French theatre audiences swell. The restrictions on establishing a private venue were lifted in 1864 and boulevard theatres began to proliferate. The masses, egged on by a bit of disposable cash and a smattering of education, sought out drama in all its forms. Enthusiasm spread beyond the capital and most cities and large towns had a theatre by the end of the century.

Putting on a show: Parisian cabaret

It all started in the cafés of Paris in the 1850s. Some began staging modest concerts by local singers, the audience paying simply for the price of a drink. Before long a stage was installed to accommodate a small band and a chorus of girls. The Second Empire penchant for a good time saw the cafés expand into the music halls that would later flourish in the permissive atmosphere of the *belle époque*. Les Folies Bergère opened in 1869 with a repertoire of *chanson*, operetta, dancers and acrobatics. At the turn of the century, the cabarets attracted a bohemian clientele, drawn to watch the socially motley crowds as much as the paid

entertainment. Toulouse-Lautrec famously painted the action at Le Moulin Rouge while a young Picasso sipped his drinks in the atmospheric gloom of the Le Lapin Agile in Montmartre. The 1920s heyday of music hall saw stars like Josephine Baker and Mistinguett (real name Jeanne Bourgeois) become part of the floorshow. Mistinguett, the first to wear the large showgirl headdress, apparently insured her legs in 1919 for half a million francs. Later in the 20th century, as the music hall tradition evolved the girls became increasingly central to the evening's entertainment and nude dancers a staple of the shows. Many of the historic cabarets, including Les Folies Bergère and Le Lapin Agile, are still going strong, thanks largely to the tourist dollar.

The rise of the directors

Claudel and the Symbolist playwrights carried serious French theatre into the 20th century. Their work filtered through to a new generation of dramatists in the 1920s, writers enamoured with allegory and the poetic potential of theatre. Jean Giraudoux was one of the best. He turned from novelist to playwright, transferring a lyrical, dramatic style to the stage in plays like *Amphitryon 38* (1928), so numbered because he estimated his to be the 38th stage version of the Greek comedy. The multi-skilled Jean Cocteau was another, using his talents as a poet to rework classic tragedy with *Orphée* (1927), which he later made into a film.

Playwrights began collaborating with a new breed of theatrical directors between the wars. Jacque Copeau set the tone as a director unimpressed with showy, profit-driven boulevard theatre, preferring to build his legend on reduced sets that wouldn't cloud imaginative writing. Director Louis Jouvet formed a dynamic partnership with playwright Giraudoux, staging elegantly decorated productions packed with colourful speech. Jouvet also joined with three other Parisian directors to form Le Cartel des Quatres, a clique that fought the invasion of cinema and commercialized theatre with success during the 1930s.

Stage fright: Surrealism and Theatre of Cruelty

While Giraudoux, Copeau and co diverged from the past, they weren't truly avant-garde. That label stuck instead to playwrights like Roger Vitrac. He smeared the Surrealist ethos across the stage in comedies packed with grotesque scenes. His finest play, *Victor ou les enfants au pouvoir* (1928), a monstrous twist on the traditional drawing room farce, has become one of the most prized of 20th century French theatre. Vitrac's psychologically troubled friend Antonin Artaud came up with a new theory of theatre in the 1930s: Theatre of Cruelty sought to break the traditional 'false reality' spoken word format of theatre. The term 'cruelty' referred to crushing this projected reality rather than anything specifically painful. Vitrac hoped to unlock the audience subconscious through gesture, lighting and noise; to inflict and elicit raw emotion.

An ill wind

In Vitrac's surreal *Victor ou les enfants au pouvoir,* the lead character is a six-foot tall nine-year-old boy who meets his death in the play. Vitrac choose to embody the grim reaper in a sophisticated lady with violent flatulence.

Theatre under Occupation

Theatre attendance rose dramatically in Occupied France and stage entertainment played an important part in maintaining morale in Paris and the provinces. The Germans employed the Comité d'Organisation des Entreprises as a puppet for governing theatre.

Jean Cocteau's *Le Bel indifférent*, staged in 1940, was written for and starred Édith Piaf. The psychological drama, a monologue featuring a woman on the phone, was a huge hit.

Marcel Marceau had the only speaking part in Mel Brooks' film *Silent Movie* (1976). His dialogue comprised a single word, 'non'.

The strong stage management required helped to elevate the director's role further. Artaud's work went largely unappreciated before his premature death in 1948 but would prove vital to the evolution of modern theatre.

It's the quiet ones you have to watch: French mime

Mime originated in ancient Greece but for most the silent art, in its latter day form, is intrinsically French. It arrived in the country in the 16th century, introduced by Italian actors, but it wasn't until Jean-Gaspard Deburau unleashed his pasty-faced Pierrot routine on early 19th century Paris that it found its familiar modern form. Étienne Decroux took up the imaginary baton in the 20th century and began pushing mime further, eager not merely to replace words but to express real emotion and thought. He did so expertly in Carné's film, *Les Enfants du paradis* (1945). Another mime artist, Jean-Louis Barrault, appeared in the same film. He would later direct the Théâtre de France, helping to enliven post-war theatre with a mix of classics and the avant-garde. He was sacked in 1968 for offering an opinion on the student protests in Paris. In 1947 Marcel Marceau created Bip, he of the stripy jumper and flowered hat. He also developed a series of *mimodrames* like *Le Manteau* (1951) and *Les trois Perruques* (1953). Meanwhile, Jacques Lecoq's famous school in Paris became like the Sorbonne of physical theatre, mime at its core, in the later 20th century. The physicality of mime plays an important role in contemporary theatre, with directors like Jean Vilar and Ariane Mnouchkine using it within new work and also as a training technique.

Existentialism on the stage

Existentialism wafted into theatre in the late 1940s. Both Albert Camus and Jean-Paul Sartre put notions of the absurd on stage, pondering the 'why' of it all and obliquely commenting on current affairs. Sartre's *Les mains sales* (1948) and Camus' *Les Justes* (1949) give a good flavour of what they got up to. Jean Anouilh has also often been filed among the Existentialist playwrights. He was less politicized than Sartre and Camus but, like them, he broached post-war concerns about man's role in a random universe.

He accrued a remarkably varied output, moving from farce to serious drama and covering much in between. *Antigoné* (1944), a reworking of the Greek tragedy, and *La Valse des Toréadors* (1952), a sexual farce, were among his most successful. Few modern French playwrights have found such a receptive audience worldwide.

Playing the fool: Theatre of the Absurd

In the 1950s, Theatre of the Absurd (sometimes called New Theatre) took its lead from the Existentialists. Like Camus and co, the playwrights were connected by a despair at man's ineffectuality. But Theatre of the Absurd went further. Camus, Satre and Anouilh wrote about the meaning (or lack or it) in life, but strayed little from the traditional structure of the play. In contrast, Theatre of the Absurd undermined the norms of characterization, language or plot, using objects, lights, movement and stage directions – the mechanics of theatre itself – to convey a vision. It should be noted that Theatre of the Absurd wasn't an actual theatre, company or even cohesive school: the playwrights never fed off any particular allegiance. The key writers were foreign but they took root in the experimental theatres of the Left Bank, and most even had the decency to write their plays in French. Irishman Samuel Beckett wrote *En attendant Godot* (1952), shaping the genre with a pared down, repetitive and deliberately unsatisfying plot. Romanian Eugéne Ionesco contributed with *La Cantatrice chauve* (1950), laced with apparently meaningless dialogue and set on a kind of loop – the author described it as an anti-play. French playwright Jean Genet was associated with Theatre of the Absurd through his disregard for conventional language, although his politicized plays have also been linked to Theatre of Cruelty.

> Samuel Beckett was decorated with the Croix de Guerre for his work with the French Resistance.

Man of the people

Actor and director Jean Vilar had a massive impact on modern French theatre. He wanted to produce theatre for the masses, accessible across the whole country. In 1947 he established the Festival d'Avignon, staging sparse open-air productions in the Palais des Papes. Given the directorship of the Théâtre National Populaire (a state subsidized company) in 1951, Vilar was revolutionary in laying on quality classics that the people could understand and afford. The Festival d'Avignon remains the leading annual French theatre festival.

Sun rises on new era

Under the influence of figures like Vilar, creative clout moved from playwright to director. The visual and aural bias of Theatre of Cruelty and the earlier rise of Le Cartel des Quatres contributed to the shift. Directors in the 1960s began reworking the classics or creating their own theatre, often built around improvised rehearsal. The Théâtre du Soleil, both company and venue, broke new ground under director Ariane Mnouchkine in the mid 1960s. Based in an old warehouse on the edge of Paris, they operate like a worker's co-op, producing theatre with a dynamic leftie edge. *1789* and *1793*, dramas that cast a historical light on May 68, were two of the biggest French plays of the '70s. Directors like Antoine Vitez put the classics under the knife in the '70s and '80s – some critics decried the corruption of Racine and Molière, others applauded the injection of new life. Vitez also worked with contemporary writers on progressive new theatre. More recently Patrice Chéreau has been a big directorial force with innovative, energetic interpretations of Genet, Chekhov and others. Today, creative power is gradually moving back towards the writer although collaboration remains important.

Funding frenzy: the boulevard takes a back seat

The gulf between private and state-funded theatre is wider in France than in most countries. Although hugely popular before the Second World War, boulevard theatre has struggled in recent decades, reliant on star names cast in romcoms to pull in the crowds. The small experimental theatres that spawned Theatre of the Absurd rarely risk anything so avant-garde today. Nearly all of the 50 or so private French theatres are in Paris. Some benefit from meagre government handouts, but the big money goes to state theatre. This is where modern French drama finds its experimental edge. They're an important part of *l'exception culturelle*, drawing financial support to produce new work. Of the five national state theatres, four are in Paris – Comédie-Française, Théâtre de l'Odéon-Théâtre de l'Europe, Théâtre de la Colline and Théâtre National de Chaillot. Only the Théâtre National de Strasbourg resides outside the capital. Government funds also fuel 44 Centres Dramatiques Nationaux around the country. While the five nationals have their own specialities – for example, l'Odéon regularly hosts foreign productions – each state theatre is required to stage a healthy stew of reinvigorated classics and contemporary work. Ticket prices are fixed to lure the punters.

1. Identity:
the foundations of
French culture   2. Literature
and philosophy   3. Art, architecture
and design   **4. Performing arts**   5. Artists of stage,
cinema, photography
and fashion   6. Media and
communications   7. Consuming culture:
food and drink   8. Living culture:
state of the nation

Curtain call: big names in contemporary theatre

The directors' dominance and a taste for foreign theatre haven't helped French playwrights over the last three decades. Only a handful have accrued acclaim or longevity. Michel Vinaver has been lauded since the 1970s, tinkering with dramatic structure and portraying a disjointed reality in plays like *Portrait d'une femme* (1984). Bernard-Marie Koltès was a big name in the 1970s and 80s and remains much performed since his death from AIDS in 1989. He wrote poignant, socially aware plays that dealt with relationships and contemporary life, often working in collaboration with director Patrice Chéreau. Yasmina Reza scored a more commercial success with *'Art'* (1994), the witty exploration of male friendship that scooped a cherished Prix Molière and found translation in over 20 languages.

Five modern French plays that played to a packed house

Topaze (1928). Marcel Pagnol.
Elegantly sidestepping the avant-garde, Pagnol wrote about everyday life, as in this astute portrayal of a naïve young schoolteacher.

La Guerre de Troie n'aura pas lieu (1935). Jean Giradoux.
A story of love and war from the master of allegory, in this instance alluding to impending conflict in Europe.

Becket (1959). Jean Anouilh.
The giant of modern French theatre gave a historically shaky rendition of medieval murder in Canterbury Cathedral but still won a Tony Award for its Broadway incarnation starring Anthony Quinn and Laurence Olivier.

Dans la solitude des champs de coton (1985). Bernard-Marie Koltès.
Simile-sodden dialogue between a mysterious Dealer and his Client from the biggest French playwright of the late 20th century.

'Art' (1995). Yasmina Reza.
The biggest popular hit of recent French theatre is pleasingly conventional in its analysis of three friends arguing about a painting.

1. Identity
the foundations of
French culture

2. Literature
and philosophy

3. Art, architecture
and design

4. Performing arts

5. Arbiters of style
cinema, photography
and fashion

6. Media and
communications

7. Consuming culture:
food and drink

8. Living culture: the
state of the nation

The Lully soap opera Jean-Baptiste Lully's wife Madeleine bore him ten children, yet he couldn't help going after other women and young men, cultivating a scandalous reputation for sodomy. He died aged 55 after refusing the amputation of a gangrenous foot, injured when he hit himself with a conducting staff.

Lift off with Lully

The birth of French opera is usually attributed to one man. Jean-Baptiste Lully, court composer to Louis XIV, combined music, dialogue and dance in *comedies-ballet* (with the help of Molière) before cooking up the *tragédie en musique* (later called *tragédie lyrique*) in the 1670s. The *tragédies* were a distinctly French affair (even though Lully was from Florence), successfully rebuffing the boisterous advances of early Italian opera and using the French language. Plots often had classical roots, were divided into five acts and usually enjoyed after a prologue that glorified the king. Lully wrote the tunes while poet Philippe Quinault, and sometimes playwright Corneille, penned the words. Ballet was usually a key feature. The tragedies set the format for French opera for a century, establishing a balance between libretto and music. Of Lully's 13 *tragédies* (a misleading title, as some were almost jolly), *Armide et Renaud* (1686), a story of love in the first Crusade, is considered his *chef d'oeuvre*.

Jean-Philippe Rameau chose his librettists well: Voltaire wrote the text for *La Princesse de Navarre* (1744).

Finding new forms: Rameau and Gluck

Jean-Philippe Rameau built on Lully's foundation and was attacked for distorting his predecessor's style. Yet their work wasn't vastly different, with Rameau maintaining the tenets of the *tragédie en musique*. A musical theorist, Rameau only began writing opera in his late 40s yet still churned out dozens. Rameau was an expert at delivering intense tragic emotion through music, as seen in his first opera, *Hippolyte et Aricie* (1733). The German Christoph Willibald Gluck has been credited with maintaining Lully's style, soaking up elements of the *tragédie en musique*, but also with pre-empting the great operatic composers of the 19th century. He went to Paris in the 1770s under the patronage of his former student, Marie-Antoinette. Gluck challenged the Italian tradition: music should serve the libretto by expressing the emotion of a scene and the flow of the opera shouldn't be broken by the different elements of song, music or dance – they should all dissolve into one form. Many of these ideas had already been trumpeted by philosopher Jean Jacques Rousseau, who composed his own uncluttered opera, *Le devin du village* (1752). Gluck's first Parisian composition, *Iphigénie en Aulide* (1774), proved a hot potato but set the form for modern opera.

Opera light

Opéra-comique emerged in the 18th century, born of vaudeville and the *comédies-ballets*. *Opéra-comique* wasn't always humour-led, although the libretto usually featured a more contemporary, sometimes satirical subject than the *tragédie en musique*. Crucially, it was opera that included spoken dialogue. Pierre-Alexandre Monsigny, known for his grasp of a perky melody, was an early leader. After the Revolution, François-Adrien Boïeldieu pushed *opéra-comique* further. *La Dame blanche* (1825), with a Eugène Scribe libretto based on stories by Sir Walter Scott, was considered his best effort. His use of a ghostly Scottish backdrop foresaw the Gothic leanings of Romantic opera. Later on, Bizet's *Carmen* (1875) drove around in an *opéra-comique* chassis, albeit with a more serious engine. The genre's spiritual home, the Théatre de l'Opéra-Comique, was established in 1717 and survives today at the Salle Favart, Paris.

Big it up: Romantic opera

With *opéra grande,* the French use of drama in opera reached new heights in the 19th century. Grandiose sets, sumptuous costumes and flouncy historical tales saw opera fall head over heels for Romanticism. Rossini got in early with his final opera, *Guillaume Tell* (1829), composed for the French stage, but it took the German Giacomo Meyerbeer to successfully blend the vivid vocal parts, ballet and raging music that would bring Parisian audiences to their feet and cost a fortune to put on stage. His wordsmith was playwright Scribe: they took lavish productions to the Paris Opera, including the hugely popular *Les Huguenots* (1836); its portrayal of the St Bartholomew's Day Massacre displaying a bloodlust typical to Romantic opera. Hector Berlioz later composed and wrote the lyrics for the most brilliantly outlandish slice of *opéra grande* with *Les Troyens* (1856-58), recognized as a peak of Romantic opera but also as the ultimate realization of Gluck's ideas on the homogenous

operatic form. Other French composers taking a stab at
Romantic opera included Camille Saint-Saëns (*Samson et
Dalila* (1877)) and Jules Massenet (*Manon* (1884)).
The latter was known for a lightness of touch that some
deemed mawkish.

Twists on Romanticism

Charles Gounod upheld the Romantic trend, albeit
infused with *opéra comique*, composing the mighty
French opera *Faust* (1859) and also *Roméo et Juliette*
(1867). The lyrical *Faust* proved such a departure for
Gounod that some questioned if the work was actually
his. The composer even challenged one inquisitive critic
to a duel that never saw the light of dawn. Gounod
was good, but amid the 19th century flowering of
French opera George Bizet left the greatest legacy.
Carmen (1875), an idiot's guide to falling for a fiery siren,
borrowed the passionate emotion and evocative locations
of Romanticism yet added a realist edge with its daring
libretto. Essentially, with its use of dialogue, *Carmen* was
serious *opéra-comique* and was duly premiered at the
Théatre de l'Opéra-Comique.

Offenbach and the operetta

While Romantic opera flourished in the 19th century,
a new pint-sized humorous cousin, the operetta,
found an even wider audience. As *opéra-comique*
became increasingly serious, operetta filled the light
entertainment vacuum, carrying elements of satire, farce
and parody in its mix of dialogue, song, music and dance.
Hervé (real name Florimond Ronger) was among the first
to compose operetta. He went on to write over 100, the
most famous of which was *Mam'zelle Nitouche* (1883).
However, as with Gluck and Meyerbeer in opera proper,
French operetta's lama, Jacques Offenbach, came from
over the Rhine.

1. Identity,
the foundations of
French culture
2. Literature
and philosophy
3. Art, architecture
and design
4. Performing arts
5. Artisans of style,
showbiz, pornography
and culture
6. Media and
communications
7. Consuming culture:
food and drink
8. Living culture: the
state in the nation

Offenbach wrote more than 80, including *La Belle Hélène* (1864) and *Orphée aux enfers* (1858) that made famous use of that Parisian dance craze, the cancan. Henri Meilhac and Ludovic Halévy became legendary as Offenbach's libretto writing duo. Operetta sobered up a little after the Franco-Prussian war when Charles Lecocq took the helm – *La Fille de Madame Angot* (1872) was by far his most popular effort. The genre proved the forebear of musical comedy, a form for which modern France has shown strangely little appetite.

20th century blues: modern French opera

The most successful French opera of the 20th century arrived early on and little that came afterwards rivalled its pedigree. It was Claude Debussy's only opera, yet *Pelléas et Mélisande* (1902) was a virtuoso effort. The story of doomed medieval love is often seen as a French response to Wagnerian opera. Like Wagner, Debussy gave the music a lead role, yet he used it more subtly, teasing out the nuances of Maurice Maeterlinck's Symbolist play. It has often been described as an Impressionist opera. Ravel was the other big classical cheese to flirt with opera. The one-act comic opera *L'heure espagnole* (1911) was a first foray; the second, *L'enfant et les sortilèges* (1925), had a libretto by author Colette.

Such collaborative work spawned much of the French operatic activity in the 20th century. Composer Darius Milhard worked with dramatist and poet Paul Claudel on the opera *Christophe Columb* (1928), while Henri Poulenc's *La Voix humaine* (1959) drew on a play by all-rounder Jean Cocteau. The latter work takes the form of a woman's last phone conversation to her cheating lover. As with all of Poulenc's work, the emotionally harrowing monologue serves to emphasize the tonal rhythms of the French language. He's a rare success story in post-war French opera. Critics remain undecided on Olivier Messiaen, who wrote both score and libretto for *Saint François d'Assise* (1983), a work that took eight years to complete and five hours to watch. The composer's love of birdsong found its way into the music, inspiring leitmotifs that denote particular characters. Today, there is little in the way of contemporary French opera. Instead, the opera houses continually revive and reassess the classics or turn to foreign composers for those rare new works.

Where the French watch their opera
The French National Opera traces its origins back to Lully and the Académie
Royale de Musique, a kind of governing body entrusted to Lully by Louis XIV.
In 1875 the company got its flamboyant HQ, the Opéra Garnier. The curtain
went up on a second national stage for opera in 1989 – the 2,700-seat Opéra
Bastille stages bigger productions, although runs under the same Opéra
National de Paris company as the Garnier. The Théâtre de l'Opéra-Comique
is still going while the Théàtre du Châtelet, run by the City of Paris, is the
place to see more contemporary work. Out in the provinces, opera-goers can
choose from ten consistent companies, with Lyon, Strasbourg and Toulouse
traditionally among the best. For opera with atmosphere, head to the annual
Chorégies d'Orange, held each summer in the Roman theatre of Orange,
Provence.

Lording it: early movers

The Italians and their pervasive Renaissance may claim the invention of ballet, but the French nobility weren't far behind with *ballet de cour*, a popular 16th century hotchpotch of poetry, music, art and dance. Flamboyant sets and costumes were employed for the aristocratic audience at court. It led to Jean-Baptiste Lully's *comédie-ballet* (in this instance *'comédie'* essentially meaning drama) with its elements of speech and music.

Lully teamed up with Molière on a series of dramatic productions, of which *Le Bourgeois Gentilhomme* (1670) proved a high point. With Lully by his side Louis XIV did much to promote dance, even starring in many of the early works choreographed for court. Indeed, he may have acquired the 'Sun King' tag after prancing as a high-heeled Apollo in a piece by Lully.

Leave it to the professionals

When Louis XIV created the Académie Royale de Danse, a professional dance company, in 1661, the free-for-all ethos of courtly dance began to ebb and ballet was increasingly staged in the theatre. The Académie survives today in the guise of the Paris Opéra Ballet. The first Académie director, choreographer Pierre Beauchamp, was also the first to record the five classic feet positions of ballet. In 1681 he used professional female dancers in ballet for the first time in *Le Triomphe de l'Amour*, a joint effort with Lully. Prior to that, women had been played by men in masks, big skirts and hefty corsets – the constrictive weight of costuming was apparently given as a reason for not getting women involved sooner.

The first ballet
Le ballet comique de la reine, its story based on the Greek fable of Circe, is often considered the first ballet. Composed and choreographed by the Italian Balthasar de Beaujoyeulx, the five-hour performance piece got a first airing at the Palais du Petit Bourbon, Paris, in 1581, as organized by Catherine de' Medici.

The language of ballet
In 1700, Raoul Auger Feuillet published *Choréographie, ou l'art de décrire la danse*, notating dance in a way that remains relevant today. The language of ballet, essentially French, was already in place by the early 18th century with words like *jeté, pirouette* and *chassé*.

Nice movers: the early
stars of dance
Mlle de Lafontaine, star
of *Lully's Le Triomphe de
l'Amour*, was the world's
first prima ballerina.
She wore the moniker
reine de la danse before
withdrawing to life in
a convent. Marie Sallé
became famous in the
early 18th century for
an expressive portrayal
of character, while her
rival, Marie Camargo
was known for a dazzling
entrechat. Both helped
to simplify costumes and
shorten cumbersome
skirts, although neither
did without the *calcons
de precaution,* worn
underneath the skirt
to avoid inadvertent
exposure. Gaétan Vestris
and his son, Auguste,
were among the main
men of 18th century
ballet. Daddy was known
as *le Dieu de la Danse*
while his pride and joy
first danced with the
Paris Opéra aged 12
and went on to lead the
company's troupe for
36 years.

France, the home of classical ballet

In 18th century France, ballet found its feet as a serious
art form to rank alongside opera. Jean-Georges Noverre
did much of the legwork. He published his *Lettres sur
la danse et les ballets* in 1760, honing the *ballet d'action*
style that suggested character and emotion were to be
found through expressive movement, not elaborate
sets and costumes. Before *ballet d'action,* dancers
were burdened by brutish wigs, hooped skirts (on both
sexes) and heeled shoes. Noverre also choreographed
more than 150 ballets, none of which survive. His
protégé, Jean Dauberval, had more success in leaving
a stagebound legacy: *La Fille Mal Gardée* (1789), first
performed by the company of the Grand Théâtre de
Bordeaux, is the oldest ballet still in repertory.

Fairytales: Romantic ballet

France remained guardian of world ballet throughout
the first half of the 19th century, the escapist texture
of Romanticism lending itself well to the form. Two
particular works endure: *La Sylphide* (1832), a tale of
fairy love that kept leading ballerina Marie Taglioni on her
toes with extensive use of the new *en pointe* technique,
and *Giselle*, conceived by poet Théophile Gautier and
choreographed by Jean Coalli and Jules Perrot. Both
were launched in Paris. Later on came *Le Corsaire*
(1856), based on Byron's poem about a pirate. Adapted
by celebrated choreographer Joseph Mazilier, the ballet
apparently drew Napoleon III and Eugénie to its first
three performances at the Paris Opéra. In the second half
of the 19th century the hub of ballet moved east,
in particular to Russia and Denmark.

1. Identity,
the foundations of
human culture   2. Literature
and philosophy   3. Art, architecture
and design   **4. Performing arts**   5. Artforms of sight:
cinema, photographic
and fashion   6. Media and
communications   7. Consuming culture:
food and drink   8. Living culture: the
state of the nation

Russian invasion: 20th century ballet

For France, ballet came in from the cold in 1909 in the shape of Les Ballets Russes. Sergei Diaghilev's avant-garde troupe gyrated provocatively and caused a storm in Paris. It was an all-star affair: Cocteau helped on the libretto, Braque and Picasso got involved with the sets, Vaslav Nijinsky (sometime lover of Diaghilev) danced and choreographed and Satie, Debussy and Ravel were among the composers. Diaghilev's Modernist approach brought a new sexuality to the primness of ballet, as seen in the riot-invoking *Le Sacre du Printemps* (1913), set to a violent Stravinsky score. The original company died with Diaghilev in 1929, its assets seized by creditors, but would prove the pivotal ballet movement of the 20th century. Ukrainian-born dancer and choreographer Serge Lifar, among the Ballets Russe corps, went on to revitalize the Paris Opéra in the 1930s. He remained there until 1959, apart from a three-year banishment incurred for collaborating with the Nazis. The Russian flavour of Parisian ballet continued under Rudolf Nureyev. He defected in 1963 and found his way to the Paris Opéra Ballet 20 years later where he brought a modern touch to the classics and finally widened the repertoire to include contemporary work.

New moves: modern French dance

While Russia may have provided much of the recent personnel, France has long considered itself the custodian of classical ballet. In fact, such was ballet's deep-seated primacy that new forms had a hard job breaking through. When French modern dance did finally take centre stage in the early 1980s, inspired by American practitioners and by healthy state patronage, it shone. Choreographer Maurice Béjart had done much to pave the way, blending ballet and modern dance for packed theatres in the 1970s.

Père shaped: the father of classical ballet
When the focus of ballet switched from France to Russia, it took French choreographer Marius Petipa with it. The so-called 'father of classical ballet' made the Imperial Theatre in St Petersburg home for much of his career, carving classics like *Sleeping Beauty* (1890) and *The Nutcracker* (1892) and brilliantly revamping giants like *Swan Lake* (1895)

Principal dancers at the Paris Opéra Ballet are traditionally called *Étoiles*.

Bend it like Sylvie
The most famous French dancer of recent times has been Sylvie Guillem. The unnervingly limber Guillem controversially left Nureyev's Paris Opéra Ballet in 1989 and joined the Royal Ballet in London. Many have since adopted Guillem's flexible technique, which she employs in both classical and contemporary dance.

In 2004 the Ministry of Culture opened a new purpose-built Centre National de la Danse on the outskirts of Paris. Studios, theatres and lecture halls make it a veritable factory of dance.

The number of professional dancers in France has trebled since 1987.

Working from Belgium and then Switzerland, he reworked the likes of *The Nutcracker* (1998), turning it into a semi-autobiographical work set in his native Marseilles. Roland Petit, with his angular, theatrical choreography also did much to further post-war modern dance, collaborating in one instance with Pink Floyd. His best work unfurled with the esteemed Ballet National de Marseille.

Jean-Claude Gallotta has been a significant choreographer for two decades, producing modern work with his Groupe Émile Dubois in Grenoble. His recent *Trois Générations* (2004) featured three different age groups performing the same choreography in succession. Gallota exemplifies the talent found within regional dance in France. The major cities boast progressive troupes, nurtured by generous funding from the Ministry of Culture. Lyons' opera house boasts the most successful company outside Paris. Dance festivals also flourish out in the provinces. Every summer, Montpellier has one of the biggest fests in Europe, while the Hivernales in Avignon offers a bubbling soup of contemporary dance each February. The Biennale de la Danse de Lyon brings together the likes of ballet and breakdance every other September.

Keeping it local: French folk dancing
As well as funding radical contemporary work, significant dollops of governmental cash are set aside to keep regional folk dancing alive. The French provinces harbour hundreds of very local dance traditions and the movers and shakers in one village may do it differently from those in the next. Brittany has a strong heritage of Celtic style dance, closely woven to its native music: most dances are group affairs, carried out in a circle, as with the *Hanter Dro*, or in a line that roams around the room to the sound of Breton pipes. In the centre of France the varied 17th century peasants' *Bourée* of both Berry (arms held by the side) and Auvergne (get those arms up) remains popular. At village festivals in Provence and Languedoc, people often join hands in a chain to skip the medieval *farandole* accompanied by drum and flute.

Laughing matter: what do the French find funny?
France enjoys a laugh as much as the next nation. In
conversation, their humour may be guided by wordplay and
wit, distinguishing it from the cynicism, ironic or punchline-
driven modes of other Western nations, yet, as a cultural
package, be it in sitcom, film or stand-up, French comedy
also explores the universal themes, from politics to sex,
scatology to religion. The French comic tradition has
a rich ancestry: Rabelais, Molière and Beaumarchais
all contributed to the development of humour through
literature and drama. The stage played a crucial role: farce,
classical comedy, vaudeville, burlesque – all have their
elements of comedy. Indeed, the French word *comédie*
once simply meant 'drama', while *comédien* still translates
directly as 'actor'. However, in the 20th century the French
nurtured a clutch of comedians in the modern sense –
comics who emerged through stand-up, television and film.

Three 20th century heroes of comedy
The first great post-war funny man was Jacques Tati.
He began as a mime artist in the 1930s but, like many
modern French comedians, found success making films.
He played the pipe-smoking mac-wearer Monsieur Hulot
in a number of movies that were heavy on visual gags and
light on dialogue. In the likes of *Mon Oncle* (1958), Tati
used the character's buffoonery to mock modernity. He's
been described as an early Mr Bean – who, incidentally,
the French seem to adore. Ask a French person who
their greatest comedian is or was, and they're likely to
mention Coluche. He began on café stages in Paris in
the late 1960s and graduated to television in the 1970s.
While Coluche often appeared in a clown suit, his act was
based on aggressive satire that picked apart politicians,
the clergy and the petit bourgeoisie. By 1980, he was
campaigning to be the next French President – a race

1. *Identity:
the foundations of
French culture* | 2. *Literature
and philosophy* | 3. *Art, architecture
and design* | **4. Performing arts** | 5. *Arbiters of style:
cinema, photography
and fashion* | 6. *Media and
communications* | 7. *Consuming culture:
food and drink* | 8. *Living culture: the
state of the nation*

Mon Oncle, in which Jacques Tati teases post-war France for its consumerism, won an Oscar for Best Foreign Language Film in 1958.

In 1985 Coluche set up Restos du Coeur, a charity that still gives out free meals to the homeless and unemployed.

he dropped out of despite (or perhaps because of) encouraging support. France was stunned by his death in a motorcycle accident in 1986. Pierre Desproges also died prematurely, succumbing to lung cancer in 1988. He was a supremely eloquent misanthrope, offering mock despair about every aspect of life in expertly polished French on radio and TV. Books like *Vivons heureux en attendant la mort* (Enjoy life while you wait for death) (1983), hint at Desproges' style.

Agenda benders: crusading comedy

Other artists have followed the example of Coluche and Desproges, stirring controversy with routines that swing aggressively from right to left. The leading provocateur of the last 30 years has been Guy Bedos. A French Algerian, Bedos launched his left-wing routine in Parisian clubs in the late 1960s before graduating to TV where a talent for pithy insight on current and social affairs still makes the masses laugh. Bedos' comic opposite, Thierry Le Luron, rose to fame in the 1970s, often using impressions to lampoon politicians before his death from illness aged 34. Many of Le Luron's quarry, including Jacques Chirac and Valery Giscard d'Estaing, attended his funeral. In the 1980s and 90s the rubber-faced TV puppets of *Les Guignols de l'info* clawed at politicians and other public figures to widespread delight. Today, the limits of French political comedy are further stretched by a comic known as Dieudonné. The former left-wing anti-racist has found both outrage and support for his increasingly anti-Semitic routines. In 2003, he ended a TV appearance dressed as an Orthodox Jew with a Nazi salute and three years later was fined for making anti-Semitic comments.

Women in French comedy

French comedy has traditionally been dominated by men. The few women who broke through postwar rarely did so as solo acts: Sophie Daumier, who perfected a sniping nuptial routine with Guy Bedos in the early 1970s, was about as independent as most comediennes got. However, over the last 20 years significant progress has been made in the café theatres of Paris and on television. Sylvie Joly had audiences rapt in the 1980s with a bleakly funny repertoire on married life and parenthood. Muriel Robin has emerged more recently, also finding humour in life as a French female, although in her instance as an empowered, post-modern woman. *Les Vamps*, aka Dominique De Lacoste and Nicole Avezard, have wowed post-millennial audiences with character comedy from two sharp-tongued headscarf wearing old dears. Like their male counterparts, successful contemporary French comediennes have moved lithely between stage and screen. And, again in common with the blokes, many have made the move to serious drama: Muriel Robin earned a Best Actress César nomination for her titular performance in *Marie-Line* (2001), a film about one woman's efforts to help illegal immigrants.

Comic relief: toilet humour
The French might pride themselves on an appreciation of witty repartee, but where do you think the phrase double-entendre originated? The smell of Rabelais and his 16th century musings on toilet habits and bedroom shenanigans lingers on with comedians like Vincent Lagaf' and Jean-Marie Bigard, the latter ranting about everything from homosexuals and blonds to Belgians.

Coluche won a César for his serious role as an alcoholic petrol pump attendant in Claude Berri's dark *Tchao Pantin* (1983).

Where the French watch their comedy

French comedians rely less on an established circuit of stand-up clubs than their British or American equals. Yes, there are places where you can go and watch a 'one man show' (as the French call stand-up) – the famous café theatres of Paris, like Le Point-Virgule or Le Bout, or larger venues like the Olympia music hall – but most punters chew on comedy served from an extensive televisual buffet. Having begun in TV or radio, the big French stars often develop their cachet through appearances in film. Tati and Coluche both took the film route while modern figures like Christian Clavier (*Les Visiteurs* (1993)) and Alain Chabat (*The Science of Sleep* (2006)) muddy the waters between acting and comedy.

Sublime to ridiculous: the current funny crop

The French comedy scene is in rude health, thanks mainly to its large slice of telly time. Some entertainers echo the greats of times past: the ludicrous situation comedy of Moroccan Gad Elmaleh recalls Tati's style. Others, like Michaël Youn, who pushes his public into laughter with *Jackass*-style absurdity, offer something more edgy. Youn entered the national consciousness in 2001 on early morning TV by running naked in the streets while commentating through a megaphone. However, by relatively general consent, the funniest man in modern France is Jamel Debbouze. If you've seen the film *Amélie*, you'll recognize Jamel as the shy grocer boy. He does the lot – stand-up, television and film – but is most often seen on his own TV show, the *Jamel Comedy Club*, on which he compères for a raft of new young talent. Jamel's trademark quickfire patter feeds on his everyday life, his family and growing up among the *beur* (French of North African descent) communities of Trappes, a Parisian suburb.

Jacques Tati

Arbiters of style: cinema,
photography and fashion

5 Arbiters of style: cinema, photography and fashion

5.1 Cinema

Cinema has been integral to French cultural identity for over a century. Often deemed the seventh art, film is cradled within *l'exception culturelle*, ensuring that new work doesn't necessarily have to justify its existence through box office receipts.

"THE CINEMA IS AN INVENTION WITHOUT A FUTURE."

Louis Lumière. (The inventor of film assumed that people would quickly tire of moving images.)

French films comprise 4% of the world cinema market.

Viewing habits
The old custom of tipping the usherette in French cinemas has died out since the introduction of the minimum wage.

In 2004 the French government legalized the use of mobile phone jamming technology in cinemas after complaints from film-makers that mobiles were killing ticket sales.

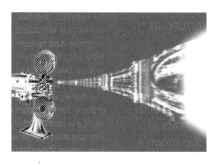

Also in 2004, French police discovered a fully-equipped cinema in the catacombs (which run for 150 miles under Paris) beneath the Trocadero complex.

More people – about 175 million a year – go to the cinema in France than in any other European country.

The pioneers of cinematography were French, rapidly raising the medium from curiosity of the day to a vital mode of creative expression. Then came the first epics, battle-strewn reflections on French history that sprawled across several hours. However, it was the intellectualization of film in the late 1950s and early 60 that would become French cinema's defining hour. The progressive techniques and ideas that flowered under the New Wave proved so influential that the genre still casts a cerebral shadow over French cinema today.

Who goes to the cinema in France?
Cinema audiences declined steadily through the 1970s 80s and 90s, and have only recently begun to increase When teenagers and young adults go to the cinema they usually go to watch an American film and the quantity of home-grown output doesn't always equate to high box office takings; indeed a large proportion of the 200 French films mac every year go straight to television. But the scene is far from gloomy. Around one in three films shown in French cinemas is made domestically - a significantly higher proportion than in other European countries – and work retains an admirable degree of immunity from market forces. Output remains remarkably diverse and small *art et essai* cinemas manage to survive, often showing programmes dedicated to specific actors, directors or genres. Paris remains the hub: in the capital's cinemas you can choose from over 300 films a week.

The bigger picture
Le Grand Rex in central Paris is Europe's biggest cinema with 2,750 seats.

But scale comes second to style: the real excitement lies in the Art Deco façade and Baroque

décor. You can even ta a behind the scenes to

178

Light show

When Auguste and Louis Lumière switched on their cinematograph (an invention that filmed, printed and projected images) in the basement lounge of a Parisian café in 1896, the viewers apparently leapt for cover. The world's first film audience feared *L'Arrivée d'un train en gare de La Ciotat* (1895) would chug straight off the projection screen and into their midst. Yet within 12 years, Paris had over 100 cinemas and film already carried huge cultural significance. The Lumière brothers were prolific, producing over 1,400 short films. Ostensibly they documented French life at the turn of the century, capturing their father's factory, washerwomen or horse drawn wagons. Yet they also tailored perspective and portrayed depth, paving the way for the motion picture as an art form. Creative growth was matched by the Lumières' fiscal development: the brothers accrued a large fortune as their cinematography company evolved.

New directions: early filmmakers

France proved a rich source of early film-making. Georges Méliès was the first director to employ special effects, perhaps most famously in *Le Voyage dans la lune*, in which a spaceship embeds itself in the moon's face. Méliès is also credited with launching the horror genre in *Le Manoir du diable* (1896), a two-minute film that terrified its novice audience. While the Lumières and Méliès created basic film narrative, the silent epics of the 1920s established a French movie industry. Abel Gance found an international audience with *J'Accuse* (1919). Filming on the battlefields at the end of the First World War, Gance created a three-hour epic that railed against the conflict's mechanized slaughter. He later made *Napoléon* (1926), a vast six-hour film that proved revelatory in developing montage and hand-held camera techniques.

Down at heel

While the Lumière brothers made a fortune from film, Georges Méliès was less prosperous. Despite producing the first science fiction and horror films, Georges was declared bankrupt in 1913. With the outbreak of the First World War, the French army seized most of his stock of 500 films and melted the celuloid down to make army boot heels.

Reel experiences

For the full 'birth of film' experience, visit the Institute Lumière in Lyon. Here, in the atmospheric basement of the family's grand Art Nouveau -inspired villa, you can watch the Lumières' short films. The Institute also boasts a comprehensive museum and the world's first film set, restored beyond recognition in the mid 1990s. La Cinémathèque Française in Bercy, Paris, harbours the world's largest collection of film, costumes and cameras. Four screens show classic films of every description.

The first movie moguls

In 1896 four brothers, Charles, Émile, Théophile and Jacques Pathé, founded the Société Pathé Frères in Paris. Six years later Pathé got their hands on the Lumiere brothers patents and began making their own cameras. Studios and a chain of cinemas quickly followed. In 1908 Pathé invented the newsreel and by the following year had 200 movie theatres in France and Belgium.

Poetic Realism

The bittersweet, doom laden love stories that flourished in the 1930s are often loosely grouped under the heading of Poetic Realism. Although their diversity creates a somewhat intangible genre, Marcel Carné's classic *Hotel du Nord* (1938) is often cited as a distilled example. The film opens with two young lovers checking into a hotel with the intention of committing suicide.

"I JUST WANTED TO MAKE A MOVIE, EVEN A PLEASANT MOVIE, BUT A PLEASANT MOVIE THAT WOULD AT THE SAME TIME FUNCTION AS A CRITIQUE OF A SOCIETY I CONSIDERED ROTTEN TO THE CORE..."

Jean Renoir on
La Règle du jeu

Daddy's boy

Jean Renoir first appeared in public as the boy with golden curls in his father's (Jean Auguste Renoir) oil paintings. Jean would later sell his father's work to finance his early film projects.

Keeping it real

While the advent of recorded sound boosted French cinema's taste for the historical epic, the wider growth in social awareness also crept grittily onto the silver screen. Indeed, the open wounds of the First World War and the looming spectre of further conflict ushered in an edgy wave of satire and Realism in the 1930s.

In 1931, former journalist René Clair made *À nous la liberté*, a somewhat surreal musical comedy that portrays an ex-con groping his way up the capitalist ladder. Initially controversial for its grim portrayal of factory life, the film really hit the headlines when Charlie Chaplin was accused of pilfering its gags for *Modern Times* (1936). The respective production companies instigated a lengthy dispute, much to the embarrassment of Clair who was actually a huge Chaplin fan. Celebrated playwright Marcel Pagnol was less provocative. He made the transition from stage to film with ease in the early 1930s, writing and producing *The Marseilles Trilogy* (*Marius* (1931), *Fanny* (1932) and *César* (1936)) based on one of his own plays. Preoccupied with the human condition, Pagnol shot poignant films on location amid the towns and fields of his beloved Provence.

In 1937, Jean Renoir made *La Grande illusion*, a biting account of the First World War based around his own experiences of the trenches. Renoir went on to become a leading figure in the Realist trend that flourished until the late 1950s. He directed and appeared in *La Règle du jeu* (1939), an unflattering dissection of French society and, in particular, a moody and capricious upper class. Derided by audiences, banned by the government and then temporarily lost, the film has only enjoyed critical acclaim since its re-construction in 1959.

Filming under occupation
Les Enfants du paradis
was voted Best French
Film of the 20th Century
by a gaggle of film
literati in 1995. Written
by Jacques Prévert and
directed by Marcel Carné,
the tale of unrequited
love in 19th century Paris
was shot during the Nazi
Occupation. Many of the
1,800 extras used filming
as a cover for Resistance
activity.

The five golden age films you need to watch

La Kermesse héroïque (Jacques Feyder 1935).
The French-made period comedy, directed by a
Flemish realist, won awards in the USA and started
riots in Belgium.

La Femme du boulanger (Marcel Pagnol 1938).
Pagnol's stunning use of the Provencal landscape
reaches its height.

La Règle du jeu (Jean Renoir 1939).
Vicious social comment forewarning of further war
in Renoir's finest work.

La Belle et la bête (Jean Cocteau 1946).
The poet pushes the boundaries of technology and
surrealism in a film starring his male lover, Jean Marais.

Les Enfants du paradis (Marcel Carné 1945).
Frequently cited as the best French film ever made.

Leading man
Jean Gabin was the
leading actor of pre-
Second World War French
cinema. He starred in
two of Renoir's best films,
La Grande illusion and
La Bête humaine (1938).
When war broke out
Gabin fled to Hollywood,
began a turbulent affair
with Marlene Dietrich and
then returned to France to
fight for De Gaulle's Free
French Forces, earning the
Médaille Militaire and a
Croix de Guerre. In total
he made 95 films over six
decades.

1. Identity
the foundations of
french culture

2. Literature
and philosophy

3. Art, architecture
and design

4. Performing arts

**5. Arbiters of style:
cinema, photography
and fashion**

6. Media and
communications

7. Consuming culture:
food and drink

8. Living culture: the
state of the nation

5.1.4 Capturing the mood: New Wave

Five actors who defined New Wave

Jean-Paul Belmondo
Became the face of New Wave cinema after starring in *A bout de souffle*.

Jean-Pierre Léaud
Appeared in five Truffaut films, initially playing the director's young alter ego in *Les Quatres cents coups*.

Jeanne Moreau
Best remembered for her magnetic role in *Jules et Jim*, Moreau also appeared in Louis Malle's *Ascenseur pour l'échafaud* (1958), for which Miles Davis did the soundtrack.

Corinne Marchand
The beguiling subject of Agnès Varda's *Cléo de 5 á 7*.

Jean-Louis Trintignant
Bookended the New Wave era with romantic leads opposite Brigitte Bardot in *Et Dieu... créa la femme* and Anouk Aimée in *Un homme et une femme*.

The rise of the *auteur*

The New Wave (*Nouvelle Vague)* of film that emerged in the late 1950s revolutionized French cinema. Convention was discarded in favour of hand-held cameras, unknown actors and themes drawn from real life. A lingering shot of a couple meandering down a Parisian street or an abruptly edited Existential conversation suddenly became fair filmic game. New Wave wasn't a formalized movement, more the work of like-minded directors embracing a wide variety of subject matter. In common, their approach was that of the *auteur*: each film resonated with the personal vision and concerns of its director.

How New Wave evolved

Claude Chabrol's 1958 film *Le Beau Serge*, a story of alcoholism and moral decay in a rural town, is often branded the first New Wave film, although Roger Vadim's *Et Dieu... créa la femme* (1956), which famously unleashed Brigitte Bardot on the world, had set the tone a couple of years earlier with its verve and sharp photography. Chabrol formed a New Wave triumvirate with François Truffaut and Jean-Luc Godard, all three of whom cut their cinematic teeth writing for *Les Cahiers du Cinéma*, a then ground-breaking magazine which remains in print today. They loved the work of Jean Renoir, but also wrote passionately about the great Hollywood directors like John Ford and Alfred Hitchcock. Godard was the most radical, famous for using jump cuts, chopping out the unwanted sections of scenes that were filmed in one long take.

Cinema Vérité

New Wave directors like Goddard were inspired by Cinema Vérité and the unscripted docu-films that first made use of small cameras and real locations in the 1950s. Jean Rouch, dubbed the father of Cinema Vérité, began using hand-held cameras when his tripod fell in the Niger river. In France, the movement is usually referred to as *cinéma direct*.

François Truffaut first coined the phrase *la politique des auteurs* in an essay of 1954.

"A FILM SHOULD HAVE A BEGINNING, A MIDDLE AND AN END... BUT NOT NECESSARILY IN THAT ORDER."

Jean-Luc Goddard

His debut film, *À bout de souffle* (1960), proved seminal, more for its technique, use of pastiche and protracted philosophical dialogue than for its portrayal of youth on the run from the law. Truffaut paid more conventional homage to American thrillers in films like *Tirez sur le pianiste* (1960), but is perhaps best remembered for *Jules et Jim* (1962), a love triangle that became the popular apotheosis of New Wave. In *Hiroshima mon amour* (1959), Alain Resnais brought his experience of documentary making to bear on a haunting love story set in the aftermath of the nuclear bomb, while Claude Lelouch gave a New Wave edge to more traditional romantic fare in *Un homme et une femme* (1966), winner of the Palme d'Or at Cannes in 1966. While the *auteurs* had been inspired by American directors, Hollywood soon reciprocated, assimilating elements of the French New Wave into its films; Francis Ford Coppola, Martin Scorsese and Quentin Tarantino have all acknowledged their debt.

Un homme et trois femmes

Roger Vadim, director of *Et Dieu... créa la femme* became as celebrated for his pulling power as for his movies.

At various times he was married to Brigitte Bardot and Jane Fonda, and also fathered a child with Catherine Deneuve.

The ten New Wave films you need to watch

Et Dieu... créa la femme (Roger Vadim 1956).
A 22-year-old Brigitte Bardot smoulders through the first cinematic exploration of youthful amorality.

Le Beau Serge (Claude Chabrol 1958).
The story of a young man's return to his decaying hometown is often touted as the first New Wave film.

Les Quatres cents coups (François Truffaut 1959).
Truffaut's semi-autobiographical masterpiece about a juvenile offender in Paris.

Hiroshima mon amour (Alain Resnais 1959).
A war-torn love story that broke new ground in its use of sequencing and flashback.

Le Feu follet (Louis Malle 1963).
One of Malle's earliest and best films studies an alcoholic writer in the depths of despair.

A bout de souffle (Jean-Luc Goddard 1960).
Anarchic and hugely influential in its use of jump cuts and extended scenes.

Jules et Jim (François Truffaut 1962).
A turbulent love story New Wave style.

Cléo de 5 à 7 (Agnès Varda 1962).
This rare female take on New Wave studies a woman awaiting the results of a cancer test. Better than it sounds...

Le Mépris (Jean-Luc Goddard 1963).
Brigitte Bardot and Jack Palance star in one of Goddard's best: a subversive story of broken marriage.

Les Parapluies de Cherbourg (Jacques Demy 1964).
The lighter side of New Wave: a musical starring Catherine Deneuve, set largely in an umbrella shop.

Un homme et une femme (Claude Lelouch 1966).
Moody silences and sexual tension in a wet and windy Deauville.

1970 to 2000:
The ten films you need to watch

Le genou de Claire (Eric Rohmer 1970).
The breakthrough movie for a New Wave old boy was his fifth, exploring a married man's temptation by another woman, or more specifically her knee.

La maman et la putain (Jean Eustache 1973).
A monumental love triangle often viewed as the formal end of New Wave.

L'argent (Robert Bresson 1983).
Bresson's final film saw him return to themes of corruption and redemption, creating a rare moment of minimalism in 1980s cinema.

Un dimanche à la campagne (Bertrand Tavernier 1983). A gentle, humanist portrait of family life. Brilliantly humdrum.

Shoah (Claude Lanzmann 1985).
The Holocaust documented through eyewitness testimony alone. Unforgettable, and not only because of its length (nine hours).

Jean de Florette/Manon des Sources (Claude Berri 1986). Neighbourly tensions with a stunning Provencal backdrop; among the most popular French films of the last 30 years.

Au revoir, les enfants (Louis Malle 1987).
Drawn from Malle's experiences as a child under Nazi occupation and often cited as the director's best film.

Nikita (Luc Besson 1990).
The slick Besson thriller that blends French style with Hollywood gloss.

La Haine (Mathieu Kassovitz 1995).
An emotive 24 hours in *la banlieue*. Won a César for Best Picture.

L'Humanité (Bruno Dumont 1999).
The last genuinely original work of the 20th century, centred on an emotionally scarred policeman, won the Grand Prix at Cannes.

In the wake of New Wave

By the early 1970s New Wave had hit the rocks. The spirit of May 1968 linge and cinema, like the nation in general, struggled with identity and direction. The *auteurs* continued to make some noteworthy contributions: *La nuit Américaine*, Truffaut's comedy about fi making, starring Jacqueline Bisset, wo an Oscar for Best Foreign Film in 1973 However, *La maman et la putain* (1973 was perhaps the creative high point of the 1970s. Jean Eustache's engrossing three and a half hour film is laced with pondering dialogue as a young philosopher struggles with his love for two different women. Television, video and Hollywood began to buffet the indigenous film industry in the 1980s a the French state duly stretched its poli of subsidization. Derived in part from a tax levied on ticket prices, the financi encouragement has maintained the prolificacy of home-grown cinema ever since – only India and the USA have produced more films.

Vive la difference

The last two decades of the 20th centur spawned various genres – flouncy peric dramas and slick urban thrillers among them – but were best defined by spora individual brilliance and directorial motif: Claude Berri remade Marcel Pagnol's *Manon des Sources* (1986) to huge acclaim in the mid 1980s, also filming t prequel, *Jean de Florette* (1986), which Pagnol was planning to shoot when he died. The bucolic allure of Provence has never been more vivid. Luc Besson successfully straddled the Atlantic with

1. Identity:
the foundations of
French culture
2. Thought
and philosophy
3. Art, architecture
and design
4. Performing arts
5. Arbiters of style:
cinema, photography
and fashion
6. Media and
communications
7. Communication:
food and drink
8. Living culture:
state of the natio

polished, edgy films exploring the margins of society. In 1985 he made *Subway*, a black comedy about the subterranean characters of the Paris Métro, garnering 13 César nominations, and by the early 1990s was making English language movies like the highly acclaimed (and censored) snapshot of the thinking man's hit man, *Leon* (1994).

Love and hate in the 90s

Diversity ruled in the 1990s. Historical drama flourished briefly; Gerard Depardieu won Best Actor at Cannes by a nose for his portrayal of *Cyrano de Bergerac* (1990), a film that also scooped ten Césars. Depardieu also starred in *Germinal* (1993), Claude Berri's take on Zola's bleak novel, while *La reine Margot* (1994) gave a bloody twist to Dumas' story of courtly life in the 16th century. Claude Sautet's final film, *Nelly et Monsieur Arnaud* (1995), was a beguiling, ambiguous love story about a young woman and a retired businessman. *Delicatessen* (1991), a surreal black comedy set in a post-apocalyptic future, and *Indochine* (1992), starring Catherine Deneuve as a plantation owner in Vietnam, are indicative of the '90s' diversity. There was, however, one film that really stood out as being of its time: the searing tension of *La Haine* (1995) was revelatory in dissecting social exclusion and racial tension on a Parisian housing project.

1970 to 2000: Five great actors

Catherine Deneuve
Broke through New Wave style in *Les Parapluies de Cherbourg* and has been making movies ever since. Best roles in *Le Dernier métro* (1980) (César for best actress) and *Indochine*.

Gerard Depardieu
Drew on his own juvenile delinquency for *Les Valseuses* (1973) and went on to Hollywood success. French films like *Jean de Florette* and *Cyrano de Bergerac* remain his best.

Daniel Auteuil
The most versatile French actor of his generation, Auteuil often plays the outsider. His finest work includes *La reine Margot, La séparation* (1995) and *La veuve de Saint Pierre* (2000).

Emmanuelle Beart
The epitome of aloof French beauty starred in *Manon des Sources* and *Nelly et Monsieur Arnaud*. Shares a child with Daniel Auteuil, co-star in *Manon* and the excellent *Un coeur en Hiver* (1992).

Juliet Binoche
Got her big break in André Téchiné's *Rendez-vous* (1985) and then secured stardom in absorbing homelessness flick *Les amants du Pont-Neuf* (1992). The *Trois couleurs* (1994) trilogy and *La veuve de Saint-Pierre* (2000) are also among her best.

Hail César
In an era when France consistently fought against the dominance of Hollywood, it seems entirely apt that the Académie des Arts et Techniques du Cinema should create their own Oscars. The César Awards have been held in the Théâtre du Châtelet since 1976. The gongs, made from compacted pieces of metal, were designed by sculptor César Baldaccini.

Close to the bone
The success of *La Haine* raised widespread debate about police brutality. Kassovitz' story resembles actual events in 1986 when Malik Oussekine, a 22-year-old French Arab, was beaten to death by police at a university demonstration. Prime Minister Alain Juppé reportedly ordered his cabinet to watch a special screening of the film.

Cinéma du Look
The visually slick films of Luc Besson *(Nikita)* and Jean-Jacques Beineix *(37°2 le Matin* (1986)) in the early 1980s are sometimes collectively termed *Cinéma du Look*, referring to work that draws on the aesthetics of music videos and advertising. Deemed derivative of American culture, the genre is regularly lambasted by film critics.

"CINEMA IS STILL A VERY YOUNG ART FORM WITH EXTRAORDINARY TECHNIQUES AND VERY IMPRESSIVE SPECIAL EFFECTS BUT SOMETIMES IT SEEMS THE SOUL HAS BEEN TAKEN OUT OF THINGS."

Catherine Deneuve

Laughing gear: three contemporary comedies

Le Goût des autres
(Agnès Jaoui 2000).
Wry, culture clash
humour built around an
industrialist's attempts
to keep up with a young
actress; a big critical
and popular success
that earned an Oscar
nomination.

Taxi trilogy
(Luc Besson 1998-2003).
Three films that combine
car chases in Marseille
with fast paced repartee.
The second sold over ten
million tickets.

*Les Bronzés 3:
amis pour la vie*
(Patrice Leconte 2006)
Comedy with a *Carry On*
flavour that broke box
office records on its
opening weekend

Home advantage

Having ebbed consistently for three decades, cinema
audiences in France are tentatively increasing again.
Films are still being made in large numbers – pushing 200
a year – and, much to Hollywood's chagrin, legislation
continues to lend a hand. The major TV channels allocate
a proportion of their income to film (historically Canal Plus
has given most) and the tax on box office receipts still
generates substantial cash for new work. Governmental
loyalty to *l'exception culturelle* tugs French cinema in
different directions but seems to maintain its reasonable
health. Many directors still make cerebral – distinctly
French – films, while others are happy to put a Gallic spin
on the Hollywood blockbuster. The genuine American
article still remains popular with the people who actually
go out and watch films.

Modern movies

The continuing global significance of French cinema
is born of standout, individual films that blend popular,
critical and financial success. *Le Fabuleux destin
d'Amélie Poulain* (2001) is the best example. Audrey
Tautou's elfin altruist revived the gentle humanism of
Truffaut, albeit wrapped in the humour and Surrealism
that director Jean-Pierre Jeunet previously brought to

In 2005, approximately
172 million cinema tickets
were sold (slightly down
on the previous year),
39 percent of which
were to see French
films. American movies
accounted for about
half of the market.

DVD sales in France are
the lowest in Europe.

Amélie trivia
Nino, the shy object
of Amélie Poulin's
affections, is played
by Mathieu Kassovitz,
director of 90s discourse
on *banlieue* tension,
La Haine.

When film-maker Serge
Kaganski suggested that
Amelie's Montmartre
lacked racial diversity,

likening it to an advert
for the National Front,
Amelie director Jeunet
replied with equal maturity
that Kaganski was
"wallowing in bitterness
like a pig in its own shit."

Jean-Pierre Jeunet turned
down an offer to take the
helm for *Harry Potter and
the Order of the Phoenix*
(2007).

Bird watching
Le Peuple Migrateur
(2001) and *La marche de
l'Empereur* (2005), both
stunning documentaries
on bird migration, enjoyed
marked box office success.
The latter was released in
America as *March of the
Penguins*, dubbed with a
far less anthropomorphic
narrative.

1 Identity:
the foundations of
French culture

2 Language
and philosophy

3 the architecture
of design

4 Performing arts

**5. Arbiters of style:
cinema, photography
and fashion**

6 Media and
communications

7 Consumer culture:
food and drink

8 Living culture: the
state of the nation

Delicatessen. First time director
Christophe Barratier scored a
similarly big surprise hit with *Les
Choristes* (2004), stretching *Amélie's*
sentimental glow with the story of a
provincial teacher who used choral
singing to inspire his pupils in 1948.
Perhaps predictably, both films have
endured a mild backlash from critics
unimpressed by the sanitized subject
matter. Critics had more to mull over
with *Code inconnu* (2000), a winner
at Cannes. Directed by Austrian
Michael Haneke and starring Juliet
Binoche, the film has been dubbed
both masterpiece and meaningless
essay with its disordered fragments
of disparate lives. *La Pianiste* (2001)
was a more consistent critical
triumph: Isabelle Huppert gives
a remarkable performance as the
middle-aged piano teacher with a
sado-masochistic private life. More
recently, *L'Enfant* (2005), Palme d'Or
winner at Cannes, has added to the
body of contemporary French cinema
exploring the social margins. Directed
by the Belgian Dardenne brothers,
LEnfant harnesses the realities of
life on the streets for a young couple
with a baby.

"OUR GENERATION IS NOT LIKE THE 1960S, OBSESSED
WITH READING *CAHIERS DU CINÉMA*... FOR ME THE
BEST DIRECTORS ARE THE ONES WHO ALLOW YOU TO
SHARE EMOTIONS."

Christophe Barratier, director of *Les Choristes*

The ten 21st century films you need to watch

Le Pacte des loups (Christophe Gans 2001).
Typical of Gans' talent for genre bending, this period
fantasy box office smash confirmed audiences'
appreciation of Hollywood gloss and was a rare French
hit in America.

À ma soeur! (Catherine Breillat 2001).
A 12-year-old girl bears witness to adolescent sexual
awakening in a powerfully shocking film.

Le Fabuleux destin d'Amélie Poulain
(Jean-Pierre Jeunet 2001). Nine million tickets sold
and 13 César and five Oscar nominations for the most
successful French film ever made.

Sur mes lèvres (Jacques Audiard 2001).
Beautifully wrought study of a deaf girl dragged into
crime. Emmanuelle Devos won Best Actress César for
the role.

Etre et avoir (Nicolas Philibert 2002).
This captivating documentary about a teacher and his tiny
Auvergne school was a surprise cinematic hit.

8 Femmes (François Orzon 2002).
A whodunit featuring Deneuve, Béart, Ardant and five
more, made by a leading auteur of contemporary cinema.

Bon voyage (Jean-Paul Rappeneau 2003).
Classy, murderous humour set amid the Nazi occupation
of Paris, starring Gerard Depardieu, Isabelle Adjani and
Virginie Ledoyen.

Un long dimanche de fiançailles (Jean-Pierre Jeunet
2004). The follow up to Amélie had state funding pulled
because of foreign Warner Bros input; still proved a
global hit.

Les Amants réguliers (Philippe Garrel 2005).
Critically lauded vision of student strife in May 1968
filmed in black and white.

Joyeux Noël (Christian Carion 2005).
The story of First World War soldiers who ceased firing
on Christmas Eve 1914 to play football and bury the
dead was a critical and popular success.

1. Identity:
the foundations of
French culture

2 Literature
and philosophy

3. Art, architecture
and design

4. Performing arts

**5. Arbiters of style:
cinema, photography
and fashion**

6. Media and
communications

7. Consuming culture:
food and drink

8 Living culture: the
state of the nation

5.1.7 Outside looking in: global interest in French film and France as a location

Exporting French cinema

While Hollywood makes itself comfy in the majority of European cinema seats, France attempts to return the favour by selling films beyond her borders. In 2005, over 70 million filmgoers around the world paid to go and watc a French film; a stat which, while dwarfed by American movies, remains considerably higher than other Europear contributors. However, few of these tickets were bought in Britain or the US. French films accounted for 2% of all UK cinema tickets (double the usual) while Hollywood grabbed 62%. Gone are the days of New Wave, when cerebral French cinema could rely on a faithful English-speaking audience. Instead, the Gallic flicks that have done well in Britain and the States since the 1970s tend to confirm our romanticized notions of France: peasant charm in *Jean de Florette* (1986), for example, or costum drama in *La reine Margot* (1994). In recent years, oversea success has come more obliquely via Hollywood remakes such as *Three Men and a Baby* (originally *Trois hommes et un couffin* (1985)) and *Sommersby* (*Le retour de Marti Guerre* (1982).

On location: Hollywood in France

France has traditionally had more reward in catching America's eye as a film set. *Bonjour Tristesse* (1958), starring Deborah Kerr and David Niven, was one of the first to exploit the aesthetics of the Côte d'Azur; *French Connection I* and *II* (1971/75) and *Swordfish* (2001) made more gritty use of the Med coast in Marseilles and Nice respectively. D-Day epic *The Longest Day* (1962), starring Wayne, Micham, Fonda et al, was filmed on the beaches Normandy where the allies landed in 1944. More recently, *The Bourne Identity* (2002) was shot largely on location in France, featuring a raft of Parisian landmarks from the

Landscape painting

Many of the locations used in the Kirk Douglas does van Gogh biopic *Lust for Life* (1956) served as a muse for the artist himself, not least Arles and Saint-Remy in Provence. While director Vincente Minnelli used original van Gogh paintings in the film for added authenticity, he was also happy to spray paint a section of field yellow in an effort to match Vincent's vibrant colours.

Trench footage

In 1916 the British government commissioned American director DW Griffith to shoot *Hearts of the World*. Filmed in the trenches of northern France, it was made to prompt American intervention in the First World War. Lillian Gish starred and Noel Coward made his first film appearance, aged 18.

Talking in Code

In 2005 *The Times* reported on a meeting between Jacques Chirac and *The Da Vinci Code* director Ron Howard in which the French president reportedly suggested Sophie Marceau – best friend to Chirac's daughter and a stout supporter of his 2002 presidential campaign – for the part of Sophie Neveu. Chirac allegedly also hinted that the Louvre would become more available for filming were Jean Reno – playing Bezu Fache – to get a pay rise.

Jardin de Tuileries to the Grande Arche de La Défense. *The Da Vinci Code* (2006) also made use of Paris for the murderous goings on at the Musée du Louvre, while Sofia Coppola's *Marie-Antoinette* (2006) exploited Versailles' opulence. A previous American take on *Marie-Antoinette* (1936), one of the first Hollywood movies to shoot in France, also filmed in the palace.

189

Three film festivals you probably haven't heard of

Festival d'Anères, held each May in a small Pyrenean village, is dedicated solely to silent film. Movies made between 1895 and 1929 (when talkies arrived) are screened to the accompaniment of live music.

Festival du Film Policier de Cognac finds the small town best known for its brandy indulging in a long April weekend of detective movies from around the world.

Festival de Films de Femmes de Créteil is the largest European festival dedicated to films made by women. Held every March on the south eastern edge of Paris.

Cannes: the daddy of film festivals

The French affection for cinema has given birth to a wealth of film festivals. In Cannes we find the biggest annual global gathering of film industry insiders, while beyond, at less prestigious (but no less valid) events, world cinema is served up for public consumption. Today, Le Festival International du Film de Cannes can feel like a 12-day publicity stunt; the red carpet a very plush treadmill trudged by any star with a new movie to plug. Each May, 10,000 industry folk broker new deals behind the scenes in the Marché du Film while the lucky few with a pass sit through the 20 or so films entered in competition for the Palme d'Or. The majority of work is shown out of competition, brought to Cannes because it's *the* place to find an influential audience. It hasn't always been so glitzy. The first festival in Cannes was scheduled for 1st September 1939, organized by government minister Jean Zay (1904-44) in response to Mussolini's fascist film fest in Venice. An aged Louis Lumière was booked to preside. When Hitler invaded Poland, the party was postponed and the subsequent hiatus was only resolved with the inaugural festival in 1946. Various categories, competitions and workshops have been added to Cannes through the years but the main prize remains the Palme d'Or, awarded to the film perceived to best further the cinematic art. Recent winners have included *Pulp Fiction* (Quentin Tarantino 1993), *Secrets and Lies* (Mike Leigh 1996) and *Fahrenheit 9/11* (Michael Moore 2004). Since its creation in 1955, the Palme d'Or at Cannes has only gone to a woman once – to Jane Campion for *The Piano* (1993).

mike leigh picking up a Palme D'or

"THE FESTIVAL IS AN APOLITICAL NO-MAN'S-LAND, A MICROCOSM OF WHAT THE WORLD WOULD BE LIKE IF PEOPLE COULD CONTACT EACH OTHER DIRECTLY AND SPEAK THE SAME LANGUAGE."

Jean Cocteau

Best of the rest of the fests

Other festivals are more accessible, with tickets readily available for the public. Deauville on the Calvados coast plays host to the Festival du Cinéma Américain each September, welcoming movies and stars from the States. At the opposite end of the country, the popular Festival International Cinéma Méditerranéen, held in Montpellier in late October, screens work with a Mediterranean connection. In Clermont-Ferrand, the Festival International du Court-Métra serves up a buffet of short film at the end of January. At the Némo Festival in the Forum des Images, Paris, the country's best young independent film-makers show off their work in April, while the Dinard Festival, held on the north Breton coast in early October, is dedicated to showing British films.

Stellar Performance

Each summer the capital hosts a free Cinéma au Clair de Lune season. As the name suggests, the fest serves up moonlit cinema in outdoor venues across the city. New films feature alongside some classics. If you're looking for atmosphere, you can't beat watching *Les Enfants du paradis* projected onto the side of a Parisian apartment.

Short cuts

La Jetée, home to the Clermont-Ferrand Short Film Festival offices and the Auvergne Film Commission, harbours a library of thousands of short films, many available for public viewing.

5.2 Photography

Photography began in France. In the summer of 1826 or 1827 (debate rumbles) Joseph Nicéphore Niépce coated a pewter plate with bitumen and pointed it out of his bedroom window in Le Gras, Burgundy. Roughly eight hours later he held what has been dubbed the world's first photograph (a rooftop scene), or heliograph as he called it.

Overexposure:
early erotic
photography
As soon as man
developed the
capability to take
photos, he turned his
sights to the female
form. The French
dominated early erotic
photography, printing
nudes on handily
sized postcards.
Americans on holiday
in Paris apparently
bought bucket
loads. The lengthy
exposure times on
early daguerreotypes
precluded anything
too dynamic or
interactive on the
models' part. Of
course, the moral
climate of the 19th
century dictated that
erotic images were
usually marketed as
aids for the budding
artist or simply sold
illicitly.

While *Point de vue
pris d'une fenêtre
du Gras* is widely
considered the first
photograph taken
from 'life', in 2004
the French National
Library paid €450,000
for an earlier Niépce
effort that copied a
17th century Flemish
print onto paper.

A dozen years on, Niépce's partner, Louis-Jacques-Mandé
Daguerre, took the process further. Daguerre developed the firs
widely useable photographic form, the daguerreotype. The meta
plate images, produced with a ten minute exposure, were great
for portraits and duly sold in their millions. Early daguerreotypes
of Paris portrayed empty streets: the long exposure period
magically erased anything that moved. A bit like the Polaroid of
its day, the daguerreotype produced a positive image that
couldn't be replicated. People were blown away by the accuracy
Art historians have suggested that contemporary painters, most
notably the Impressionists, may have drifted toward a more
interpretive view of the world in the face of this new 'reality'.

The new face of portraiture
As the calotype photo with its paper negative replaced the
daguerreotype in the 1850s, new techniques and figures
appeared. Gaspard-Félix Tournachon, better known simply as
Nadar, was a calotype pioneer. In particular he produced portrait
of the late 19th century French literati. Courbet, Delacroix, Duma:
and Hugo all posed humourlessly in his studio. Nadar also took t
first aerial photograph, shot from a hot air balloon tethered over
the Bievre Valley in 1858; he did the same over Paris a decade
later. Nadar was the big name in a loose school of Portraitists th
included André Adolphe-Eugène Disdéri. In 1854 Disdéri patente
the *carte-de-visite*, small card-mounted photos that became hug
popular. He also photographed Napoleon III in his Parisian studic

Drawing on painterly traditions
The calotype process saw photography up its ambitions as an
art form. Camille Corot and Jean François Millet of the Barbizon
school both used photos to further their painting skills, while
seascape snappers Gustave Le Gray and Henri Le Secq, like
Millet, both emerged from the art classes of Paul Delaroche.
At the turn of the century, Pictorialists began manipulating dark
room techniques to soften landscapes and nudes, echoing
Impressionism in the process. Robert Demachy was a leading
Pictorialist; he often retouched his photos using etching or paste
Étienne-Jules Marey was a scientist with an eye for the aestheti
He developed chronophotography, showing the movement of
animals with a series of staggered images on one plate. Marey's
deadly-looking photographic gun shot 12 images per second.

1. Identity:
the broadsheets of
French culture

2. Literature
and philosophy

3. Art, architecture
and design

4. Performing arts

**5. Arbiters of style:
cinema, photography
and fashion**

6. Music and
entertainment

7. Gastronomic culture:
food and drink

8. Living culture: the
new in the nation

Life through the lens

Rolled film, cheaper cameras and the media's love of images saw a new type of photography emerge in the early 20th century. Documentary and art began to mingle, setting the tone for the photo-reportage style that flourished in France. Jacques-Henri Lartigue was one of the first to portray everyday life using his camera. He took his first photo aged six and maintained a pictorial diary for the rest of his life. From a friend jumping into a swimming pool to a man on a motorbike, Lartigue snapped the world around him. With the publication of *Album de Famille* in the late 1960s, Lartigue's photos earned the widespread acclaim that his career as a painter had failed to muster.

The Surrealist's photographer

Paris played host to American Emmanuel Radnitzky, better known as Man Ray, in the 1920s and 30s. Inspired by his Surrealist buddy Marcel Duchamp and Eugène Atget's old photos of reflective Parisian shop windows, Man Ray developed new techniques. Solarization altered the dark and light areas of a photograph, while rayographs were created not with a camera but by placing objects on photographic paper. Inspired too by the writings of the Marquis de Sade, Man Ray doctored the female nude: *Violon d'Ingres* (1924), in homage to the painter Jean-Auguste-Dominique Ingres, saw him painting f-holes onto the print of a nude's back. His photos were shown in the first Surrealist exhibition at Galerie Pierre, Paris, in 1925.

The father of photojournalism

To the French, Henri Cartier-Bresson is the greatest photographer. The 'father of modern photojournalism' clarified the link between documenter and artist. He shot life as he saw it: people in the street, sleeping in the park, at war – all captured with his trusty 35mm camera, the perfect, unobtrusive tool for an apparently shy man. In 1947 he jointly founded the first international photographic cooperative, Magnum Photos. As a photojournalist, Cartier-Bresson travelled the world, shooting for the likes of *Life* and *Paris Match*. He documented the Spanish Civil War, the student demos of 1968 and the accession to power of Chairman Mao. He made portraits of the great and the good, from Pablo Picasso to Richard Nixon. And yet he was equally at home snapping a boy in a Parisian street or a man leaping a puddle. Cartier-Bresson's photos were received as art, and books and exhibitions flowed from the 1950s. *The Decisive Moment* (1950), a mix of treatise and images, was accompanied by the first photographic exhibition ever staged in the Louvre. In the early 1970s he gave up photography and confined himself to his first love, painting.

"IN PHOTOGRAPHY,
THE SMALLEST
THING CAN BE A
GREAT SUBJECT.
THE LITTLE HUMAN
DETAIL CAN BECOME
A LEITMOTIF."

Henri Cartier-Bresson

Social services: humanist photography

Cartier-Bresson led a wave of French Humanist photographers in the mid 20th century. Common people, in work, play and love, were the unglamorous subjects. Preoccupied with social injustice and aware that photography could influence opinion, snappers like Robert Doisneau and Willy Ronis shot many of their black and white images in the Parisian suburbs. Ronis often focussed on union activity or scenes of urban poverty, while Doisneau documented the rapidly changing life of post-war Paris. Sometimes they ventured into less gritty territory: Doisneau's *Le Baiser d'Hôtel de Ville* (1950), with its lip-locked couple oblivious to the passing world, is the most famous example.

Fashion photography

As halftone printing transformed media in the early 20th century, France took an important role in the emergence of fashion photography. *La Mode Practique* began publishing in 1892, followed in 1916 by *Vogue*; both carried early fashion photography. In the 1950s Guy Bourdin, friend to Man Ray, broke new ground in the genre. For three decades he produced iconic shots for *Vogue*. His talent was for staged drama, placing models in surreal adventures where sex and death were recurring themes.

Puckering up for posterity
In 2005 an original print
of Doisneau's *Le Baiser
d'Hôtel de Ville* sold for
€155,000. It was put up
for auction by Francoise
Bornet, one half of the
kissing couple in the photo
that was wholly staged
despite its apparent
spontaneity. Bornet came

forward as the woman
in the photo in the early
1990s after various
couples began laying claim
to being the young lovers

Photography festivals
The French interest
in contemporary
photography is nurtured
through various

progressive festivals.
The best known is
the Rencontres
Internationales de
Photographie de Arles.
Founded in 1969,
the annual summer
celebration of new
photography swamps
its Provencal host.
Every other November

Le Mois de La Photo
crams more than 70
exhibitions into Paris,
while Perpignan arranges
its September around the
Festival International du
Photojournalisme.

Yann Arthus-Bertrand

No one gives the natural world a better visual press. His first book, *Lions* (1981), established him as a wildlife photographer, but today he's best known for *The Earth From Above,* an ongoing aerial inventory of the planet. He also maintains a series of matter-of-fact portraits of French people, from porn stars to peacekeepers.

Gilles Peress

The modern embodiment of photojournalism, Peress has recorded turmoil the world over. In Northern Ireland he photographed Bloody Sunday, in Iran he reflected revolution, in Bosnia war and in Rwanda genocide. He's published books on each.

Bernard Faucon

Few can match Faucon's originality for staged, often surreal images. He often photographs children, aiming to capture the beauty of youth. The figures are strangely stilted, as enhanced by his occasional use of mannequins. Numerous books and awards have celebrated his talent.

Bettina Rheims

Rheims began by photographing striptease artists and circus performers in the studio, moved on to female nudes, parodying fashion photography with her use of 'real' people, and later graduated to official portraiture for President Chirac.

Georges Rousse

The most avant-garde of the current crop creates bizarre optical illusions that, however hard you stare, never quite make sense. He works in disused warehouses, painting parts of the building which, when photographed from a very specific point, create an unfathomable block of colour in the middle of the photo.

5.3 Fashion

Few nations can rival the French for an inherent sense of style. French women have long been the embodiment of elegance, the traditional keepers of chic. The great fashion houses of the 20th century confirmed Paris as a sartorial hub, yet the city and its well-heeled socialites have actually been hogging the global catwalk since the 17th century.

The royal rug
Louis XIV began wearing a big wig when his own luscious curls succumbed to male pattern baldness in early adulthood; the fashion was soon adopted throughout polite society. He also pioneered petticoat breaches that looked a bit like a full-on skirt.

From the reign of Louis XIV to the Ancien Régime's choppy final years, Europe looked to France for its fashion tips. In the Sun King's court, style, like everything else, was used to applaud royal greatness. Nice threads meant status, and status, among nobles vying for royal favour, was everything. Many lurched into debt trying to keep up with the latest trends, laying out vast sums on silk, gold brocade and tumbling wigs. Fashions changed rapidly and seasonal revamps, created by a growing brood of Parisian designers, became part of the calendar. Louis revelled in looking good, but the fashion industry also offered him a malleable new cash cow. Silk, lace and weaving centres sprung up and their profits bolstered royal coffers.

What was fashion like in the *Ancien Régime?*
New trends were limited to the wealthy, among whom fresh development came largely thorough materials and accessories, from fans to ribbons, jewellery to powdered wigs. The basic garb of the nobility remained quite constant: men wore a coat, waistcoat and breeches: women a long boned bodice covered by a dress and a hooped skirt ill designed for getting through doorways. Toward the end of the monarchy the bourgeoisie became increasingly fashion conscious and women began wearing the manteau, a less formal gown.

The height of fashion
As noble hairdos reached new heights in the mid 18th century, a wire cage was used to support the wearer's locks. Flowers, false birds and even toy ships were inserted as decoration.

Dressing for revolution

The cost and flamboyance of noble clothing spiralled amid Louis XV's Rococo reign. Softer materials and lighter colours fuelled foppery and frivolity among the king's small clique. Often they changed costumes several times a day; if you weren't wearing the clothes of the season, or even the day, you weren't allowed into court. The masses no doubt pondered such indulgences over their evening gruel. Marie-Antoinette and her absurdly large wardrobe later became a loathed symbol of this extravagance. Among the enlightened bourgeoisie of 18th century society, fashion became more avant-garde with styles driven by the flourishing *modistes* (designers) of Paris. Fashion journals like *Le Journal des Dames*, complete with sketches, began keeping dressmakers and fashionistas up to date.

Republican fashion: less is more

Predictably the Revolution ushered in a more restrained French style. Men wore trousers for the first time in centuries, apparently inspired by sailors' outfits, and decoration was discarded in favour of sober, darkly uniform colour. For women the puffed-out style reduced down to a much plainer dress. In keeping with the nation's new democratic ideals, a classical Greek style came into fashion with its high sleeves and waist and thin fabric. Shoes lost their heels and modest bonnets replaced elaborate headdresses.

The first queen of fashion
With Marie-Antoinette, French fashion bridged the gap between high Parisian society and the royal court. She wore what she decided was fashionable and women who could afford it followed her lead. Her breathtaking annual clothing spend went on elaborate dresses and a two-foot-high hairdo dubbed the *pouf*. She helped launch new styles like the polonaise, a risqué, ankle-revealing dress with a tight bodice. Later she wore simpler clothes as the tide of discontent rose, led in part by a penchant for role-playing a shepherdess on a specially built farm.

A sense of Worth: the first couturier
Haute couture was invented by an Englishman. Charles Frederick Worth opened his Parisian salon in 1857 and began making dresses for the likes of Empress Eugénie, wife of Napoleon III. Previously, customers had suggested dress designs to anonymous seamstresses but Worth came up with four annual fashion shows featuring live models. He elevated dressmaking from a trade to an art form. Stylistically, he flattened the hooped crinoline skirt at the front and pushed bustles out at the back, working with lavish fabrics and extravagant trimmings. Paul Poiret filled Worth's shoes in the early 20th century. He replaced the corset with the girdle and brassiere. How could he fail with a catchphrase like "I freed the bust"? Poiret introduced the hobble skirt: so tight that an *ooh la la*-inducing slit had to be cut from hem to knee. In 1906 Poiret became the first couturier to launch a perfume.

What is *haute couture?*
A term that once simply meant 'high sewing' has become a catch-all phrase for top end fashion. Yet it's more tangible than that: a fashion business is either *haute couture* or it's not, as determined by set criteria. Indeed, *haute couture* has become a legally protected tag, similar to the AOC status decreed on select French wines and foods. To be *haute couture*, a fashion house has to make it onto the annual list of the government's Chambre Syndicale de la Haute Couture. A minimum of 20 staff must be employed, and twice a year the fashion house must show a collection of work containing at least 50 different outfits for evening and daywear.

The lavish clothes rarely sell. *Haute couture* is about status and cachet, and the houses that remain within its ranks survive by selling ready-to-wear lines, cosmetics and perfumes carrying the all-important name. At present, there are around ten *haute couture* fashion houses (down from 24 in the 1980s), Chanel, Christian Dior, Jean-Paul Gaultier and Givenchy among them. Estimates suggest that only around 500 women, the majority American, actually buy *haute couture* dresses. No wonder – prices usually begin at around €30,000. *Prêt-à-porter*, off the peg, mass produced clothes, are more accessible. The *haute couture* houses often produce *prêt-à-porter* lines, paraded at Paris Fashion Weeks held in October (for spring season) and February (for winter).

A golden age: Coco, Dior et al

Coco Chanel changed everything in the 1920s, ditching elaborate gowns and confirming France as the leader of high fashion. She began with a hat shop in 1913, apparently funded by one of her various wealthy lovers, before introducing simple, sleek clothes. Chanel relaxed women's fashion, bringing liberation with shorter skirts, loose fitting sweaters and the iconic Chanel suit, and uncluttered elegance with the little black dress launched in 1926. The fragrance Chanel No.5 later became almost as famous as the clothes. In 1947 Christian Dior launched his New Look of full skirts, tiny waists and narrow shoulders. Never mind that the strictly rationed multitudes couldn't afford any of it. Hubert de Givenchy opened his fashion house in 1952 with an elegant collection that established a refined, understated style. He was the first *haute couture* designer to launch a luxury ready-to-wear collection. His finest hours came in designing for Audrey Hepburn and Jackie Kennedy. The latter famously shrouded herself in Givenchy for JFK's funeral.

In the 1960s Paco Rabanne, a Spaniard raised in France, tried to radicalize *haute couture*, fashioning metal, rubber and paper into way-out designs that did much to shape the 'who would actually wear that' response to *haute couture*. Pierre Cardin began the 1960s in similarly space age form, but later had more success bridging the gap between high street and catwalk. Algerian born Yves Saint Laurent started his career with Dior, developing the 'trapeze' silhouette in the 1950s. In 1962 Saint Laurent opened his own fashion house. He was modern but not quite as radical as Rabanne. The pea jacket, trenchcoat and, most famously, *le smoking* all came out in the 60s. By the 1980s his androgynous style was spawning shoulder pads and pencil skirts.

Kooky Coco

Gabrielle Bonheur Chanel often rewrote her mysterious past. Apparently she claimed 1893 as her birth year, making her birth certificate ten years early. Her mother, who worked in the Samur poorhouse, died when Chanel was a child, and she was raised in a Catholic orphanage where she learnt to sew. We do know that she adopted the name Coco during a brief spell as a cabaret singer in her early 20s. An affair with a Nazi intelligence officer in the Second World War later found her avoiding the limelight in Switzerland until 1954.

The trickle down effect

While the world of *haute couture* can seem like a pretentious playground for over moneyed kids, the 'trickle down' effect of high fashion shouldn't be underestimated. Ready-to-wear lines feature toned down versions of *haute couture*, while the classic ensemble worn by many French women, so attuned to fine tailoring and sleek elegant lines, has its origins at Chanel.

When Yves Saint
Laurent retired in 2002
he explained:
"I HAVE NOTHING
IN COMMON
WITH THIS NEW
WORLD
OF FASHION,
WHICH HAS BEEN
REDUCED TO
MERE WINDOW
DRESSING.
ELEGANCE AND
BEAUTY HAVE
BEEN BANISHED."

Who are the leaders of modern French fashion?

Paris has had to share its fashion crown with New York and London over the past 20 years. The media periodically predicts the death of high fashion, and admittedly the true *haute couture* houses continue to dwindle. Yet the cachet o the catwalk remains. Reducing the gulf between high fashic and the high street has helped keep the industry afloat.

Jean-Paul Gaultier has done more than most for the cause. The irreverent Gaultier began placing popular culture in the salon in the early 1980s. Underwear as outerwear (who cou forget Madonna's conical bra), punk, men in skirts: Gaultier has brought a common, resuscitative touch to high fashion. Thierry Mugler shone for a couple of decades with an angul brand of solid colours and vampish glamour. However, losse forced the closure of his salon in 2003. His ready-to-wear lines and perfume still linger. Christian Lacroix has enjoyed greater longevity. He launched his fashion house in 1987, acquiring a reputation for theatrics and for placing outlandish design in ready-to-wear fashion. Fly first class overnight on Air France and you'll get a pair of pyjamas designed and signed by the man himself.

Wacko Paco
Paco Rabanne had his first supernatural experience aged seven and has taken an otherworldly outlook ever since. In 1999 he fled Paris, convinced that the Mir space station was going to crash land on the city during a solar eclipse.

Foreign designers have helped France retain its role as a fashion capital. German Karl Lagerfeld is chief couturier at Chanel, injecting a contemporary touch to the label's sleek traditions. In the 1990s the Brits moved in. John Galliano led the charge, first at Givenchy in 1995 and a year later at Christian Dior with diverse collections in extravagant, theatrical shows. Alexander McQueen briefly succeeded Galliano at Givenchy, while another young British designer, Stella McCartney, enjoyed four years at the house of Chloé before jumping ship to Gucci in 2001. But the current darling of Parisian fashion is a Frenchman, Nicolas Ghesquière, responsible for resuscitating the Balenciaga label, blending street and traditional styles with effortless cool and introducing the globally adored skinny pants. Kate Moss, Sienna Miller and Nicole Kidman are all apparently smitten.

yves : il fume :
I have nothing in common
with the
new world of fashion
which has been
reduced to
mere
window
dressing

A sense of style

Parisian women have perfected an understated sexy chic that transcends fashion seasons. They're less inclined towards daring individualism and colour than American or British women, concerned more with the honed femininity of pencil skirts and sleek knits. The BCBG (*bon chic bon genre*) woman is another Parisian constant, wearing a kind of upper middle class uniform of mac, ballet shoes and cashmere sweater. Typically associated with the Right Bank of Paris, the BCBG's have their counterparts in the more bohemian style of the Left Bank: younger and more inventive with trainers, bright colours and jeans. In these and other styles, wider French fashion offers a gauge of social status. Among French youth the street style inspired by American rap culture and characterized by sportswear remains important.

Where do the French buy their clothes?

It would be wrong to imagine that your average Frenchwoman just pops into Chanel on the Rue du Faubourg-St-Honoré whenever she needs a new bag, cardy or fragrance. While a significant minority do indulge in ready-to-wear lines produced by designer labels, most are happy with less brand-conscious garments. Small boutiques and historic department stores like Le Bon Marché and Les Galeries Lafayette sell the big brands, but many French are happy to buy anonymous clothes at knockdown prices in chain stores like Tati, or even in the hypermarket. Others get their togs via post: La Redoute sells a mix of designer and unlabelled clothing for mass mail order consumption. The French only spend about five percent of their disposable income on clothes – less than many other Europeans.

Media and communications

6 Media and communications

6.1 Media

They don't like to brag about it too much but the French had their own version of the Internet before the rest of us. As for print media, radio and television, there is, of course, a distinctly French way of going about things that draws the observer into the nation's culture.

Good news and bad news

There is a certain sense of malaise surrounding the French newspaper industry. For a nation with such a strong historical track record, things aren't looking too rosy. The average citizen still takes a strong interest in current affairs, but the last few decades have seen them look to other sources for their daily news fix. Only around 170 out of every 1,000 French adults take a daily paper. Amongst western European nations, only Spain, Portugal and Italy fare worse. The biggest selling daily nationals, *Le Figaro* and *Le Monde*, are both struggling with a circulation around the 325,000 mark. Compare that with the UK, where around 390 of every 1,000 people take a daily newspaper and *The Daily Telegraph* knocks out around 905,000 copies a day. That's not the full story though – the regional press, by comparison, is thriving. There are three or four titles that at least rival the national press. The Rennes-based *Ouest-France* outsells both of the leading national papers by more than two-to-one with a daily circulation of over 760,000.

Daily newspapers in France: the big five

Ouest-France (circulation: 761,100). Unusual for two reasons: it's bucking the trend of declining readership and it's owned by a non-profit making organization.

L'Équipe (circulation: 358,000 (over 400,000 on a Monday)). Readership may have dipped slightly, but it seems there's enough mileage in sport alone to keep it ahead of papers with a news bias.

Le Figaro (circulation: 326,800). France's oldest daily is traditionally a right wing affair. It required subsidizing in 2004, after which it got a new parent company better known for arms sales.

Le Monde (circulation: 324,400). Traditionally text-heavy, deadly serious, slightly left-wing and internationally respected. Recent changes have seen an increase in images and graphics, and, shocker, a World Cup supplement.

Libération (circulation: 135,600). Founded by Jean-Paul Sartre and friends in 1973. Currently in serious financial strife, it has softened its socialist agenda somewhat since its inception, when all staff, from editor to tea-boy, received the same salary.

(Circulation figures from 2005)

Media moguls and government control

The loss of readership and advertising revenue has allowed big business to move in on most of the country's leading newspaper titles. The Dassault Group, for example, now has a majority share of Socpresse, the parent company of *Le Figaro*, *L'Express* and a number of other titles. Dassault is the arms company that manufactures the Mirage fighter jet – some have suggested that they didn't waste much time in warning their journalists off publishing stories that might affect France's commercial performance. The government also gets involved in the newspaper industry, with subsidies totalling around €38 million a year. These can take many forms, from reduced telecommunication costs and grants for printing plants to half price train travel and a 30% reduction on income tax for journalists. The government also controls the cover price of newspapers. One paper that slips through the regulatory net more than most is the weekly satirical paper *Le Canard Enchaîné*. The name, which translates as 'The chained up duck' is a reference to an earlier paper called *L'Homme Libre*, which was forced to close after heavy government censorship.

Freedom of the press?
Press freedom came under the spotlight in 2006 amid the uproar surrounding the decision by five French papers to reprint satirical Danish cartoons of the Prophet Muhammad. The managing editor of *France Soir*, Jacques Lefranc, was sacked as a result – the only direct editorial casualty of the whole furore. Reporters sans Frontières, an international organization promoting freedom of the press, were less than impressed.

The kids' daily
France is home to the world's first and.longest-running daily newspaper for children. Aimed at 10-14-year-olds, *Mon Quotidien* has been running since 1995 and shifts 200,000 copies a day.

1. Identity the foundations of French culture
2. Literature and philosophy
3. Art, architecture and design
4. Performing arts
5. Arbiters of style cinema, photography and fashion
6. Media and communications
7. Consuming culture food and drink
8. Living culture: the state of the nation

In contrast to newspapers, the magazine industry is doing rather well for itself. Better than that in fact, France has the highest level of magazine readership in the world. Amongst the country's estimated 7,600 titles are a number that have become internationally read and instantly recognizable. You will almost certainly be familiar with *ELLE, Marie Claire* and *Paris Match*, but the French also enjoy a vast monthly output of law, technical chidren's and even agriculture-based magazines. The periodical, it would seem, is much more the French way

Match made in heaven

The *Paris Match* blend of paparazzi photography, sex, scandal and current affairs is also faring extremely well. It's more than just an intellectual gossip mag though; *Paris Match* has recently moved more towards the *Time* model, carrying major national and international news stories, and was first to break the story that Ségolène Royal intended to run for the 2007 Presidential elections. With over 1.3 million copies circulated each week, *Paris Match* is clearly how many French like their current affairs.

Women's magazines

Fashion publishing is synonymous with the French media, most obviously represented by *ELLE* and *Marie Claire*. Although they are now published across the globe in languages from Thai to Turkish, they both have their roots in Paris. There is some confusion over which is the original. *ELLE* has been helping to define feminine fashions since 1945. *Marie Claire*, however, was established by the industrialist Jean Provoust back in 1937. It was an instant success and continued to be published each Wednesday until the occupying Germans put a stop to it. *Marie Claire* was not re-published again until 1954, when it was reincarnated as a monthly title.

From small acorns
The world's largest
and most influential
magazine publisher,
responsible for dozens
of popular titles, comes
from humble French
origins. Hachette
Filipacchi Media can
be traced back to
1822 when Louis
Hachette was kicked
out of his seminary
for reasons termed
'political'. Having
tried his hand at law,
he then established
a small educational
publishing house and
the *Bibliothèque des
Chemins de Fer*. The
publication of his first
magazine, *Le Journal
pour Tous*, was a great

success, selling over 150,000 copies a week. The
company has never looked back. Today Hachette
Filipacchi dominates the French market, boasting
ELLE, *Paris Match*, *L'Equipe* and a large share in
Marie Claire amongst its prize European assets.

Hachette job
Emile Zola, one of the great
French writers, famous for
his controversial open letter,
J'Accuse, offering comment
on the Dreyfus Affair, was
employed in the sales
department of Hachette's
publishing house before his
breakthrough.

French residents pay a TV license: *la redevance télé* costs around £80 a year and is collected alongside the *taxe d'habitation*, the nationwide occupant's tax. There are seven terrestrial channels and if you want more, you pay the price. In contrast to other Western nations, many educated or middle class French barely watch television at home at all. This, it would seem, is because a lot of French television requires little cerebral involvement.

Interference with the picture

The issue of programme standards is a fairly contentious one in France. There is a good word, *abrutissant*, which is often levelled at French programming. Essentially, it means mind numbing. There is a problem with funding at grass roots level, which means that not much good quality French material is produced. That didn't help TF1 back in 1992 though, when it was charged with not showing enough home-grown programmes. The question of content control is somewhat muddied, but the Conseil Supérior de L'Audiovisuel is charged with making sure there are appropriate levels of French language and culture on show. There is also a law preventing terrestrial channels from showing films before 11pm on a Saturday in order to protect the cinema industry. Although there was uproar at the sexual content of the French version of *Big Brother* back in 2001, there is a general a greater tolerance of adult content. Don't be surprised to see mild nudity on your screens during the daytime.

What's on the box?

TF1
Originally state-owned and license funded, now a commercial channel showing a mix of game shows, imported sitcoms and the usual major international formats.

France 2
Misleadingly named, this is the first of the state-owned channels. This is where you tend to find the best news coverage and higher pedigree programmes. They take the license fee but still make you watch adverts.

France 3
Another state-funded channel, France 3 concentrates on regional programming, anchored by a national news show from Paris. It also features plenty of old films.

Canal Plus
Privately owned and only free to view for two hours a day. After that, you'll need a decoder. Lots of imported and dubbed content, but also some good films as the company finances a wide range of film productions.

France 5
This is the state's more educational channel, filling its time with documentaries, news and current affairs.

Arte
A Franco-German channel that shares a signal with France 5 from 7pm until midnight, broadcasting a varied mix of cultural programming.

M6
Proudly broadcasting soft porn and American sitcoms since 1987. Ooh la la!

Lost and found in translation

A number of French programmes have borrowed their format from abroad. Reality TV's favourite formula, *Big Brother*, hasn't proved particularly popular in France. *Loft Story*, as the French version was called, provoked outrage with protest groups dumping rubbish bins and rioting outside the set. Some complained that the contestants were treated as 'mice' and 'chickens'. The music format has fared rather better for reality TV. TF1's *Star Academy* has spawned such chart sensations as Jenifer Bartoli and Nolwenn Leroy. It began its sixth season in September 2006, a longevity rivalled only by the Russian version. You may not have heard of Gilles Triquet of *Le Bureau*, but his particular brand of office management has a toe-curling familiarity. Following the success of *The Office* in America, adapted from the UK original, Canal Plus

decided to ship the format across the Channel. Barring a few cultural changes, it stuck pretty closely to the original script. France has never before looked so drab. The major departure from the original is the casting of respected actor François Berléand as Triquet (David Brent) rather than the standard cast of little-known actors. *Le Bureau* met with rave reviews, particularly from critics who apparently saw in Triquet a searing personification of modern France.

The world through French eyes
At the end of 2006, prompted by President Chirac's fears that BBC World, CNN et al were giving global news an Anglo-Saxon bias, France 24 was launched. Broadcasting initially in English and French but with Arabic and Spanish variants imminent, the new international news channel reaches its audience via satellite and the Internet. France 24's journalists have apparently signed a mission statement promising to "cover international news with a French perspective."

Outside looking in
Although private
broadcasting has only
been legal since 1982,
key commercial stations
RTL (formerly Radio
Luxembourg), Radio
Monte Carlo and Europe
1 have been entertaining
listeners from their bases
just outside the French
border for over 50 years.

The French tune in

Radio in France began in earnest in 1921 when a member of the *sapeurs-pompiers* read out a weather forecast and the stock market news from a studio in the Eiffel Tower. Quite why a fireman was chosen for this role is shrouded in the mists of time, but we do know that by the outbreak of the Second World War there were five million radio sets shared between 41 million citizens. Radio retains an important role in French life, and government figures suggest that most French still spend at least two hours a day tuned in.

Who controls the dial?

French radio stations are split between those in the public sector, which are controlled by Radio France, and private stations. The private stations are generally known as *radios libres*, or formally as *Radio Locales Privées* (RLPs). They are numerous, diverse and have mushroomed since the early 1980s when the French government opened the nation's airwaves to competition. Radio France is the BBCesque umbrella organization with control over the national stations. It was created in 1975 to take over the radio responsibilities of the Office de Radiodiffusion Télévision Française, a larger public body which, under a variety of acronyms, had run the country's TV and radio since the war. Separate and distinct from Radio France since 1986 is *Radio-France Internationale* (RFI), which fulfils the same role as the BBC World Service in the francophone world.

Home advantage

In 1996 a controversial new law came into effect, forcing French radio not only to make sure that 40% of the music it broadcasts is in French or French dialects, but also that half of all this French music must be from new talent or at least released within the last six months.
The aim was to help French artists and halt the spread of Americanization. The initial reaction, from the commercial stations at least, was one of horror. "Totalitarian and useless" were the words of Christian Bellanger, then President of Skyrock, a major private broadcaster.
It was assumed that the major US-controlled French record labels didn't produce enough good quality French-language music to fill airtime and meet quotas. The Conseil Supérior de L'Audiovisuel watchdogs have the power to fine or remove the broadcast license of any station not meeting the rules, so if you listen to any French station these days you'll find that, almost without exception, every second track is in French. Some argue that they were right, that there wasn't and indeed still isn't enough good quality French music to fill the schedules, particularly for the niche stations. Although some stations (those broadcasting classical music for example) are allowed to ignore the rules, the net result is that many French acts have become expert at translating lyrics written in English.

National radio stations

France Bleu
targeted at older listeners

France Culture
cultural content

France Info
news station

France Inter
general mix of music, entertainment and current affairs

France Inter Paris
a broad range of music

France Musique
classical and jazz music

Le Mouv
a pop music station

6.1.5 Overexposure: the cult of celebrity

The President's daughter
President Mitterrand was able to keep his illegitimate daughter out of the media spotlight for 20 years. It was not until 1994, when Mitterrand was approaching retirement and his influence was on the wane, that the news broke. The daughter, Marazine Pingeot, is now a novelist and television personality.

Tabloid void

France doesn't really have a daily tabloid press as such. Established weekly French titles such as *Ici Paris* and *France Dimanche* have been filling the nation's celebrity gossip hole since the 1940s, but it took the introduction of *Voici* and *Gala*, both German-owned, to turn things particularly lurid. That's not to say they're particularly intrusive by Anglo-Saxon standards. *Voici* openly admits to making things up and sets aside a budget for libel damages. *Infos du Monde* is another sensationalist weekly rag that has been running since 1994 and is doing reasonably well. While the French may consider themselves above the Anglo-Saxon clamour for celeb gossip, in truth there is a widespread interest in what the great and the good are doing in private. Magazines like *Closer*, *Voici* and *Public*, among what is known as *le press public*, have all seen rocketing circulation figures in recent years.

A private people

Although Brigitte Bardot was famously hounded by the paparazzi and attempted suicide as a result of the pressures of fame, the cause was international success and a lifestyle ahead of her time rather than anything peculiarly French. Indeed, French stars enjoy far greater levels of privacy than might be expected elsewhere, in the UK for example, and some are even said to deliberately court press intrusion so they can benefit financially from the eventual settlement. Newspapers will often have to sit on lurid revelations about the private lives of politicians because if the scandal is not deemed to be 'in the public interest' then they risk litigation - even if the facts are all accurate.

Minitel versus the World Wide Web

As a nation, the French like to do things differently. In 1983, a good decade or so before the Internet took off in the rest of the world, PTT (*Poste, Téléphone et Télécommunications*) started to hand out the first of its ground-breaking Minitel sets to their telephone subscribers. The French were searching residential phone numbers, buying tickets and checking their stocks and shares online whilst the rest of the world was still getting all clammy about the fax machine. It's difficult to see it today but these little sets were an exciting technological innovation. They never quite ushered in the new era that was expected of them though. The uptake was excellent within France itself; all you had to do was forego your free copy of the residential phone listings. However, requiring strong political will and a telecommunications company with a total monopoly to succeed, it just never spread to the rest of the world. The system is still available and is now integrated with the Internet as a whole.

From leading light to millstone

Considering that it was such a forward thinking and innovative piece of technology, Minitel didn't do much to advance the march of the information age in France. One estimate claimed that Internet usage grew 50,000 times faster in the USA than it did in France during the early to mid-1990s. The French may have been slow to log on to the Internet but they did get there in the end. Between 2000 and 2004, the number of Net users in France rose from 8.5 million (14% of the population) to 24.8 million (41%). Broadband is now widely available, you'll find Internet cafés in most towns and post offices also offer Web access. French Internet companies are also beginning to make an impression abroad; Wanadoo (a subsidiary of France Télécom) is a big success story.

Voulez-vous coucher avec moi (ce soir)?
As with the Internet, the creators of Minitel failed to predict the huge and almost instantaneous demand for personal chat and pornography. On Minitel, the latter largely takes the form of erotic message boards or *messageries roses*.

Chirac takes on Google
In 2006, President Chirac launched plans to create a European answer to all-powerful search engine giants Google. He recruited financial help from Germany but the project to create Quaero (Latin for 'I search') stalled amid concerns over Chirac's apparent determination to declare war on English language search engines and the fact that any investment (and technological advance) made would be dwarfed by the fiscal might of Google.

Loic Le Meur
(www.loiclemeur.com).
The king of French blogs
has put out interviews
with various politicians
via podcast (also available
in English).

Skyblog
(www.skyblog.com)
A bit like a French
MySpace, the single
biggest host of French
blogs provides a public
platform for around 2.5
million teens and twenty-
somethings. Used by
some as an online
allying point during the
2005 riots.

Pointblog
(www.pointblog.com).
Slick commentary on
current affairs and all
things blog based.

Cyber-café culture: the blog generation
Blogging is one aspect of New Media that the
French have really taken to their hearts. It is
estimated that between three and four million
citizens have their own blogs; a figure that
represents about 5% of the current population
and makes them the world's biggest bloggers.
The French taste for public political debate
and philosophy may be what fuels the café
culture, while their collective lack of trust in
the mainstream media probably motivates the
phenomenal success of the web log. Loic Le
Meur, the nation's *premiere blogeur* was quoted
in *Le Monde* as saying: "The French *blogosphère*
is replacing the function that used to be provided
by cafés. The French have big egos and like to
express them."

1. comedy: 2. education   3. art, architecture   4. Performing arts   5. Artistic culture: 6. Media and   7. Consuming culture: 8. Living culture: the
the foundations of and philosophy   and design   cinema, photography   communications   print and drink   state of the nation
French culture   and fashion

Blogs and politics

During the run up to the 2005 referendum on the EU Constitution, a blog run by Marseilles schoolteacher Etienne Chouard attracted over 700,000 visitors and is credited with having influenced the eventual *'non'* vote.

The only candidate not to have a personal blog in the early run up to the 2007 Presidential elections was Nicolas Sarkozy. He simply enlisted the public support of Loic Le Meur, France's most-read blogger. Ségolène Royal used her own blog *Desirs d'Avenir* to interact with the public and develop an election manifesto.

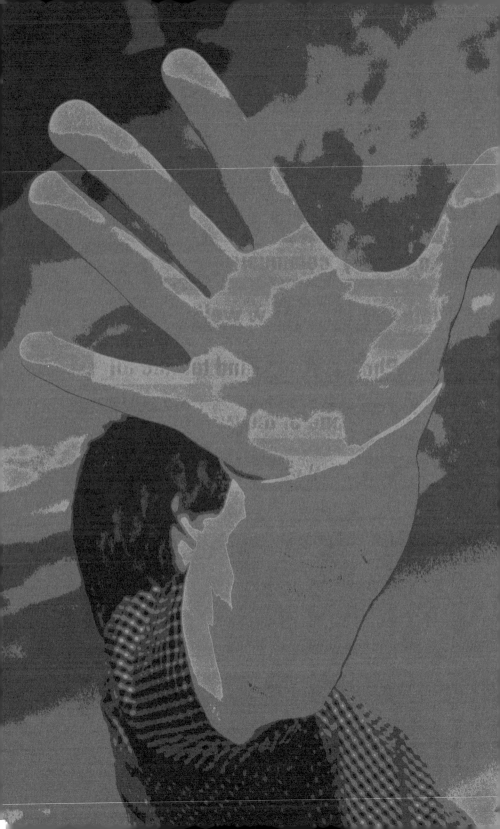

6.2 Communications

When we say 'communications' we're not talking about a few well-timed shrugs. Phones, trains and tarmac all contribute to one of the world's slickest (in parts at least) networks for keeping people connected.

Coded messages

The French postal system began using postal codes in 1964. Today, any letter addressed without a five-digit codes *postaux* is unlikely to reach its intended destination.

France celebrates the humble stamp each March with La Fête du Timbre, a nationwide weekend of philately-related events.

Delivery notes

Louis XI is sometimes credited with leading the French to the letterbox, establishing a system of relayed post horses in 1464 to carry written instruction out to the provinces. By the late 18th century, the combination of *poste aux chevaux* and a *petite poste* that moved mail more locally found most of France enjoying a delivery every two days. As trains replaced horses, the efficiency of mail carriage grew, aided by the use of postage stamps from the 1840s. Throughout much of the 20th century, post and telecoms fell under the jurisdiction of one governmental department, but in 1971 they parted company and by 1990 bore the labels of La Poste and France Télécom. La Poste carries a familiar iconography: the yellow post boxes and delivery vans with their blue logo are an unmistakable part of everyday French life. You can use the post office for banking, paying bills and, where the *Cyberposte* service operates, surfing the Net. In recent years, the service has been slammed as a lumbering dinosaur when compared to privatized equivalents elsewhere in Europe, but reform is rapidly unfurling ahead of new EU deregulation directives that come into force in 2009.

It's alright, Geoff, he said he's off to a philately-related event..

Post modern

Like the rest of us, the French are writing fewer letters than they used to. Email, telephones and the pace of modern life all share the blame. Traditionally, when they do sit down to compose formal correspondence, the French have been renowned for wordy phrasing. Today, the norm is less convoluted but you will still see the likes of 'Please be willing to accept, sir, the expression of my distinguished sentiments' used to conclude a letter. The exact wording will depend on the author's literary dexterity as well as their relationship with the recipient. When it comes to cards, the French are more likely to acknowledge New Year than Christmas.

France on the phone

France first got on the blower in 1878 and control of the fledgling telephone network fell into government hands a decade later. However, only after the Second World War did telecommunications begin playing a role in everyday life. Even then services were shoddy at best, with paltry state investment. Only major and rapid modernization in the 1970s gave France the efficient telecoms network expected of a developed nation. The industry has been partially privatized since 1998. The old state network, France Télécom, still owns the lines but call charges have been opened up to the private market. Neuf Cegetel and Bouygues Telecom have emerged alongside France Télécom as the market leaders. Both are similarly big players in the nation's burgeoning mobile phone market. Orange France, another giant in the mobile market, is owned by France Télécom. The French have embraced the cell phone with enthusiasm, enamoured in particular with SMS messaging, for which younger users are rapidly developing a thumbnail version of the French language. As with their use of the landline, the French are perhaps less likely than other Westerners to chitchat on the mobile phone, using it instead for arranging face-to-face assignations.

La Poste: mail pride

La Poste deals with around 25 billion pieces of mail each year

France has around 17,000 post offices

La Poste is the second biggest employer in France with over 300,000 staff

Signalman
Inventor Claude Chappe initiated the first telecommunications network in France with trials of his semaphore system in 1792. Essentially a series of towers with large moveable rods on top, the system was first used to send a message from Paris to Lille. Napoleon later used the relay stations to help manoeuvre troops. As for Claude, he was a sensitive soul who jumped to his death down a well, depressed when rivals began questioning the originality of his design.

In 2005 mobile service providers Orange France, SFR and Bouygues were fined more than €500 million for controlling the market by sharing commercial information.

Off the rails
Since its inception
in 1981, the TGV has
derailed three times at
speeds varying between
155mph and 186mph.
Yet the safety record is
excellent – none of the
incidents caused serious
injury to passengers.

In cultural terms, France pays its transport system due reverence. On the nationalized railways, Gallic pride swells amid enviable post-war achievement – hang the cost. But there's more to it than simply running on time (the usually tardy French are beguilingly punctual when it comes to trains): from the sleek nose of the TGV to the ornate tiling of a Métro station, the bland realities of modern travel take on a seductive *élan* in French hands. On the roads, the less winsome side of the French nature hones into view…often flashing its headlights.

Back on track: the French railways

The French rail network was all but destroyed in the Second World War, but the SNCF (*Société nationale des chemin de fer français*) bounced back with remarkable verve. The TGV (*Train à grande vitesse*) epitomizes its success. In 2006 the high-speed train celebrated its 25th birthday. It first made headlines by halving the journey time from Paris to Lyons back in 1981 and the special track required to run the TGV has since thrust out to the Atlantic, the Channel and the Med. The train has also proved a success in the export market: in 2006 Taiwan became the latest country to launch a version. Much of France's remaining rail network is served by the similarly efficient *Grand Lignes*. Alas, such an enviable rail system doesn't stop the French from descending into indignant rage at the first sign of a delay.

Underground movement: the Paris Métro

Since making its first journey in 1900, the Paris Métro has become a potent icon for its host city. Sixteen lines shunt upwards of four million passengers (expect to be jostled) between 297 stations (22 more than London) every day from 5am to about 1am. Many of the stations retain their fine Art Nouveau-led interiors, although Hector Guimard's enchanting entrance ways are thin on the ground. The RER (*Réseau express regional*) network, linking Paris' extensive suburban rail system with the Métro, was conceived in the 1960s.

Life in the fast lane: France on the road

The French fell in love with the car back in the 1960s and the infatuation has yet to stall. Nearly a third of people own at least two, which they drive around a network of tolled *autoroutes* and free *routes nationales* and *départementales*. Behind the wheel, the French have traditionally found

1. Identity,
the maintenance of
French culture   2. Literature
and philosophy   3. Art, architecture
and design   4. Performing arts   5. Ârbiters of style:
fashion, gastronomy
and fashion   **6. Media and
communications**   7. Consuming culture:
food and drink   8. Letting off steam:
leisure and sport

their most Latin form. Speeding, tailgating and a collective blindspot when it comes to pedestrians all seem to find greater expression here than elsewhere. For the inexperienced foreigner who gets in the way, vigorous hand gestures and a verbal volley can be expected. Until recently the French style of driving gave the country an unenviable road mortality rate. Only protracted government campaigns – including metal roadside figures marking where road users have been killed – have reduced the annual death toll from its early 1970s high of more than 16,000. A zero tolerance campaign focussing on lowered speed limits, tougher drink driving laws and the enforcement of seatbelt use saw deaths fall below 5,000 in 2005. By the way, when they do start flashing their lights at you it means 'get out of the way', not 'after you'.

Domestic bliss: French air travel

The French also enjoying flying, although usually only do so within the bounds of the Hexagon: no other European country has such a complex web of domestic air routes. Historically, France has played an important role in the evolution of aviation. The Montgolfier brothers invented air travel with their balloon in the late 18th century before the extravagantly moustachioed Louis Bleriot became the first person to fly a plane across the Channel in 1909. Early advances in long haul flying, reaching South America in the 1930s, furthered the cause. The 1930s also saw the birth of Air France, the country's national carrier.

Travelling by canal

For a more sedate travel experience, the French turn to their extensive canal network (although it seems far more popular with foreign tourists). Over 5,000 miles of navigable water courses through the country. Some routes boast UNESCO World Heritage status, not least the 17th century Canal du Midi linking Atlantic and Mediterranean. The Canal de Briare is similarly historic, used to connect the Loire and the Seine since 1642.

Return of the streetcar
At the end of 2006, Paris began operating a tramline for the first time in nearly 70 years. The turfed, tree-lined eight kilometre line links the 13th, 14th and 15th arrondissements, replacing an overworked bus service at a cost of €300 million. It was unveiled as part of mayor Bertrand Delanoë's efforts to get Parisians out of their cars. The capital followed the lead of cities like Strasbourg, Bordeaux and Lyons, all of which have modern tram networks.

The Procotip scheme in Marseilles was the world's first car sharing scheme. It ran for two years in the early 1970s.

Trains in France, in contrast to cars, pass each other on the left.

7 Consuming culture: food and drink

7 Consuming culture:
food and drink

7.1 Food

La cuisine. Where do you start?

Nothing is more fundamental to the French cultural experience than food. It's a sensual, sociable, twice daily homage to the aesthetics and flavours of life itself. And, despite recent swipes from a foreign media eager to perceive a decline in standards, in global terms France remains the epicurean font.

7.1.1 A national obsession: the French love of food

The first Michelin Guide was published in 1900 – it was distributed free until 1920.

Foodie bible *Larousse Gastronomique*, first published in 1938, is considered the bible of French food. A second edition, printed in 2001, includes food from around the world – even Yorkshire Puddings get a mention.

The spirit of the AOC harks back to the 15th century when Roquefort cheese production was controlled by parliamentary decree.

"WHOEVER SAYS 'TRUFFLE' UTTERS A GREAT WORD WHICH AROUSES EROTIC AND GASTRONOMIC MEMORIES AMONG THE SKIRTED SEX AND MEMORIES GASTRONOMIC AND EROTIC AMONG THE BEARDED SEX".

Or so reckoned Jean-Anthèlme Brillat-Savarin, often labelled the father of gastronomy

It is perhaps misleading to talk about a national cuisine when, like much of French life, produce and cooking are subject to extensive regional variation. True, certain staple dishes appear on most menus (*cassoulet, bouillabaisse* etc), but local landscape and climate still determine many of the dishes served up in restaurants and homes. For instance, in Brittany the sea yields clams, perfect topped with shallots, parsley, butter and breadcrumbs (*praires farcies*); while in Burgundy, the famous vineyards attract luckless snails, to be simmered in wine and then bathed in garlic and parsley butter (*escargots à la Bourguignonne*).

Attitudes to food have changed in the last 20 years. Fewer people now linger over the two-hour lunch, a reduced share of income goes on food and the diet tends to be less calorific than of old. Such are the pressures of modern life. Some cite new eating habits as indicative of the French battle between modernity and tradition. Yet the passion remains and French cooking continues to evolve. The late 20th century fad for *nouvelle cuisine* has abated, but its taste for innovation and for fine fresh produce is increasingly applied to the traditions of country cooking (*cuisine du terroir*), now back in fashion. Supermarkets have latched on to the rediscovered taste for seasonal, small-scale food production. Of course, on local market stalls and in the small town *charcuterie or boulangerie* the trend never went away.

What is *terroir?*

The word may have ancient connotations but *terroir* is a fashionable, if hard to quantify, facet of modern French cuisine. The term embraces land, climate, culture and produce, an intangible catch-all for that sense of place so important to the regions' food and wine. So, that wild boar stew from just south of Orléans only tastes as good as it does because the ingredients flourished in the physical and climatic conditions unique to the Sologne forest. More traditionally, the term *terroir* has been applied to wine, used to describe the unique combination of soil, climate and topography that generates a particular vintage.

The name game: AOC standards

One downside of having so much great food is that everyone else tries to rip if off. In an effort to safeguard regional produce from pale imitation, the French government devised the complex *Appellation d'origine contrôlée* (AOC). Any food bearing the AOC standard will have been traditionally made with ingredients drawn from a specific area and will conform to set standards. Only such produce can bear the name of its locale. Butter from Poitou-Charentes, walnuts from Grenoble and mussels from the bay at Mont St Michel all wear the AOC badge with pride. As with *terroir*, the use of standards like the AOC has lapped over from the world of French wine.

Guilty pleasures

To the gourmand's horror, France has developed an unexpected lust for American-style fast food. There's a McDonalds on the Champs Elysées and a burger joint in pretty much every town across the country. On average, French people now spend nearly 70 euros a year each on *les hamburgers*. But not everyone has developed the taste: the Astérix-moustachioed José Bové gained folk hero status in 1999 after he and fellow farmers dismantled a half built McDonalds in the town of Millau. The Americanized Buffálo Grill chain of steakhouses has also proved a resounding hit with many diners – there are more than 250 across France. Even the accusation that their restaurants used banned British beef between 1996 and 2000 hasn't dimmed their popularity.

Five key dates of French food

1533
Italian aristo Catherine de Medici marries into French royalty and, under her guidance, the Court gets passionate about its food for the first time.

1691
François Massialot reveals the recipes of Louis XIV's kitchen in *Le Cuisinier Royal et Bourgeois*, effectively launching *haute cuisine*.

1765
When Parisian soup maker Monsieur Boulanger offers customers at his tavern a choice of dishes, the world gets its first restaurant.

1902
Auguste Escoffier pens *La Grande Culinaire;* 500 recipes of the rich, sauce-based cooking that would dominate 20th century French cuisine.

1969
Food critics Millau, Gault and Gayot identify 48 chefs creating lighter food focused on fresh produce, recognizing *nouvelle cuisine* for the first time.

Carrots from Creances (Normandy)

Coco de Paimpol – white haricot beans (Brittany)

Oysters from Belon (Brittany)

The taste for beer in Nord-Pas-de-Calais seeps into the cooking pot. Chicken is braised in dark ale to make *coq à la bière* and the viscous beef stew, *carbonnade à la flamande*, wallows in the local brew.

Accept no imitations: genuine *quiche Lorraine* is simply made with flaky pastry and a filling of beaten eggs, cream and fried lardons.

i. North and North-west

Lush, fertile **Normandy**, laced with orchards and grazed by brown and white Normande cows, is the milk churn of France. The region abounds in fine cheeses such as Camembert, Pont-l'Evêque and Livarot, while rich butters and creams infuse the local cuisine. Seafood is another staple: nowhere in France catches more oysters or scallops. Normandy is also the home of *brioche*. In **Brittany,** the diet is similarly guided by fish and seafood. Towns have become famously allied to their catches: oysters in Cacale, crabs in St Malo and lobsters in Camaret. *Primeurs* (spring vegetables) grow well ahead of globe artichokes and leeks where the soil allows, and cereals are used for *crêpes* and their buckwheat cousins, *gallettes*. Saint Paulin and Campénéac, both semi-hard cheeses of monastic origin, are made here too. **Picardy** and **Nord-Pas-de-Calais** are largely overlooked in the gourmand's France, yet both harbour some worthy local fare. Cuisine from the Nord takes its lead from vegetables and fish. In Picardy, highly prized *pré salé* lamb is reared on the salt marshes of the Somme Estuary for a distinct flavour, while the region's opulent summer fruits are used to make sorbets.

ii. North-east

In **Alsace**, with its strong Germanic flavour, cuisine reaches furthest from the French norm. This divergence hasn't stopped the recent rise in popularity of the region's robust food across France. The fertile landscape is regal veg territory and, in the plains around Strasbourg, the white cabbage is king. Cured pork and sausage are also fundamental to the diet – *charcuteries* sell some 200 local specialities – while the pungent rind-washed Munster Fermier is the AOC cheese of choice. Forests yield fruits and berries that end up in breads and tarts.

In the wilds of **Lorraine** and the **Ardennes** the woodland serves up wild boar, venison and mushrooms, while carp, pike and trout are all caught in the rivers and lakes. Pork here comes in many forms, from pâté to suckling pig, salt cured belly pork to *saucisson*, but the most famous remains the dry salted, air cured *jambon d'Ardennes*.

iii. Paris and Île de France

Paris, despite what people from Lyons may tell you, is the gastronomic mecca of France. Although the city doesn't retain a definable menu of its own, it soaks up produce and culinary expertise from across the country, bringing together a wealth of excellent markets, delis, bistros and restaurants. Migrants have also brought Paris the flavours of world cuisine (especially North African and Vietnamese) – tastes that are gradually spreading out to the rest of the country. The capital's hinterland clings to its shrinking agricultural backcloth. Market gardens and orchards support fruit and vegetables, and the celebrated likes of Montmorency cherries and white Argenteuil asparagus still grow in the region, even if the towns that gave them a name have been largely swallowed by the suburbs of northern Paris. Salad vegetables provide the principle crop of the Île's main agricultural area, Seine-et-Marne, to the east of the city. Here too, the ancient province of Brie continues to make its famous cheese.

Do your chous up
The first Alsatian cabbages of the season are usually shredded in time for Bastille Day to make *Choucroute Nouvelle*. Another favourite, *Choucroute Alsacienne*, typically simmers the lightly pickled cabbage in Reisling before draping it in variations of Strasbourg sausage, pork loin, bacon and pork knuckle.

Champagne: beyond the bubbles
The Champagne region may be best known for the bubbly stuff but it also produces some fine cheeses. Chaource is the most famous. Mild, with a faint odour of mushroom, the small round AOC cheese with an edible white rind is best enjoyed after just a few weeks' aging. Another Champagne delicacy takes pig trotters on a journey through poaching, breadcrumbs and grilling.

The Gâtinais area south of Paris is renowned for its white honey and its saffron.

The king's cheese
The most famous Brie of them all, produced in the town of Meaux 20 miles north-east of Paris, uses 20 litres of unpasteurized milk to produce one 35cm wide AOC cheese.

Let them eat soup
If Paris does retain an indigenous cuisine, soup probably comes closest to fulfilling the role. *Soupe a l'oignon*, often served covered with a crust of cooked cheese *(gratinée)*, and the thick, pea-based potage *St-Germain*, are favourites.

Budding enterprise
The town of Provins produces a preserve made from the crystallized petals of the Provins Rose. In medieval times, the town was a European centre for the 'Apothecary's Rose' (one of various other names for the flower), whose oil was thought to have medicinal qualities.

Poulet de Bresse chicken
(Lyons, Burgundy and Jura)

Lentille verte du puy
green lentils (Auvergne)

Noix de Grenoble
walnuts (Alps)

Raclette (Franche-Comté
and Savoy) Traditionally, the
Raclette cheese is melted in
front of the fire (most people
now use a Raclette machine)
and then smeared over boiled
potatoes, onions and gherkins.
It's that easy.

Fondue Savoyard (Savoy)
A warm mixture of Beaufort,
Comté and Gruyère cheeses
cooked with white wine.
Simply douse your hunk of
bread in the bubbling pot and
enjoy.

Tourte au Reblochon
(Savoy) A round Reblochon
cheese baked in a pastry crust.
Reblochon was first made
when 14th century farmers
cheated the milk tax inspectors
by not fully milking their cows.
The second, secretive milking
turned out to produce great
creamy cheese.

iv. Centre and East

The realities of rural life in the Massif Central emerge in the **Auvergne**'s unpretentious cuisine. One-pot cooking blends humble ingredients like cabbage, green lentils, potatoes, bacon and game into hearty stews. Cured meats and smoked and blood sausages are local specialities. While *terroir* is similarly pivotal to **Burgundy**'s famous cuisine, recipes here enjoy the subtleties of wine, mustard and cream. The strong Burgundian cheese, Epoisses de Bourgogne, washed in the *marc de Bourgogne* spirit, is eternally popular, and the region is also home to that national treasure, *coq au vin*. In **Lyons**, French produce reaches its apex. Myriad eastern elements – from Charolais beef to Bresse chicken and, above all, *charcuterie* – collide and the city takes full creative advantage to stake its claim as the nation's gastronomic HQ. In **Franche-Comté** and the Savoyard and Dauphiné **Alps**, the upland herds produce some of the country's finest cheeses and cured meats.

Cultural icons
in the kitchen
The finest French chefs learnt their trade in the kitchens of Lyons and Burgundy. The most famous is Paul Bocuse, trailblazer for *nouvelle cuisine* in the 1970s and now guru of classic French cuisine. He was awarded the Légion d'Honneur in 1975. Paul's main restaurant is just north of Lyons; you'll know it when you see

it – it says Paul Bocuse in giant letters on the roof and a large painting of the great man grins at you from a *trompe l'oeil* window. For some, the pressure of getting it right in the kitchen proves too much. Bernard Loiseau was a famous chef from Burgundy whose reputation for perfectionism brought fame, three Michelin stars and intense critical scrutiny. In

February 2003, Bernard shot himself in the head. Many blamed unfavourable press reviews and a demotion of two points (from 19 to 17 out of 20) in the *Gault Millau* restaurant guide, but the pressures of expanding his restaurant business no doubt played a part as well.

v. West

French cooking took shape in the **Loire**'s royally connected kitchens and tradition has it that you still find the nation's purest palate amid the region's fertile landscape. In Anjou and Touraine the Loire Valley's protective climate is perfect for apples and pears, and the sandy soil ideal for asparagus. Perch, shad, zander, pike and salmon are all served fresh from the region's rivers, often bathed in a *beurre blanc* (wine, butter and shallots) or simple sorrel sauce. The Loire's legendary goat's cheeses include Crottin de Chavignol. On the coast, the peninsula of Guérande offers up a rich harvest of sea salt. Further south, the **Dordogne** dribbles foodie class. Pigs (or more likely dogs these days) snout for elusive black *truffes* and duck and geese livers are fattened for *foie gras* and *confit*. Duck and goose fat flavours everything, from soups to sautéed vegetables. Autumn brings the region a rich walnut harvest. *Foie gras*, *confit*, *cèpes* mushrooms and truffles spread into the **Borderlais** where the warm Garonne valley also supports plums, peaches and pears. Shellfish flourish on the coast west of Bordeaux, as they do along much of the Atlantic seaboard.

In *A Moveable Feast,* Ernest Hemingway commented on the high quality of the *pommes à l'huile*, a staple of Lyons cusine, at the Brasserie Lipp, Paris.

Three AOC foods from the West

Walnuts from Périgord

Butter from Poitou-Charentes

Selles-sur-Cher – Loire goat's milk cheese dusted with ash

Poitou-Charentes is famous for its sweet cantaloupe melon, the Charentais.

Fungi facts

More than half of the mushrooms consumed in France are grown in the 80km of caves around Saumur, in the Loire. Gouged from the soft tufa limestone, the caves and former quarries traditionally produce the champignon de Paris (the button variety), but today they also nurture the exotic likes of oyster and shiitake mushrooms. In the early 20th century, south-west France snuffled out around 1,000 tonnes of truffles each winter. The loss of the mature oak woodland required for truffle growth and the exodus of rural labour have helped reduce that yield to around 35 tonnes in a good year. Demand always outstrips supply, yet despite the lucrative prices paid, few farmers get involved with the notoriously hard to cultivate fungus. Everyone's heard of the famous black, winter truffles of Périgord, but the kitchen's most expensive dark matter also has a less glamorous summer cousin. The summer truffle or Truffle of Saint-Jean, harvested between June and August, is less potent in taste, smell and price.

French cuisine finds its bite in the country's south-western corner. Petulant red chillies are an essential ingredient in **Les Pays Basque**, used to flavour everything from *jambon de Bayonne* to *ttoro*, an Atlantic answer to *bouillabaisse*. Across the Pyrenees, the scrubby, sun drenched lands around the Mediterranean support a colourful crop. **Provence**, with its tomatoes, peppers, aubergines, olives and figs, enjoys a southern European diet. Traditional peasant soups and stews, often fish-based, are flavoured with the region's bountiful wild herbs. *Pieds et paquets* is famously Provençal: lambs' 'feet' and tripe 'packets' slowly cooked with garlic, wine and cured pork. **Languedoc**, similarly blessed with fresh produce, reputedly cultivates the best garlic in France, while neighbouring **Roussillon** digests paella in accordance with its Catalan spirit. In **Corsica**, rosemary, lavender, fennel and thyme, sourced in the island's wild *maquis* undergrowth, blend with tomatoes, olives and lemons to flavour mountain-reared mutton, pork and beef.

Pistou is a Provençal take on Italy's pesto sauce, made from basil, oil and garlic.

Basqueing in the heat
Piment d'Espelette is the most famous of the Basque cooking chillies. They hang in the autumn – drying in vivid scarlet clumps – from the houses of Espelette, a village close to the Spanish border. The chilli was brought to the Basque region by explorers returning from the New World in the 16th century.

Niçoise good taste
Even by southern standards, Nice is blessed with a distinct cuisine. Beside the renowned *salade Niçoise*, the city also serves up the *bagnat* (garlic, tomato and anchovies in a sandwich), *socca* (chick pea pancake), *pissaladière* (onion tart) and, during the February carnival, *ganses* (sweet fritters).

Three southern stews

Cassoulet

Languedoc's humble stew has become a French legend. Soaked haricot beans are cooked with wine, garlic, tomatoes, onions, herbs and pork (duck if your luck's in), and then topped with breadcrumbs. Three inland towns – Toulouse, Carcassonne and Castelnaudary – all claim the superior version.

Stufatu

In Corsica, the traditional peasant's casserole contains beef, mutton or wild boar, languidly cooked in wine and tomatoes to create a thick sauce. As befits Corsica's Italian ancestry, Stufatu is often served with pasta or polenta.

Bouillabaisse

Another national icon born of humble origins, the soupy Provençal stew originated among Marseilles' fishermen who would throw the small, unsellable characters of the catch into the cooking pot. Garlic, tomatoes and saffron usually find their way into the stock, served with bread and a chilli mayonnaise called *rouille*.

i. Bread

Consumed with virtually every meal, bread is integral to the French eating ritual. Freshness is calculated in hours not days, and most *boulangers* will bake at least twice a day to ensure both lunch and dinner are accompanied by fresh bread. The French like their bread crusty: the *baguette* was an innovation designed to get more crust from your loaf. Although bread consumption fell steadily in France during the 20th century (the French ከ ካ eat one fifth of the bread they did in 1900), the modern taste for *produits du terroirs* has seen baking traditions regain ground in the last decade. In bakeries across the country the humble *baguette*, its even slimmer cousin, the *ficelle*, and the fatter *pain* increasingly share shelf space with crusty and chewy *pain de campagne*, rye breads and others made with nuts, wine, olives or meat.

Until the end of the 19th century, most French bread was baked at home or in communal village bakeries with wood-fired ovens. Some of these stone-built *fours banals* have been restored and are used to bake bread during village festivals.

Rising to the occasion

Many villages and towns across France celebrate the humble loaf with an annual bread festival. La Fête du Pain Normand is typical, with traditional local bread baked in the wood-fired ovens and giant bread offerings given to the church. The feast day of Saint-Honore, patron saint of bakers, is celebrated on 16th May.

Use your loaf: five slices of bread etiquette

Don't nibble at your bread before the first course has arrived.

Use your fingers to break the bread – don't cut it with a knife.

It is okay to mop your plate with the bread.

Don't ask for butter to spread on your bread – the French rarely do.

You're unlikely to get a separate plate for bread – put it on the table.

Crumbs of comfort: bread superstition

In rural areas, some still trace the sign of the cross on their daily bread before breaking it.

The French believe that storing bread upside down brings bad luck. Medieval bakers placed bread reserved for the executioner upside down (the axeman was thought to be cursed) and the dark association has lived on.

Loaves that expand in the oven and touch each other are said to have kissed and are thought to bring good luck.

ii. *Charcuterie*

They give you a parade —

Montagne au Perche
in Normandy pays annual
homage to the *boudin noir*
(blood sausage) every
March. Over three miles
of black pudding is
purchased during the
town's three-day fair.

Bayonne in Les Pays
Basque has celebrated
its eponymous ham since
1492 with the Faire au
Jambon at Easter. A hotly
contested award is given
to the year's best producer.

Morteau in Franche-
Comté celebrates its pine
wood-smoked sausage
each August with a parade
through the town.

In France, the traditional
necessity of preserving meat
bred such creativity that it
seems harsh to describe
charcuterie as a mere staple
foodstuff. Sausages, tripe,
pâtés, blood puddings, cured
hams, terrines, rillettes:
charcuterie encompasses all
manner of meat products,
straying well beyond the
traditional pork boundaries
to embrace everything
from goose to wild boar, veal to chicken. *Charcuterie*,
like all French food, is a patchwork of regional tastes, a
mélange from which a few choice cuts have emerged as
nationwide favourites. And, in common with all traditional
French produce, *charcuterie* is also enjoying something
of a renaissance, from the *boudin blanc* (a pork or
chicken sausage) of the north to the *jambon de Bayonne*
(salted, air-cured ham) in the south-west.

then they do this – c'est la vie!

Plates of meat
You will find sausages
amid the main courses on
French menus, but most
charcuterie is served as
an *hors d'ouevres*.
A typical *assiette de
charcuterie* may feature
slices of *andouillette*
(tripe sausage), *saucisson
sec,* garlic sausage and
cured ham. Expect a
lettuce leaf and gherkin
as accompaniment.

Best of the wurst: unusual charcuterie

Jésus
air cured *saucisson sec* from Lyons supposed to resemble the swaddled baby Jesus.

Fromage de Tete
take a pig's head, strip off the meat and set it in a thick, flavoured aspic to make
a popular brawn.

Crépine
white, lacily veined fat encasing a pig's stomach, removed and often wrapped around
sausagemeat.

iii. Cheese

At first glance cheese seems emblematic of
the nation, but in truth it's a food defined by
local variation. When de Gaulle grumbled about
governing a country with 246 different cheeses,
he alluded to the trials of presiding over the
different regions and the French themselves.
The parallel is apt: mass production and regulation
attempt to harness the spirit of great French
cheese, yet consumers retain most affection for
the rule breakers, for the unpasteurized (*lait cru*)
fermier cheeses so important in the prevailing
taste for *terroir*. Today, around 500 variations of
cheese are produced in France, from the cooked
and pressed Beaufort of Savoie, to the soft
and creamy Gris de Lille, rind-washed for three
months. Factory-made cheeses are exported
around the globe; others (most will tell you
the best) are produced on family run farms, in #19
monasteries or even mountainside huts, and
sold on local markets. Certain varieties of cheese
can fall within more than one of these categories.
For instance, the anodyne factory Brie has its
cottage industry cousin.

How to find the best cheese

In all there are 41 *Appellation d'origine contrôlée* cheeses. Roquefort was the first in 1926, Banon the last, awarded the AOC in 2003. To qualify for AOC accreditation each cheese must:

Be made with milk from a set geographical area

Be produced and partly matured in that same area

Be made using traditional methods

Adhere to set size, fat content, rind and texture standards

#20

Cheese bite
Even while mealtimes shrink, cheese – the original snack – shows no signs of a dip in popularity.

Each French person consumes an average of 24.5kg of cheese per year (the Americans get through 12.3kg, the British 8.3kg).

**Getting it right:
five slices of
cheese etiquette**

Going back for seconds
of cheese is very poor
form: it's about taste,
not quantity.

When the cheese tray
comes round, only sample
up to three different
cheeses.

The biggest *faux pas* of
the lot is to cut the nose
off a soft cheese. Cut
slices from the rind of the
cheese to the centre, as
if carving up a pie.

Use wine to clean the
palate between cheeses.

Don't remove the rind
from a cheese before
serving; connoisseurs
won't be impressed.

Homage to fromage: three cheese festivals

Journées du Saint-Nectaire
The Auvergnat village celebrates its famous *pâte pressée* cheese over two days
in June with demonstrations, tastings and competitions.

Foire aux Fromages in Livarot
In praise of the Norman rind-washed Livarot, an AOC cheese known as 'the colonel'
because of the sedge reed bands traditionally used to maintain its round shape.

Reblochon Festival in La Clusaz
On one day in August the Rhône-Alps village celebrates its mountain cheese by cooking
up Reblochon in a giant copper cauldron, to be eaten freshly moulded.

As gastronome Brillant-Savarin once commented:
"A MEAL WITHOUT CHEESE IS LIKE A
BEAUTIFUL WOMAN WITH ONLY ONE EYE."

Less is more

The French society that stopped for two hours at lunch and longer for dinner has gone. Rural communities may still find the time, but for many the working day doesn't accommodate such indulgence. *Nouvelle cuisine* played its part in the change: four cardio-squeezing courses of heavy food every night, just hours after the same at lunch, slipped from fashion. And yet eating in France remains fundamental to the nation's culture. A social meal, with the family group at its core, still stretches on for hours. Also, despite the growth of ready meals, fast food and lunch on the run, unprocessed foods continue to take precedence. Indeed, the young Parisian professional living miles from the nearest whiff of country air is increasingly engaged by *terroir*. Amid the oft-quoted identity crisis of contemporary France, such good honest produce offers a rare chance to connect with *la France profonde*.

Where do they put it all? The French Paradox

The English-speaking media often ponders the French Paradox. That is, how do French women remain so trim on a diet of wickedly rich food? Similarly, when saturated fats are consumed with abandon, why are heart disease levels lower and life expectancies higher than in other Western countries? Various theories have been put forward, but the simple truth seems to be that they eat less. Portions are smaller and, in contrast to the British and Americans, the French rarely snack outside meals. The healing properties of red wine are also thought to play a role in reducing heart disease.

Just over 10% of the French population is deemed clinically obese – half the figure of the UK and a third of that for the USA.

Making a meal of it

Breakfast
often just a bowl of *café au lait* and butter and jam on yesterday's bread. *Croissants* and *pains au chocolats* tend to be eaten at weekends or on special occasions.

Lunch
while still considered the main meal by some, in urban areas the midday *grande bouffe* generally loses out to something in a *baguette*, a *croque monsieur* (ham and cheese toastie) or, deep breath, a hamburger.

Dinner
the French still enjoy an ornate evening meal when opportunity allows. It won't begin until eight but, once it does, expect a minimum of three courses washed down with different wines (all of which will be French). If a main meal was taken at lunch, dinner is more liable to be a salad or quiche.

By law, all French restaurants have to display their menu outside.

The cultural significance of French food emerges in its connection with important dates:

Twelfth Night
the three kings are remembered with a *galette des rois,* a cake containing a *fève* – a dried bean, almond or coin depending on which part of France you're in. Whoever chomps on the lucky charm is crowned king or queen for the day.

Mardi Gras
Shrove Tuesday ushers in an evening of pancakes and fritters.

April Fool's Day
the French give chocolate fish as gifts, and also surreptitiously glue paper fish on each other's backs.

Christmas
the Yuletide blowout traditionally unfurls on Christmas Eve after families return from midnight mass. Typically it begins with oysters, followed by *foie gras* terrine and sourdough bread. The main course has traditionally been turkey stuffed with chestnuts, although capon is increasingly popular today. A cheese course comes next before the obligatory cake and cream log, *bûche de noël,* brings down the curtain

Behavioural problems: dinner with the neighbours

An invitation to dine at someone's house is rare in the city – you're more likely to be lured out to a restaurant (and whoever invites usually pays). In rural areas, however, neighbours or friends may well invite you for a meal *chez nous*. Etiquette dictates you keep to certain rules. Arrive 15 minutes late – they will be expecting it and may get flustered if you turn up while they're still preparing food. Don't wander into the kitchen unless directly invited – it's the veritable inner sanctum. Finally, a gift isn't obligatory, but a plant, book or something similar will be appreciated. Don't take wine unless you're an expert; don't take non-French wine unless you want to be shown the door. Ideally, take a wine from the region you're in or, if in doubt, a bottle of champagne.

A raw deal: vegetarianism in France

Nearly all main dishes served up in French restaurants are meat-based; anything green usually only appears as an accompaniment. In accommodating vegetarians French eateries lag a couple of decades behind the UK and USA. However, the situation is improving – restaurants increasingly offer a vegetarian option on their menus and the Alliance Végétarienne says it knows of more than 180 vegetarian restaurants in France.

Fishy Fridays
Southern France retains the tradition of eating *morue* (salt cod) on a Friday and on certain feast days. Often the dried fish is mashed with olive oil, milk and garlic to form a *brandade de morue.*

While the taste for organic food (labelled *biologique*) grows in France each year, it accounts for less than 2% of food sales.

Small is beautiful

The French have struck a food-buying balance that eludes most Western countries. Cavernous supermarkets have become a familiar facet of French life, yet the march of progress hasn't completely crushed traditional shops and markets underfoot. Queuing in the *boulangerie* or browsing the market stalls remain important daily rituals for many. Some French shoppers, as in other countries, are happy to dine on whatever they can pluck from the supermarket shelf but, for most, convenience still plays second fiddle to traceable, artisanal produce.

Getting Fresh: French markets

Every French town or suburb has at least one food market a week, often more. Produce is local and seasonal, and some of the stalls will be staffed by the producers themselves. But browsing the market is about more than buying food: it's a social experience, a place to catch up on gossip where no self-respecting French woman would be seen without her make-up. As for how to behave, watching the old dears is your best bet. They always know the best stalls, where invariably they will prod and sniff the produce before parting with any cash. Most markets are open by 8am and finished by 1pm; avoid the first hour or two, unless you want to compete with local restaurateurs.

Life on the shelf: French supermarkets

They're huge, cheap and sell a lot more than just food. Clothes, bikes, furniture – the giant French *hypermarché* hovering on the edge of town offers everything under one roof. Food may be sourced more locally than in their British or American counterparts, but it remains mass-produced. While increasing numbers of French – the majority indeed – do their food shopping in supermarkets, many will simply stock up on non-perishables, heading instead to the market or to smaller shops for bread, vegetables, meat and cheese. Nevertheless, many small shops have perished as out-of-town stores draw customers away from town centres.

Cornering the market
Different regions and seasons throw up markets dedicated to particular foods:

Aix-en-Provence
Garlic market every weekend in July.

Lalbenque
Truffle market in the Lot held every Tuesday, December to March.

Marseilles
Fish market unravels on the Quai des Belges each morning.

Farm fresh
If you can't wait for the farmer to come to market, go to him. Many farms sell direct to the public: everything from eggs to *foie gras,* honey to snails can be purchased where you see a *vente directe* sign.

7.2 Drink

Say what you like about New World wannabes, about pomposity or price – France remains the seat of world wine. For the French, oenology takes its place alongside literature, philosophy or cinema as a cultural deity. And then there's the apéritifs, digestifs, beer, cider…

Pre-Roman Vines, probably introduced from ancient Greece, established wine as a daily part of Gaulish life.

Roman Gaul Wine regions emerged, setting the grape growing boundaries that remain little changed today.

Middle Ages onwards Monastic orders played an important role in developing the winemaking process.

Mid 17th century The advent of corks encouraged mass wine consumption.

Late 18th century Revolution took vineyard ownership out of Church hands and passed it, fragmented, to the peasants.

Mid 19th century The phylloxera aphid decimated vineyards. Some grape varieties were lost altogether – only resistant vines brought in from California saved the industry.

1935 The *Appellation d'origine contrôlée* (AOC) classification system was introduced.

Like food, wine is a part of the daily ritual, entwined with customs, festivities and local identity. However, falling exports and shifting drinking habits in France and elsewhere are pressuring the wine industry to adapt. Today, after decades of mechanization, intensification and chemicals, French vineyards are retreating back to the basics of painstaking labour, of hand-picking and sorting, re-establishing the role of the vine in producing high quality wine. In touch with the wider reawakening of rural identity and the faith in *terroir*, the distinct local qualities of French wine are becoming more important than ever.

The wine classifications: what do they mean?

Vin de table. Apart from the prohibition of naming grape origin on the label, there are few laws governing *vin de table*. Accounting for about a quarter of French wine, most *vin de table* is of average quality, although a handful of gems – unable to negotiate the strict AOC regulations – can be found.

Vin de pays. Encompasses about 150 wines of particular regional significance. Originally a humble classification, today many *vin de pays* carry a higher price tag than their AOC cousins. The label tells you where the wine is from, production methods and main grape variety used.

Vin délimité de qualité supérieur (VDQS). A small clutch of wines that fall between *vin de pays* and AOC conforming to rules of production, grape variety and yield. The VDQS classification was due to be phased out a few years ago, but new members are still being created.

Vin d'appellation d'origine contrôlée (AOC). AOC classified wine should only come from the region, town or vineyard on the label. Unfortunately, duplicitous winemakers, often blending in non-AOC varieties, and the complexities of the AOC system itself have devalued its worth.

Grape provenance

While New World wines are free to experiment with new blends and to plant on virgin soil, centuries of development and classification in France have created very strict rules about wine origin and content. Thus, champagne may only contain Chardonnay, Pinot Noir and Pinot Meunier grapes, while you won't find a Cabernet Sauvignon grape in the vineyards of Burgundy.

The main grape varieties

French wines, in contrast to New World varieties, tend to be named by location rather than grape variety. Indeed, today many people only know the famous French grape varieties through their usage on New World wine labels.

Red

Grape	Region	Flavours
Cabernet Sauvignon	Bordeaux (Medoc)	Blackcurrant, green pepper, dark chocolate
Pinot Noir	Red Burgundy, Champagne, Loire, Alsace	Black cherry, strawberry
Merlot	Bordeaux (St Emilion and Pomerol)	Plum, blackberry, mint
Syrah	Rhône Valley, Languedoc-Roussillon	Blackberry, pepper, smoky

White

Grape	Region	Flavours
Chardonnay	White Burgundy (Chablis, Mâcon), Champagne	Fruit, nutty
Sauvignon Blanc	Loire Valley, white Bordeaux, Bergerac	Fresh, gooseberry
Riesling	Alsace	Apple, spice, floral
Chenin Blanc	Loire Valley	Apple, honey, cinnamon
Sémillon	White Bordeaux	Lemon (when dry), honey, peach

To the horror of many French vintners, some New World producers are adding oak chippings to wine fermenting in steel barrels in a shortcut to that wooden barrel matured flavour. Such practices are illegal in France.

An industry under threat

There's no denying that the advent of New World wines has dramatically changed the world market for French wine. French vintners have sometimes described Australian or American wines as industrial and mass-produced, dismissive of new blends using historic grape varieties. Other makers, however, have been keen to learn from Chile, South Africa, Australia and the rest, bringing new techniques back to France. One thing is certain; the French wine industry is being forced to change in response to cheaper wines from overseas.

Huge EU subsidies have traditionally protected French wine, with Europe's vast annual wine surplus bought up and distilled into industrial alcohol or fuel. In June 2006, the EU decided to drain the wine lake by paying vine growers to grub up a proportion of their plants. Many now fear for their livelihood.

Bottling up frustration: wine terrorism

The Comité Régional d'Action Viticole (CRAV) has brought an aggressive edge to the battle against foreign competition. Centred in Languedoc-Roussillon, CRAV members have torched cars, planted bombs and hijacked foreign wine tankers in protest at cheap imports. In 2005, dozens of winemakers in balaclavas smashed vats in an export depot near Montpellier, destroying 100,000 litres of wine.

If you see the phrase *Fût de Chêne* on a label, the wine has been matured in an oak barrel.

Be a cultural connoisseur: how to read a French wine label

French wine labels are nothing if not quirky. They vary widely between the regions. Some declarations of grandeur, like the phrase *grand vins* on Bordeaux wines, are unregulated and effectively meaningless. Others, like the *grand cru* on certain Alsatian wines, give a guide to quality. The name of the wine – a vineyard, estate or a brand – will appear, as well as the vintage. If you're lucky you may even get the constituent grape varieties noted.

There are, however, certain things that must be listed on all labels:

Bottle size
(37.5cl, 75cl or 150cl)

Name and address of the producer (often an abbreviation or pseudonym)

Alcohol content

Classification
(AOC, VDQS etc)

Place of origin (those that don't can only be classified as *vin de table*)

Warning to pregnant women (in 2006 a new law demanded that all wines sold in France carry a message about the dangers of drinking alcohol while pregnant)

The Parisian vineyard

In Montmartre, in the busy heart of central Paris there's a vineyard. Vigne du Clos Montmartre is the last patch of a formerly extensive area under vine. A large party accompanies the annual autumn harvest, which produces about 500 bottles of white Gamay-based Vin de Clos. The wine is put up for sale at auction and the proceeds go to help Montmartre's elderly residents.

Bordeaux

The world's largest fine wine region fills 750 million bottles each year (give or take). Over 13,000 vineyards spread out from the city of Bordeaux, their wines distinguished by the area's subtle variations in climate and soil. North-west of the city, on the Gironde estuary's left bank, the Médoc region is the prima donna of world wine. Médoc reds like St Julian, Pauillac and Margaux are dominated by the smoky, blackcurrant twangs of Cabernet Sauvignon. South of Bordeaux, the gravelly Graves region supports similar reds and a few notable whites. On the Gironde's right bank, Merlot grapes fair better in the clay soils of St Emilion and Pomerol while Entre-Deux-Mers produces famous AOC whites. South of Bordeaux, the world capital of sweet white wine is found in Sauternes where once every three years or so the weather delivers the perfect level of noble rot for a heavenly elixir.

In 1663 Samuel Pepys recorded drinking a bottle of red from the estate of Chateau Haut-Brion (or Ho Bryan to use Pepys spelling), from the Médoc, in the Royal Oak Tavern, London.

Find the wine festival
Marathon du Médoc: in one of the world's stranger celebrations of wine, Bordeaux fans – most in fancy dress – run 26 miles through vineyards and past historic wine chateaux in September. Aid stations feature cheese and wine tasting, prizes are given in wine and non-participants can, of course, pass the time exploring local vintages.

Shaping up the bottle
Wines from Bordeaux are easily recognized by their straight, high-shouldered bottle.

1152
Eleanor of Aquitaine married Henry Plantagenet, heir to the English throne, and the Bordeaux clarets found an appreciative Anglo-Saxon market that has remained faithful ever since.

17th century
Dutch drainage engineers helped expand the Borderlais land under vine, particularly in the Médoc.

1855
The Bordeaux Classification structure was launched, grading the best estates into a two-tier system of *grand crus*, based on the market price of their wine. The system remains in use today, albeit with more symbolic than actual relevance.

1869
Phylloxera crippled the region's wine industry, which only recovered fully in the early 20th century.

Identity
a foundations of
ench culture

2. Literature
and philosophy

3. Art, architecture
and design

4. Performing arts

5. Arbiters of style:
cinema, photography
and fashion

6. Media and
communications

**7. Consuming culture:
food and drink**

8. Living culture: the
state of the nation

ii. Burgundy

Legendary but unpredictable, the spiritual home of both Chardonnay and Pinot Noir is subject to the climatic vagaries of its northerly latitude. Most of the estates here are small (about ten acres), family run affairs dwarfed by the heavyweights and big business of Bordeaux: often a winemaker will take grapes from a vineyard carved up by dozens of different smallholders. Growers must also work within strict legislation demanding that many Burgundian wines are pressed from a single grape variety. When grower, grape, maker and vintage are married successfully, Burgundy makes sublime wine – all you have to do is find the right one. The great dry whites of Chablis, reds and whites of the Côte d'Or and cherry twang of Beaujolais – made solely from Gamay grapes – all reside within the region.

9th Century
Charlemagne apparently selected the slopes of Corton on which to plant his vines, observing that the winter snows melted here first.

Pre-Revolution
Most vineyards in Burgundy were owned by the Church.

1789
Revolution and the divisive inheritance laws of the *Code Napoléon* (1804) fragmented Burgundy's vineyards into a complex patchwork of small plots.

Breaking Burgundy down

Burgundy, like most French wine regions, operates its own classification system alongside the AOC:

Regional
Labelled *Bourgogne Rouge* or *Blanc*, the lowest level of Burgundy wines could come from anywhere in the region.

Village
A wine made only from grapes grown within the boundaries of a certain village.

Premier Cru
Both the village and vineyard name will appear on the label, although some wines are drawn from a mixture of *premier cru* vineyards within one village.

Grand Cru
The cream of the crop can simply carry the name of their vineyard without mentioning the village name.

Oil-burning stoves were traditionally laid out amid the vineyards of Chablis to protect from frost. Today, growers are more likely to use water sprinklers. The water creates a protective layer around the new shoot or the fruit – the water freezes rather than the grape itself.

Find the wine festival Fête de la Pressée: in Chenove, near Dijon, September brings the harvest and a festival that dusts off a 13th century press to squeeze the first grapes of the year.

Shaping up the bottle
In Burgundy the bottle of choice is a portly fellow with gently sloping shoulders reaching down almost to the hip.

iii. Alsace

Sheltering behind the Vosges Mountains, the north-eastern hub of French wine is unique in various respects. The varietals used give much of the region's white wine a perfumed, fruity yet dry taste, alien to most of the country. Similarly, in contrast to colleagues in the other major *appellation contrôlée* regions, Alsatian vintners tend to print a grape name on the label, identifying by variety rather than location. Nearly all the wine produced in Alsace is white, with only a few pockets of Pinot Noir bucking the trend. Gewürztraminer, Riesling and Muscat are three big names – each a bit dryer in Alsatian hands than you might expect.

8th century
Wine was already playing an important role in the Alsatian economy.

12th century
Cultivation began to move from red to white grapes and a cultured grape stock was established.

Early 17th century
The 30 Years' War put the mockers on the region's fledgling wine industry and newcomers, given land by Louis XIV, diluted vineyards with new grape varieties.

Post-Revolution
The situation deteriorated further with lands divided and further fresh planting.

Post-First World War
Alsace worked hard to re-establish its quality vines, emphasizing the four main varietals.

Alsace wine: a question of perception
Alsatian wines have long been revered inside the wine trade, and yet outside the region the public remain strangely unenthusiastic. The Germanic names put many off, unaware that the French variants of Riesling, Gewurztraminer and co don't harbour the sweet pungency of their Teutonic cousins.

Label conscious: classifications in Alsace
Alsace has been granted *appellation contrôlée* status as a whole, indicating that any wine produced here carries the AOC mark. Where a grape is mentioned on the label, the wine will be made purely from that variety. A total of 50 *grand crus* display the name of their vineyard. A few of the region's cheaper wines are blended, in which case the word *Edelzwicker* may appear on the label. Sparkling wines carry the name *Crémant d'Alsace*, while *Vendange Tardive* indicates a wine, often sweet, produced from grapes left on the vine for a late harvest.

Around 80% of Alsatian wines are varietals, pressed from a single grape type.

Find the wine festival Foire Régionale des Vins d'Alsace: this week-long fair in Colmar celebrates wine made across the region; perfect for washing down the distinctive Alsatian cuisine also on show.

Shaping up the bottle Instantly recognizable, the Alsace bottle is tall and slender with a subtle slope to the shoulders.

iv. Champagne

It all begins innocuously enough. Chardonnay, Pinot Noir and Pinot Meunier grapes (and those three alone) are blended to make a still, often sharply acidic wine. A measure of *liqueur de tirage* (sugar and yeast) is added to the bottles, which are then stored for a second fermentation. *Remuage*, gradual turning over a two-month period, brings any yeasty bits to the top before the neck is frozen and the sediment removed (a process called *dégorgement*). A *liqueur d'expédition* (wine and sugar) is then added and a cork quickly banged in to round off the process. Essentially, this complicated, fascinating procedure, the *méthode champenoise*, unfurls because Champagne struggles to produce a good still wine so far north. That said, the quality of champagne remains dependent on the blend of grapes used.

Champagne history uncorked

Antiquity
Pliny recorded winemaking in the Marne in the First Century AD.

Early 17th century.
Sparkling wines were discovered by accident, probably in southern France, when wine shipped in barrels underwent a second fermentation process.

17th century
Still wines from Champagne battled those of Burgundy for the export market in northern Europe.

Late 17th century
The Benedictine monk Dom Pierre Pérignon pioneered the blending of different wines to make champagne. Contrary to popular belief, he was actually trying to produce a still wine.

1818
Widow Clicquot's cellar master perfected the process of *dégorgement.*

1836
M. François, a pharmacist from Châlons-sur-Marne, established a means of judging how much *liqueur de tirage* was required to create the right level of fizz.

1941
The Comité Interprofessionnel du Vin de Champagne (CIVC) was established to protect and promote the drink.

Five bubbly facts

About 270 million bottles of champagne are produced each year

The area around Épernay supports 62 miles of wine cellars

The Champagne region cultivates 30,000 hectares of vines

Two thirds of the annual champagne output is consumed within France

In 1919 the Treaty of Versailles asserted that champagne could only come from this region (alas the US senate never ratified the treaty, so 'champagne' is still produced in the States, although it can't be sold in the EU under that name)

Find the wine festival
Festival of St Vincent: the champagne houses parade, concerts are held and festive dinners take place in Epernay and the surrounding villages each January.

Shaping up the bottle
Chunky glass, gently sloping shoulders and a deep punt are all designed to cope with champagne's pressure situation.

The two main types of champagne

Non-vintage champagne blended from wines produced across various years, using the same proportions each time to create a consistent taste immediately identifiable with the producer. Can only be sold after 15 months of aging.

Vintage champagne a blend of wines all taken from the same year's harvest, deemed sufficiently good to declare a 'vintage'. A vintage year usually equates to about five years in every ten. Must be aged for three years before being sold.

v. The Loire Valley

As the longest river in France, the Loire's corresponding wine region snakes along a considerable course. Viewed in their full extent, the vines curl all the way from Muscadet territory on the Atlantic coast to the Côte d'Auvergne encircling Clermont-Ferrand. Wines produced in the Loire reflect this scale with an impressive variety: dry, sweet, red, white, still and sparkling can all be tasted amid the country's most charming vineyards. Yet, despite such diversity, many outside France associate the Loire solely with the Sauvignon Blanc grape, pressed into affordable dry to medium dry whites like Sancerre and Pouilly Fumé. Alas, as similar New World wines grown in a more reliable climate make inroads into the global market, the Loire's rather mixed, unpredictable bag of wines struggle to maintain their overseas audience.

Late 4th century
St Martin encouraged viticulture in Touraine to supply religious communities with wine.

582
Bishop Gregory of Tours wrote of the vineyards at Sancerre in his *Historiae Francorum.*

Late 10th century
Benedictine monks planted Cabernet Franc vines in Bourgueil, where notable reds are still being made from the same grape variety.

12th century
The region's wine trade was already well-established, not least through export to England.

16th century
Sauvignon Blanc vines began to play a significant role in the Loire.

Mid 19th century
Phylloxera ravaged the Loire vineyards.

Find the wine festival
The medieval village of St-Aubin-de-Luigné in Anjou holds a festival celebrating its local specialities – wine and eels – each July.

Shaping up the bottle
Wine bottles in the Loire take a similar form to those in Burgundy, bearing gently sloping shoulders.

vi. Rhône Valley

Another region, another global superstar – wines from the Rhône Valley grace the upper echelons of any wine list. Nurtured by warm climes on well drained slopes, it's no surprise that this ancient corridor of oenological nirvana produces 450 million bottles a year. The region harbours a distinct north/south split, ruled from above by the big Syrah grape and from below by Grenache-led blending. Unlike most of the country's wine producing regions, the Rhône Valley has entered the 21st century in rude health, the voluptuous character of its wines a match for any overseas competitors. In the valley's northern reaches, the small Côte Rôtie *appellation* produces meaty single estate reds, while Condrieu offers peachy whites made from Viognier grapes. At the southern end, Châteauneuf-du-Pape carries its reputation well, making use of up to 13 grape varieties – Grenache and Syrah at their heart.

A regional *appellation*
The catch-all Côte du Rhône AOC covers all of the wines produced along the Rhône Valley's length. However, in truth, the majority of grapes squeezed into Côte du Rhône will come from south of the region. Quality varies dramatically, although the best (and most expensive) have traditionally come from the Côte du Rhône-Villages (labelled as such), arranged in clumps around Orange and Avignon.

Marcel's magic
Côte Rôtie, where the warm sun nurtures the aggressive Syrah, translates as 'roasted slope'. Over the last 20 years, producer Marcel Guigal has propelled the *appellation's* rise in profile and value almost single-handed, making and promoting single estate wines.

Find the wine festival
Bau des Vendanges: Avignon pays homage to its local wines at the start of the grape harvest in early September.

Shaping up the bottle
Bottles in the Rhône Valley are similar to those in Burgundy although the girth is often subtly thinner. Many also carry a coat of arms embossed on their neck.

Rhône Valley wine history uncorked

Antiquity
The Rhône Valley was probably the first region of France to make wine, the vines brought to the area via Marseilles.

71AD
Pliny recorded the superior quality of the red wines from Vienne, a town at the northern end of the valley.

Middle Ages
The growth of monasticism in the region expanded the land under vine as monks began producing their own wine.

c.1320
Pope Jean XXII built a holiday home in the southern Rhône, planted a few vines and, within a couple of decades, the reputation of Châteauneuf-du-Pape began gathering momentum.

1923
In response to cheap imitation, Baron Leroy came up with a series of rules for the production of Châteauneuf-du-Pape, effectively initiating the AOC system.

vii. Unsung heroes: five other French wine regions

Languedoc-Roussillon

The vast area of vines (the largest in France) curving round
the Med is beginning to shed its reputation for perpetual
underachievement. As the rise of New World wines
continues, Languedoc-Roussillon offers an affordable
French alternative. Indeed, many of the makers responsible
for raising the region's profile learned their trade in Australia
and California. At present, quality remains incredibly varied
and the area's woolly *appellation* zones offer little in the
way of a reliable guide.

What to drink: Corbières and Fitou are two of the big reds,
produced from Carignan loaded blends. The Coteaux du
Languedoc and Roussillon areas have been making wine for
well over 2,000 years; the latter has gained a reputation for
producing some dazzling reds and rosés, while the former
also seems on the up with its Carignan-Syrah blends.

Jura and Savoie

Jura has pulled back from the brink as a wine region,
gradually clawing back the land under vine after decades
of decline in the 20th century. However, it remains a
region where wine (and idiosyncratic grape varieties) has
progressed little in centuries.

What to drink: the area is famous for *vin jaune*, a yellow
wine made from the Savagnin grape with its nutty hint
of sherry. Here too you find *vin de paille*, a sweet white
traditionally made by drying the grapes out on straw. Both
are something of an acquired taste. Arbois and Côte du
Jura are the main growing areas, producing *vin jaune*, *vin
de paille* and a few Pinot Noir-led reds. The scattered Vin de
Savoie *appellation*, harbouring a light white made from the
Jacquère grape, is about as close as wine gets to the Alps.

1. Identity:
the foundations of
French culture | 2. Literature
and philosophy | 3. Art, architecture
and design | 4. Performing arts | 5. Arbiters of style:
creative photography
and fashion | 6. Media and
communications | 7. Consuming culture:
food and drink | 8. Living cultures: the
state of the nation

Provence

From the Rhône delta around to Nice, Provence harbours some rewarding wines, most of them overlooked outside the region.

What to drink: Coteaux d'Aix-en-Provence and Côtes de Provence are the largest *appellations*. Both are dominated by fruity reds, made with Grenache grapes in Aix and Carignan in Côtes de Provence; certain vineyards have also taken to bolstering their wines with Cabernet Sauvignon but are forced to sell them as mere *vin de table* in accordance with AOC rules. Côtes de Provence is also home to some famous rosé wines, again with the Carignan grape at their heart. The rosés' colour and taste are achieved by reducing the amount of time the wine spends in contact with the grape skins.

Corsica

In wine, as in most things, Corsica is something of a law unto itself. Italian grape varieties play an important role in wines for which AOC status seems to have been granted arbitrarily.

What to drink: Vin de Corse is an *appellation* applying to the entirety of Corsica and is thus largely obsolete as an indicator of quality. Meaty, herb tinged reds, dry whites and full-bodied rosés all fall within its bounds. Other AOC regions are more precise: Patrimonio reds blend Italianate grapes for wines with longevity and clout, while the whites are made exclusively from herby Vermentino grapes. Vermentino is used in Ajaccio whites too, although here the blended reds, led by the Sciacarello grape, take precedence.

South-west

Large co-ops and tiny smallholders operate side by side in the south-west. Bordeaux's domineering grape varieties overlap into the vinous mélange, yet you also encounter little known local varieties making distinct if untrendy wines.

What to drink: While Bergerac is still regarded as the cheaper sibling of Bordeaux, its reds are granted increasing prestige. The tannic 'black wine' of the Cahors *appellation* is produced from the Malbec grape, although today many makers moderate the brooding red with Merlot. At the foot of the Pyrenees, the dry and sweet whites of Jurançon carry a pineapple bouquet. A few miles north, the Madiran *appellation* produces a bullish red traditionally made with the Tannat grape.

Castelain
Brewing in Benifontaine near Lens, this family firm produces various *bières de garde.*

Kasteel Cru
An Alsatian brewer producing a *blonde* beer fermented in much the same way as champagne; renowned for its sharp white foam.

Deux Rivières
A popular Brittany brewer that includes *Coreff*, a highly fermented stout-like brew, among its output.

Kronenbourg
The famous Alsatian brewer easily outsells any other in France. Founded in 1664, a year used to name its premier beer, today Kronenbourg is owned by Scottish and Newcastle Breweries.

Les Trois Brasseurs
Actually a pub in Lille that brews its own *blonde, ambreé* and *blanche* beers.

Beer

While French beer has always lived in the shadow of wine, the wider renaissance in artisanal produce has seen microbreweries mushroom of late. But it's a long road back – the French brewing industry declined steadily throughout the 20th century. The thousand or so regional breweries in existence in 1900 went flat in the competition with a clutch of industrial pilsner-style beer producers, Kronenbourg and Pelforth among them.

Two decades ago the decline slowed. It's not that more people are actually drinking beer in France (that figure dips year on year), rather that those who do enjoy ale are seeking out the smaller brewers. The growth of these microbreweries has been spearheaded in Alsace and Nord-Pas-de-Calais (where monks began brewing in the Middle Ages), the traditional heartlands of French brewing and beer drinking. In Alsace, the German love of *blonde* beers seeps into the region's drinking habits, while in Nord-Pas-de-Calais the local brews have a distinctly Flemish twang. Brittany has also joined the microbrewing fraternity over the last decade with a handful of producers, while the brewpub phenomenon (whereby bars brew their own) creeps through the north. All over France, the English style pub is making a gradual appearance.

Guarding tradition
Many of the small breweries in Nord-Pas-de-Calais produce *bière de garde* (beer for keeping). Traditionally brewed in spring, the beer was stored in champagne-style bottles, continuing to ferment until uncorked in summer to quench the farmhands' thirst. *Bière de garde* is often richly amber, blessed with a spicy, some say biscuity taste.

The first brewery in Alsace was founded in Strasbourg in 1260 by Arnoldus Cervisarius.

Cider

Find an orchard in France, from Picardy to Les Pays Basques, and it's highly likely that someone nearby will be making cider. However, the undisputed home of French cider is the north-west. Brittany boasts a sizeable cider industry, but general consensus states that the Normans of Pays d'Auge, with their AOC status, make the best. In contrast to the US and Britain, France has spawned few industrial giants in cider production. Like French wine, cider often originates from single estates: some small farms may well sell you *cidre fermier* direct. If the label says *cidre bouché*, the drink, bottled like champagne, will have undergone a second fermentation. *Cidre doux* is a weak sugary drink, rarely stronger than 3%, while *cidre brut* is a strong, dry variant of 5% or more. Brittany and Normandy also produce *poiré*, pear cider, in large quantities.

When phylloxera devastated French vineyards in the mid 19th century, cider honourably stepped into the breach – Norman cider production quadrupled between 1870 and 1900.

Breton cider is traditionally served in handled ceramic cups.

Five popular *apéritifs*

To really appreciate seven courses of fine French food you must, of course, entice the gastric juices out with an *apéritif*. Many of the famous French pre-dinner drinks have evolved into popular tipples, sipped irrespective of food.

Pastis: The Midi's favourite only became popular after 1915 when absinthe was banned and makers concocted a wormwood-free substitute. Star anise became the governing flavour. Provence harbours many artisanal variants: some blend more than 70 herbs and spices to get the right anise flavour.

Dry vermouth: Vermouth is actually Italian, but dry vermouth has its origins in France. In the early 19th century, traders found that white wine became fuller and developed an amber colour when barrels were exposed to the sun and spray of sea travel. Today the effect is achieved by leaving oak barrels out in the Mediterranean glare for a year. The addition of herbs and spices gives a nutty flavour. Noilly Prat is the big name.

Kir: A DIY apéritif, kir is made with *crème de cassis* topped with white wine. Dijon mayor Félix Kir pioneered the drink after the Second World War, serving it up at official receptions. Various kir variations exist: the most famous, Kir Royale, uses champagne.

Pineau des Charentes:
Fresh, unfermented grape juice is blended with cognac or *eaux de vie* and then aged in wooden barrels for a sweet, fruity taste. Apparently discovered by accident in 1589 when a winemaker put new grape juice into a barrel containing cognac. Today, the genuine Charentes variety has AOC status.

Pommeau: A bit like pineau but with apples. Unfermented cider is mixed with year-old Calvados and left to age in a barrel for over two years. The richly coloured result has a smooth sweet vanilla taste. Both Pommeau de Bretagne and Pommeau de Normandie have AOC status.

Toulouse-Lautrec
and
drinking
companion

Five popular *digestifs*

Like their pre-meal companions, *digestifs* aren't the staple of after dinner rumination they once were. However, many still take a little something with their coffee, or at any other convenient time.

Cognac: The original masterclass in distilling grapes twice takes place in the Charantais department. Distillers' cellars are rich in the aromatic fug of *la part des anges* (the angels' share) that evaporates into the atmosphere. The youngest, labelled VS, must be at least two years old, VSOP four years old, and the finest, XO, a minimum of six years. In truth, many cognacs produced in each classification are much older. Two of the most famous were initiated in the 18th century by an Irish mercenary, Richard Hennessy, and a Channel Islander, Jean Martell.

Armagnac: Gascony's answer to cognac isn't quite as famous. It lacks the internationally renowned merchants, instead boasting some fine small-scale *fermier* brandies. While cognac has two distinct distillation periods, Armagnac matures in one continuous process.

Calvados: An apple brandy produced predominantly in Normandy's Pay d'Auge, in the Calvados *département*, by distilling cider. Double distillation takes place in giant copper cauldrons before aging slowly smoothes out the wrinkles in wooden casks. The youngest, *trois étoiles*, is a minimum of two years old, but the best are much older, sometimes aged over decades.

Eaux de vie: The so-called waters of life are basically fruit brandies, and thus technically include cognac, Calvados and Armagnac within their ranks. However,

"NECTAR OF THE GODS":
Victor Hugo on cognac

Grape expectations
Cognac must be made from at least 90% Ugni Blanc, Folle Blanche, or Colombard grapes. Armagnac uses the same varieties.

Shots from the hip
In recent years, cognac has developed a certain cachet among the stars of American hip hop. Busta Rhymes and P Diddy acknowledged their appreciation in *Pass the Courvoisier* in 2002. Sales of the brandy apparently soared.

The elder statesmen of brandy
The signing of the First World War armistice on board a train in the forest of Compiègne on 11th November 1918 was reputedly sealed with the supping of a fine Martell cognac.

The hole truth
A traditional Norman supper is interrupted by the *trou Normand* (Norman hole), a tot of appetite-stimulating Calvados enjoyed between courses. Today the *trou Normand* often comes in the shape of an apple sorbet bathed in Calvados.

1. Identity: the foundations of French culture
2. Literature and philosophy
3. Art, architecture and design
4. Performing arts
5. Arbiters of style: cinema, photography and fashion
6. Media and communications
7. Consuming culture: food and drink
8. Living culture: the state of the nation

Manet's *Le Buveur
d'absinthe* (1859)
portrayed a man with an
absinthe bottle at his feet
and a menacing shadow
at his back. The painting
was rejected by the Paris
Salon.

In Degas' painting
L'Absinthe (1875-76) a
woman stares out blankly,
apparently stupefied by
the green fairy. The work
found its way to Britain
where it was roundly
booed at Christies and
slated for showing a
drunken woman.

During his Blue Period,
the 23-year-old Picasso
painted his friend *Angel
Fernández de Soto* (1903),
a drug enthusiast with an
eye for the ladies, looking
rather glum next to an
empty absinthe glass.

One of life's few pleasures
for Robert Jordan, hero of
Hemingway's *For Whom
the Bell Tolls*, is a canteen
of absinthe.

typically *eaux de vie* will refer to the fiery, clear
aperitifs made with plums, pears, cherries, raspberries
and other fruits. Each region has its own variations,
although the artisanal *eaux de vie* of Alsace are
particularly renowned.

Marc: Another *eau de vie*, this time made by
distilling the grape pulp (pomace) left over from wine
production. Some makers even throw in the grape
stalks. The most popular versions are made in eastern
France, from Marc de Gewürztraminer in Alsace, to
Marc de Champagne and Marc de Bourgogne.

Fairy liquid: the artist's choice
Absinthe is a bitter anise flavoured spirit, of which
the supposedly mind-bending wormwood is a minor
constituent. It takes the nickname *la Fée Verte* (the
green fairy) from its emerald colour. Originally a Swiss
elixir, absinthe was first produced in France in the early
19th century. It became hugely popular, to the extent
that France was knocking back over 35 million litres
annually by 1910. The corresponding social ills of this
mass consumption and the growing belief that absinthe
created psychosis and criminality led to its prohibition
in many European countries – it was banned in France
in 1915. This ban hasn't been officially repealed,
although you can now widely buy and drink absinthe
in France. The bottle will be labelled *spiritueux à base
de plantes d'absinthe* – spirit with a wormwood base
– rather than merely absinthe. While the accusation
that absinthe is more harmful than any other drink with
an equally high alcohol content remains unproven, the
drink's cultural prestige is undeniable. Manet, Degas,
van Gogh, Toulouse-Lautrec and Picasso all drank and
painted it, while Oscar Wilde and Ernest Hemingway
lauded its effects in print.

Drinks order

Carthusian monks near Grenoble have made the beguiling green Chartreuse liqueur since the 18th century. It's not the kind of tipple you can brew up at home – the recipe takes 130 different herbs, flowers and various secret ingredients and blends them with a wine alcohol base. Various imitators, including the French government, have tried and failed to reproduce Chartreuse. Only two monks, so the monastery blurb suggests, know the recipe. A sweet yellow Chartreuse is also available. The green original has strong literary connections: Gatsby drank a bottle in F Scott Fitzgerald's famous novel, while Hunter S Thompson, himself a Chartreuse drinker, spiked his work with the green stuff.

Water

No one has taken to bottled water quite like the French. In 2005 the Parisian authorities handed out free designer carafes in a bid to draw people back to the tap, but they had their work cut out – France produces and drinks more bottled water than anywhere else in the world. *Eau de source* is simple spring water, while *eau de mineral* may have health benefits – a *declarée d'intérêt public*, granted by the Ministry of Health, will indicate as much on the label. Of course, the French have their favourites.

Five bottled French waters

Badoit
Gently carbonated, France's best-selling sparkler was first bottled in St Galmier, Massif Central, in 1838. Owned by French food giant Groupe Danone.

Evian
Nowhere sells more still bottled water than the spa resort of Évian-les-Bains on the southern shore of Lake Geneva. Another one owned by Groupe Danone.

Volvic
Percolated through cracks in the Auvergnat granite over thousands of years and then bottled, Volvic has a light mineral content. Guess what – owned by Groupe Danone.

Perrier
The highly carbonated Perrier is bottled at source in Vergeze, Languedoc. Bizarrely, the bubbles and the water are captured separately from the same source and then reunited in the bottle.

Vittel
Often chosen for its low sodium levels, this still water comes from the spa town of the same name on the Lorraine side of the Vosges Mountains.

Tea on trial

Tea was hugely popular among the ruling elite of Bourbon France. Indeed, it was the French enthusiasm for tea, taken with milk, that launched the famous British thirst for a cuppa in the mid 17th century. However, the Revolution soon killed off the popularity of a drink associated with the aristocracy.

It came from the east

The French appreciation of coffee took off in the late 17th century after Suleiman Aga, Turkish ambassador to the royal court, served it up to Louis XIV. Paris was duly smitten within a few years.

Hot drinks

When the French order a coffee they expect a small cup of espresso, referred to as *un express* or *un petit noir*. For breakfast they may slurp a large cup or bowl of *café au lait*. In between, there are various subtleties of size and content; a *café crème* (just ask for a *crème*) is an espresso with milk or cream, a *noisette* the same but with a smaller dash of milk. If you want it decaffeinated, ask for *déca*. Tea is usually served black or, if requested, accompanied by milk or a slice of lemon. Herbal teas, particularly camomile, are popular as *digestifs*. Hot chocolate continues to be a popular breakfast drink.

When do the French drink?

Drinking habits are rapidly evolving in France but traditional practices remain relevant. *Café au lait* and hot chocolate are still the breakfast drinks of choice, and the traditions of a mid-morning coffee shot remain intact. When it comes to lunch and dinner, wine no longer sits at the head of the table: more and more people, in particular young adults, drink only water as an accompaniment to food. Dining is more likely to unravel with the help of wine in a restaurant, sipped alongside the ubiquitous bottle of water. The evening rituals of the *apéritif* and *digestif* are less prevalent than of old, and when time does allow for a drink either side of the meal, these days the French are just as likely to drink whisky as anything peculiar to France. When taken, spirits are enjoyed in moderation – usually no more than two. Similarly, a wine glass is never filled to the brim. Coffee is still standard at the end of a meal, although increasing numbers are sipping on infused teas.

Where do the French drink?

Many may still grab an early coffee from their neighbourhood café on the way to work, and the traditions of sitting in a city centre café for hours on end haven't died altogether (thanks in part to widespread unemployment amongst graduates). Cafés, bars and wine bars all cater for evening drinkers in towns and cities. In villages, the café provides a hub for any late drinking. However, people don't go to cafés and bars in droves anymore. Better living standards are encouraging people to stay at home of an evening – many used to go out simply to escape the drab living conditions in the house or apartment. When they do go out, 21st century urbanites are often more inclined to chat over a soft drink than a glass of wine. Out in the regions, change has been less swift. The tradition of drinking cheap, rough red wine in the local café remains an important, albeit diminishing, routine for older generations.

A quick pick-me-up
Traditionally, the French worker or peasant would have a glass of wine or a spirit at the café first thing in the morning, taken as fortifier for the day ahead.

Paying for location
If you go for a drink in a French bar, standing at the bar to sup will make whatever you order a bit cheaper. Choosing a table indoors raises the price, and a table outside inflates it even further.

The legal drinking age in France is 16.

Stemming the flow
Strict advertising laws
have helped reduce
alcohol consumption in
France. The Évin Law
(named after the then
Health Minister, Claude
Évin) of 1991 banned
most booze ads from
television and sporting
events. In recent years
wine growers have
taken to the streets
in protest, decrying
the law as obstructive
to promoting quality
regional produce.
They argue that wine is
a cultural phenomenon
above the trivialities of
market forces. Sadly,
drinkers don't seem to
be following their cue.

Over-55-year-olds
consume the most
alcohol in France.
Adults aged 25 and
under drink the least.

Changing tastes: alcohol consumption

Alcohol consumption in France is decreasing.
Sales of wine have shrunk dramatically in the last 20
years, while beer and spirits have struggled to hold
their ground. Health conscious young adults and
progressively tighter drink driving laws have been
blamed. However, while the French drink less, they're
spending more on what they actually consume,
seeking out higher quality AOC wines from small-scale
producers. But let's not get carried away. Even though
French wine consumption has halved over the last
40 years, it would be wrong to envisage anything like
widespread abstention. France remains one of world's
leading consumers of alcohol. The rituals of episodic,
heavy drinking among older generations have brought
their own severe health problems – alcohol abuse
remains the third largest cause of preventable death.

Sobering thoughts

Being publicly drunk in France isn't acceptable.
At almost any level of society, within any age group,
open displays of intoxication are frowned upon.
In France, drinking machismo comes from being able
to remain in control irrespective of how many you've
knocked back. In contrast to other northern European
nations, most notably Britain, French youngsters
are taught how to drink sensibly and to remain
within certain boundaries. Consistently high levels of
consumption may continue to be a scourge in terms
of liver cirrhosis, and alcoholism is no small problem,
but the French have yet to embrace binge drinking.

1. Identity: 2. Literature   3. Art, architecture   4. Performing arts   5. Screen, image,   6. Media and   7. Consuming culture: 8. Living culture: the
the foundations of and philosophy   and design   cinema, photography communications   food and drink   status of the nation
French culture   and fashion

Attitudes to drink driving
Wine producers in France have blamed strict drink driving laws on falling sales – in 1995 the legal blood alcohol level was reduced to 0.5mg/ml (it's 0.8mg/ml in the UK). But with ingrained drink driving habits responsible for a third of deaths on the French roads, the government had to act. Since 2002 the drink driving laws (along with other laws of the road) have been rigorously enforced in line with a new system of penalties. Annual road deaths have duly fallen by nearly 2,000. As with drinking habits in general, young French adults are far less likely to offend than older generations.

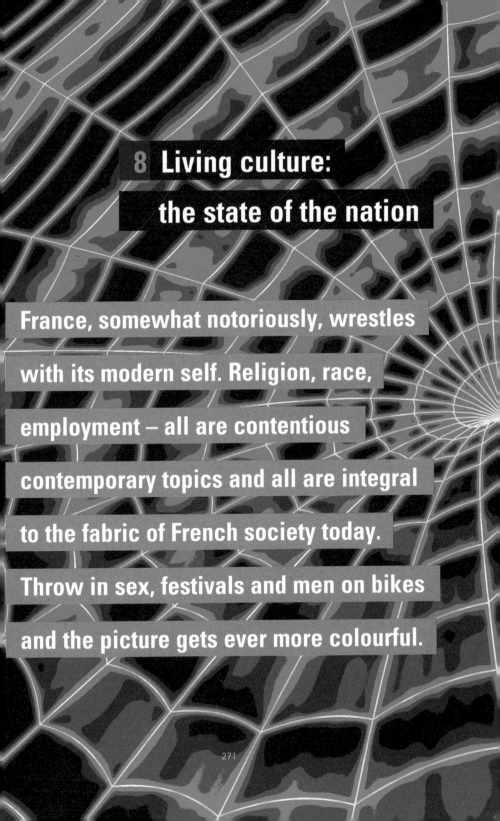

8 Living culture: the state of the nation

France, somewhat notoriously, wrestles with its modern self. Religion, race, employment – all are contentious contemporary topics and all are integral to the fabric of French society today. Throw in sex, festivals and men on bikes and the picture gets ever more colourful.

The old status quo

Under the *Ancien Régime*, French society was divided into 'estates'. By the time the Revolution beckoned, the First Estate was made up of roughly 100,000 members of the Catholic clergy and the Second Estate by around 400,000 members of the nobility. Both groups, comprising little over 2% of the population, were exempt from taxes and between them controlled most aspects of French life. The remaining peasants and bourgeoisie shouldered virtually the entire financial burden of running the nation with very little say in decision making.

Social standing: class conscious France

Today, society is broadly divided into the working class, the bourgeoisie and the intellectual elite, although each group is intricately layered. Much greater stock is put on intellectual and academic prowess in France than in other Western nations, with income and occupation no longer a real guarantee of social standing. Indeed, the intellectual elite tends to sneer at the commercial obsessions of the bourgeoisie. The peasantry, once a class apart, has all but gone, redistributed in other sectors. Disparities of wealth are perhaps more pronounced than the pioneers of *égalité* would prefer. In some ways the upper echelons of the bourgeoisie have replaced the nobility that fell apart during the Revolution (although remnants of the old aristocracy cling on), while the efforts of successive regimes have failed to substantially reduce a sizeable French underclass. The class structure isn't particularly fluid either: few move up or down the scale and the numbers of working class folk finding their way into traditional elite professions like medicine or law remain small. That's not to say there's an unsettling friction between classes – any disgruntlement is usually channelled instead towards the government.

Breaking the code: family life

The family unit is still important to French society even if it isn't the all-powerful rock it once was. Despite a shift towards more shared roles, the father usually remains at the head of the household. In 1804 the Napoleonic Code set in law the father's right to make decisions about members of his family, particularly regarding the supremacy of his opinion over that of his wife. French family life revolves around mealtimes and parents and their children can still spend several hours a day eating, drinking and talking together. Extended families will also spend a lot of time together, often congregating on weekends as well as for key occasions like weddings and christenings. They even get together on March 5th for the Fête des Grand-mères (Grandmother's Day).

However, although decline is less marked than in Anglo-Saxon nations, the traditional family unit is nevertheless being eroded in France. Divorce rates have rocketed in the last 50 years while the 1990s saw the number of single parent families rise by 22% and the number of people living alone by 25%. France has the lowest marriage rate in Europe and the PACS (*Pacte civil de solidarité*) has undermined this further. Passed in 1999, this is a law allowing a civil partnership, with accompanying legal rights, between any two individuals.

Life as a Frenchwoman

With the *Code Napoléon* effectively enshrining in law the dominance of the male until the mid 20th century, French women have had to struggle against a strong current of inequality. They didn't get the vote until 1944 and have only begun to gain any semblance of parity with men in recent decades. Between 1968 and 1993 the number of females in full or part-time employment grew at over ten times the rate for men, leaping from 5.2 million to 8.7 million. Today, women in France enjoy a number of benefits absent elsewhere in Europe. For example, the maternity leave entitlement is 16 weeks, at 84% pay, and childcare is heavily subsidized. However, change was comparatively late in coming and there are still yawning chasms between women and men in terms of earning potential and career advancement. A married woman did not have full control of her earnings, or even the legal entitlement to seek employment, until 1965 and the École Polytechnique (the country's leading business school) did not admit women until 1972. Even today, a woman can expect to earn around 20% less than her male equivalent compared, for instance, with around 12% less in the UK. In 2006 the government proposed legislation that would lean on companies to reduce this pay gap.

Numbers game
Counting first, second
and third generation
settlers, estimates
suggest that around
one fifth of the French
population is immigrant.
The majority are from
other European countries,
most notably Portugal,
although in recent years
the majority of new
arrivals have come from
North Africa.

The children of immigrants
become French citizens
at the
age of 18, as long as
they've been raised on
French soil.

Multicultural France

Large numbers of immigrants from former French colonies in North and West Africa and South East Asia made France their home in the second half of the 20th century. However, to offer any concrete analysis on the racial make up of France is impossible: there are no official figures on racial breakdown – such sub-cultures aren't counted as separate groups within a society built on the concept that everyone is equal and everyone is French. Immigrants are expected to adapt to the French way of life and theoretically there is no such thing as racial profiling, there are no quotas for ethnic minorities and positive discrimination is unheard of. In practice, championing equality over diversity has proved problematic. Widespread rioting triggered by racial tension, tied into economic imbalance and perceived police brutality, has crippled France on more than one occasion.

The melting pot: alienation or integration?

The statistical void makes it hard to assess whether immigrants or their children have really integrated into French life – we don't know who they marry or where they live. For instance, while *les banlieues* are sometimes described as 'Arab ghettos', we have no accurate information on their ethnic composition. What we do know is that the *beurs*, the children of North African immigrants, have pushed their own lively culture into the French mainstream. Comedian Jamel Debbouze, footballer Zinedine Zidane and author Mehdi Charef exemplify how *beurs* have impacted at a national level. Yet life for most second or third generation North African immigrants is far from rosy. They're far more likely to be unemployed, working in low-skilled jobs and to be stopped by the police. In autumn 2005, the *banlieue* of Clichy-sous-Bois in eastern Paris saw youths of North African descent rioting with police after two teenagers were electrocuted while allegedly trying to evade a notoriously intensive police ID check. The violent unrest rapidly spread to HLMs throughout France, where nightly riots induced the government to declare a state of emergency on 8th November.

1 Identity   2 Literature   3 Art, architecture   4 Performing arts   5 Artisans of style,   6 Media and   7 Consuming culture: 8. Living culture: th
the foundations of   and philosophy   and design   cinema, photography   communications   food and drink   state of the nation
French culture   and fashion

The faithful few

La Déclaration des droits de l'Homme et du citoyen established a shaky freedom of religion in early republican France before a law passed in 1905 went much further, cementing the concept of *laïcité*. A tough word to translate, *laïcité* draws a clear line between state and religion. It doesn't imply state hostility toward religion, merely that worship in France is deemed a matter for the individual. As with race, it can be hard to paint an accurate picture of religion in modern day France because the relevant questions are not posed in the national census. However, estimates suggest that 85% of the population is Roman Catholic, 10% Muslim, 2% Protestant and 1% Jewish. In real terms, fewer French than ever actively pursue a religion. Less than one in ten go to church each week, while only half of people tying the knot choose to do so at the altar.

Conjugal carry on

The French model of Catholicism harbours some unique traditions, not least the wedding ceremony. Today, thanks to the distinction between religion and state, anyone wanting a religious wedding has to get married twice: once for the state and once for God. When the bride eventually gets to the church service, she often has to cut her way to the altar through white ribbons tied across her path. She may also have to walk across laurel leaves outside the church. The final vows are taken underneath a white silk canopy, which is deemed to protect the couple from evil. *Chiverie* is the wedding night tradition of disturbing the new couple by making a racket with pots and pans until the groom invites the revellers in for drinks...or possibly a slap.

Headscarf headache

While the French state guarantees the individual's freedom of worship, a 2004 law banning the wearing of conspicuous religious symbols from state schools caused huge controversy. Large Christian crosses and Jewish skullcaps fell under the law's remit, yet most attention fell on the right of Muslim girls to wear the traditional hijab. Although the law passed with a landslide and is backed by around 70% of French voters, debate still rages as to whether the French system has created true equality, or simply inhibits multiculturalism and the rights of the individual.

Alsatian alibi

Bizarrely, the *laïcité* law doesn't apply to all areas of Alsace-Lorraine because the region was under German rule when the legislation was passed in 1905.

"THE REPUBLIC NEITHER RECOGNIZES, NOR SALARIES, NOR SUBSIDIZES ANY RELIGION."

Taken from the *laïcité* law of 1905

Assumption of the Blessed Virgin Mary *(L'Assomption)* 15th August: France shuts down for the day to enjoy a sizeable feast.

All Saints Day *(La Toussaint)* 1st November: Celebrated in tandem with *le jour des morts* on the 2nd November: a time for the family to gather at the graveside of their dearly departed.

Christmas Day *(Noël)* 25th December: The big day in France tends to be overshadowed by a Christmas Eve feast.

Boxing Day *(Deuxième jour de Noël)* 26th December: A holiday in Alsace-Lorraine only; the rest of France goes back to work.

Festival of the Three Kings *(La fête des rois)* 6th January: Epiphany sees the French tucking into *galettes des rois*.

Candelmas *(La chandeleur)* 2nd February: Countryfolk take a blessed candle home from church and pretty much everyone cooks up a pancake or two. If you can toss the first one over a wardrobe, your harvest will apparently be abundant.

Shrove Tuesday *(Mardi Gras)* February: The coming of Lent is marked by a carnival atmosphere. Nice is particularly famous for its parade.

Easter *(Pâques)* March/April: Church bells fall silent for two days before Easter Sunday as Christ is mourned. Traditionally, children venture into the garden to watch th bells 'fly back' from Rome, where they usually find a stash of chocola eggs. Then it's off to church.

Ascension *(l'Ascencion)* early/mid May: Alongside Labour Day and Victory Day makes May a very good month for public holidays

Pentecost *(la Pentecôte)* late May/early June: City folk typically decamp to the country. Whit Monday *(Lundi de Pentecôte)* was controversially voted off the public holiday calendar in 2005 by parliament in an effort to raise publ funds for the elderly. Many still fail to show for work.

Cultural liberalism in France

While religious and ethnic demographics in France are poorly documented, there have been several surveys into the moral state of the nation. What has emerged is that the French are a fairly liberal lot. Homosexuality has become widely accepted over the past 20 years. Indeed, civil partnerships between same sex couples came into law as part of the PACS, putting France some six years ahead of the UK in this respect. Euthanasia, abortion and suicide are also surprisingly widely accepted notions. In relationships it would seem that both wife and mistress are less willing to put up with the infamous three-way French marriage and that monogamy is increasingly prized. The rise in cultura liberalism in France has coincided with a decline in traditional spirituality. Roughly a third still believe in a traditional concept of God while another third explicitly disbelieve it, but the real growth area concerns the less specific belief in an un-named higher being.

France is on her Fifth Republic, the constitution of which was pushed through by Charles de Gaulle in 1958 and revised in 1962. It's still based largely on the core principles of the Revolution with the key difference between Fourth and Fifth Republics being increased power for the President. The role of President remains a powerful one today.

The structure of power

The President, elected by popular vote every five years, chooses the Prime Minister to head the government, who in turn selects his *conseil des ministres* (cabinet). *Conseil des ministres* members don't have to be MPs, they may be high flyers in fields like business or law. Below this hierarchy lie two legislative houses. *L'Assemblée Nationale*, elected by the people every five years, carries most power with its 577 seats. *Le Sénat* has less clout: its 321 members (all aged over 35) are elected by *L'Assembleé Nationale* and by local government, itself elected by the people. The President has the power to dissolve *L'Assemblée Nationale*.

Local government operates on a three-tier system. The country is divided into 22 *régions*, four overseas *départements* and the French overseas territories. Each *région* is subdivided into *départements*. The 100 *départements* are themselves carved up into more than 36,000 *communes*, each with an elected mayor. The theory is that nobody is more than a day's travel away from their *département* capital. This set-up was established in 1982 to push aspects of government out from Paris to the elected, and relatively independent, council of each *région*.

Provincial legacy
When the regions of France were established in 1982, efforts were made to mirror the historical provinces with each region embracing a common cultural heritage.

End of the affair
In 2000 the Presidential term was reduced from seven to five years, bringing it into line with the *Assemblée Nationale* lifespan and ending the tricky periods of 'cohabitation' in which a President had to select a Prime Minister from an opposing political party.

Going to the polls

The French are always willing to debate a political point. Sometimes they may not be willing to actually vote on it but, as they will tell you, inaction itself can be a political statement. Across the board they are a politicized people and have a number of key issues on their agenda. Immigration, nationalism, unemployment and the disenfranchised suburban youth are all perennially contentious issues. The role of women is still very much up for political discussion in France, and the emergence of a genuine female political heavyweight in the Socialist Party's Ségolène Royal has helped to keep it thus. The French electorate are known for their protest votes. In May 2005 they sunk the proposed EU constitution, using the referendum to register dissatisfaction with their own right-wing government and its failure to deal with economic languor. Three years earlier, Jean-Marie Le Pen was voted through to the final round of Presidential elections on the back of similar grievances.

Party time

France has a melange of different political parties. These are the main five:

Union pour un Mouvement Populaire
these moderate right-wingers formed from a merger of Gaulist and centre right parties and carry significant power. In 2005 the party provided the President, the Prime Minister and the speakers of both houses.

Parti Socialiste
has existed in one form or another since the beginning of the 20th century. This leftist party enjoyed its best period under François Mitterrand, although won the 1997 general election supported by a left-wing coalition.

Parti Communiste Français
popularity has declined since the end of the Cold War, but the Communists were able to form a coalition government with Mitterrand's socialists in the early 1980s.

Les Verts
born from a merger between the *Parti Ecologiste* and the *Confédération Ecologiste,* the Greens formed part of a coalition government in 1997. Alas, they've struggled for influence in recent years.

Front National
the rabidly right-wing FN was founded in 1972 by Jean-Marie Le Pen who, despite widespread outrage at many of his ideas, does surprisingly well at the polls. He famously made it to the last two of the 2002 Presidential vote.

How green is France?

Environmental debate has featured in French life since the 1960s, spurred initially by the government's taste for nuclear power. The sizeable French civil nuclear programme (no other country is so reliant on nuclear power for its electricity) has always provoked vocal opposition, although little debate in government. Subsequent decades have found the French protesting about pollution, urbanization and the loss of natural habitat. However, among the populace the battle lines can be foggy: many French still talk of an emotional connection to the land (*la France profonde*) and decry the modern pressures on green space, yet they worry more about losing a traditional way of life than the environment (many fiercely defend their right to hunt for example). In general, environmental issues have been slower to concern the wider public here than in other Western nations. On a political level, the various green parties in France are often too busy fighting each other to make much of an impact. However, mainstream politicians eager to show off their green credentials are dragging France into the global debate: in February 2007 President Chirac opened a world conference on environmental issues in Paris by calling for a green revolution and warning that "soon will come a day when climate change escapes all control."

Parklife
The first French national park, Parc National de la Vanoise, was created in the Alps in 1963. Six more followed (one is in Guadeloupe), bolstered by more than 40 regional parks.

France has the world's sixth largest economy, with a GDP of €1.7 trillion.

The day job: what the French do for a living
Although they are prolific agricultural producers, the primary group, which includes farmers and fisherman, accounts for only 3% of the workforce. The secondary group, industry, represents a quarter of all French employees. However the scale of the tertiary sector, which accounts for the remainder of the workforce, means that the French service industry is the largest in the world.

Sources of wealth

After 1945, the state looked to protect the nation's fragile assets and nationalized the coal industry, the larger banks, some industrial companies and the distribution of gas and electricity. Later, the advent of the EEC opened huge new markets to French companies. The European Common Agricultural Policy was particularly key in modernizing the agricultural industry, and also freed up large sums of cash for the government to invest in other industries. France is now the biggest agricultural producer in the EU. Other major industries are telecommunications, arms, nuclear power (which provides 80% of the country's electricity) and tourism. France also has some of the largest, most influential banks in Europe. When La Banque National de Paris (BNP) merged with Paribas back in 1999, it formed the third largest bank in the world.

Attitudes to money

It's refreshing to note that the French are still refusing to wholly immerse themselves in the consumer culture of the 21st century. They don't like to talk about money, frown on ostentatious displays of wealth and treat credit cards with a degree of suspicion. Until recently it was fairly common practice amongst peasants and bourgeoisie alike to hide their savings in a sock (*les bas de laine* means the bottom of the wool).Credit cards were slow to catch on because the old French way is to accrue as great a stockpile of savings as possible and to spend it, grudgingly, on essential items.

Work in progress: employment in France

There are two sides to the French employment coin. On the one side, employees have enviable working conditions and legal rights, but on the other there is rampant unemployment, particularly amongst the under 25 age group (among whom unemployment is around double the national average). If you are in work, you can expect five weeks of annual leave, ten public holidays and a legal maximum 35-hour week. However, if you're amongst the unemployed, who consistently account for about 9% of the potential workforce, things are not so rosy. Any moves towards liberalizing the strict French employment laws and, through it, finding a path to reduced unemployment, have met with stiff resistance. In 2006, an attempt to relax the rules on hiring and firing young workers sparked protests and devastating riots across the country. The proposed legislation was duly scrapped. *Le salaire minimum interprofessionel de croissance* (SMIC) sets a minimum wage for workers. For part-timers unable to reach this level of income, living solely off state benefits can bring greater reward.

The nation's ills: healthcare

The French are justly proud of their healthcare system In 2000, the World Health Organization declared it to be the best in the world. In fact, it is so well funded that there is little difference in the quality of care or the length of waiting times between public and private treatment. When healthcare is needed the French, depending on means, pay upfront, but are promptly reimbursed for most or all of the cost according to services used. There is a set tariff for every medical treatment, which is applied to all *conventioné* doctors

Taxing subjects
There are so many exemptions to income tax in France than only about half the working population actually contributes. Apparently one millionaire a day leaves the country, fleeing the treasury's punishing wealth tax set at 60% of earnings. Many, including former racing driver Alain Prost, tennis champion Amelie Mauresmo and singer Johnny Hallyday have made for Switzerland.

Keeping it civil
More than a quarter of the French workforce is employed by the state. Working in the French public sector brings enviable perks: jobs are almost guaranteed – you can be moved but not laid off – and pensions and holiday entitlement generally exceed those in the private sector.

The French pop more pills than anyone else in the world.

The grey area
The proportion of the population aged over 60 is increasing exponentially but fortunately, for the time being at least, the relative wealth of the retired population, who actually command a higher average income than those still in employment, is helping to stabilize the economy and support younger family members. Retirees own 40% of personal wealth in France.

and hospitals. Medical practices that describe themselves as *non-conventioné* can charge what they like. Unfortunately, the high standards of the French health service may prove unsustainable. It digs an enormous hole in public finances (around 9% of GDP goes on health) while the scandals over mismanagement and inefficiency mount by the year. Shortcomings in the system were brutally exposed in 2003 when around 15,000 mostly elderly people died in a heatwave.

Feeling the benefit
Workers pay a sizeable portion of their salary directly to the complex *La Secu*, as the government's *sécurité sociale* pot is known. It covers pensions, healthcare, dole and housing and family benefits. Employers are also expected to make sizeable contributions to the *sécurité sociale* coffers. Most people now take up the option of supplementing healthcare insurance through payment to *mutuelles* organizations.

Napoleon's code

In 1804 Napoleon unveiled the *Code Civil des Français*, widely known today as the *Code Napoléon*. It remains the cornerstone of French civil law. Written by Jean Jacques Régis de Cambacérès the code replaced the varied regional civil laws of the *Ancien Régime*, favouring instead the national, moderately liberal themes set in motion by the Revolution. It echoed the Emperor's personal mix of conservatism and radicalism. The code extended to all French territories and was also adopted by countries within the sphere of French influence. Although some sections have clearly been revised, Napoleon's Code still features large in French life.

A tangle of red tape

The bloated bureaucracy of the French civil system is legendary, and the state influences almost every area of daily living. Citizens carry an array of cards, ranging from their national identity card to driver's licence and car registration details. When documents need to be updated or permission is required for some aspect of life, the French trudge to the *Mairie* and come face-to-face with *l'administration*. French civil servants (*les fonctionnaires*) are notoriously rigorous when it comes to checking documentation, which frequently leads to long hours spent queuing, followed by further form filling. French bureaucracy is becoming increasingly available online, so everything from the payment of taxes to registering a child for school can be carried out via a personal Internet portal.

Core principles of the *Code Napoléon*

All of France and its territories were to be governed by one civil code

All (male) citizens were equal in the eyes of the law

The man was the undisputed head of the household

Religious freedom and property rights were guaranteed

Playing away at home
The *Code Napoléon* introduced new divorce laws to France. At the time they were relatively liberal; however, while both parties could claim divorce on the grounds of adultery, the woman could only do so if the man had actually enjoyed his extra marital fun within the family home.

Napoleon's other code
In 1808, Napoleon introduced a new criminal law code, the *Code d'instruction criminelle*, gently patronizing the concept of fair inquisition and trial. The protocol has experienced far more amendment than its civil cousin during the last two centuries.

Three blue lines

The police, or *le flic*, in France are divided into three elements:

Police Nationale
controlled by the Interior Ministry with responsibility for policing Paris and towns and cities with a population over 10,000.

Gendarmerie Nationale
The 'gentleman at arms' who patrol the country-side and smaller towns are actually part of the army.

Corps Urbain or Police Municipale
Employed by medium-size town halls to deal with small-scale crime.

Laws to be broken

In France there is a general recognition that the country's excessive legal system makes all areas of law enforcement hard going. With more than 9,000 laws and 127,500 decrees applied to its citizens, it's little wonder that everyone from judges to the man in the street admit they have trouble keeping up with changing legislation. Perhaps it's not surprising therefore that the French look for shortcuts whenever possible. They've even got a name for their collective disobedience: *Système D* is the method applied to pretty much any walk of life, from securing an appointment with someone at the *Mairie* to getting a bargain at the shops, that allows you to outwit rather than actually cheat the system. The *D* stands for *débrouillard* – 'unscramble'.

Crime in France

Statistics suggest that France, like most of the Western world, is becoming a more violent place in which to live. The traditional concerns of the French criminal mind, fraud and theft, are increasingly nudged aside by armed robbery, rape and murder. New laws and no-nonsense policing are attempting to tackle the problem. While the run down HLM projects of French cities have become notoriously hard to police, in truth the majority of France is no more dangerous than the rest of Europe. The media, often drawing inflammatory links between immigration, unemployment and crime, have done little to ease people's fears.

Les banlieues: a law unto themselves

When the right won power in 2002, Interior Minister Nicolas Sarkozy's determination to reintroduce a police presence in tough neighbourhoods led to a sharp rise in violence, particularly against the police. In October 2005 this violence exploded: police statistics estimate that 9,193 cars were burnt and 2,921 arrests made during 21 nights of rioting. At the end of 2006, Sarkozy drew up tough new legislation in response to the riots a year before. Repeat offenders now get longer sentences and the minimum age of detention has been lowered to 13.

Ripping yarns: three French serial killers,

Joseph Vacher Sometimes referred to as the French Ripper, in the last decade of the 19th century Vacher stabbed and disembowelled 11 people in southern France. He was eventually caught when a victim fought back.

Thierry Paulin (suspected). In the mid 1980s, the Beast of Montmartre brutally murdered several old ladies in Paris. The prime suspect, Paulin, confessed to 21 killings but died of AIDS before going to trial.

Patrice Alègre Between 1992 and 1997, 115 women and girls in the Toulouse area disappeared. The ensuing investigation saw police canteen worker, Alègre, convicted of five murders and six rapes.

Wheels of justice
The Police Nationale are divided into different wings. One branch can be seen rollerblading through central Paris on a Friday night, policing weekend revellers. Another, the Compagnie Républicaine de Sécurité (CRS), has carved an unenviable reputation for quelling rioters with a heavy touch.

Cut that out
The guillotine was last used in France by executioner Marcel Chevalier for the despatch of convicted murderer Hamida Djandoubi in 1977. The execution took place behind the closed doors of Baumetes Prison in Marseilles, and capital punishment was finally abolished in France four years later.

8.6 French lessons: education

Schoolchildren undergo national examinations every year. Those who don't make the grade may be held back a year.

Most French schools don't have a uniform.

Schoolchildren begin learning a first foreign language in their first year at collège, from age 11, and can then take a second two years later.

France spends roughly 7% of its GDP on education.

15 million people, a quarter of the French population, are students.

Numbers game
French school years count down: six to seven-year-olds in the first year of education are in year 11, while 17-year-olds find themselves in the première grade, prior to the final, exam-heavy terminale year.

Keeping to the rules

The rigidly structured and centralized French education system has changed little in decades. From a comparatively early age, French infants enter a set up that ostensibly favours intellectual rigour over individual expression. And, in a country where qualifications, not experience, lead to the right job, the importance of formal education and acquiring the right bits of paper remains huge. Despite attempts to challenge the educational status quo, powerful forces remain aligned against change. Strikes by teachers, accompanied by protesting parents and even students, are a common occurrence when change is proposed. Many teachers believe that the centralized form of administration, in which the country's largest employer, the Education Ministry, is almost wholly responsible for appointing teaching staff, maintains equality even though it may hinder certain progressive elements. Despite the studious approach, standards and literacy have apparently slipped in recent years.

School years

Most French children aged two to six attend écoles maternelles, state-funded nursery schools that, while ungoverned by formal tuition, introduce toddlers to social awareness, basic learning and the nation's characteristically flowing style of handwriting. At the age of six, children begin formal education at école primaire. Lessons soon fall into the intense and rigid French education model, although most schools offer respite midweek with a lesson-free Wednesday. Collège (secondary school) beckons at age 11. Children usually begin lessons at around 8am, attending until 4.30pm. In addition to the annual 900 or so hours they spend at school, it's not unusual for children to get on with homework after an early evening snack.

At 15, most take an exam which, if passed, sets them up for three years at *lycée* studying for *le baccalauréat*. The rest usually end up at technical college. Everyone must remain in some form of education until aged 16.

Bac breaking work

Getting *le baccalauréat*, or *le bac* as it's often called, is everything to French children and their concerned parents – all the studious graft of a French childhood winds up to this pivotal test. Created under Napoleon, *le bac* is an exacting exam that usually takes place over two to four days in June, with some 20% failing to make the grade. Students can choose a particular type of *le bac* to concentrate on, supplemented by a broader range of subjects, including philosophy, science and maths. Even those of a literary mind may opt for the science-led '*Bac S*', such is the subject's traditional prestige and career-opening potential. It's only a slight overstatement to say that success in *le bac* can dictate a student's eventual place in French society, although considerable further study usually lies ahead for those who pass.

Degrees of separation: higher education

France's state funded higher education sector is a dual system, comprising over 80 standard universities and many more highly prestigious *grandes écoles*. The latter, individually geared to specific professions, act as breeding grounds for the French establishment, responsible for churning out future leaders in the often interchangeable fields of politics and industry. As such, competition to enter the small *grandes écoles* is extremely fierce. In comparison, a qualification from the overcrowded universities doesn't hold the same kudos, and many graduates struggle to find a career opening after graduation.

Pushy parents
French parents place huge importance on their children's education and, as with many countries in western Europe, will consider moving house to ensure their child attends the best possible school. The choice is varied and not simply state biased: private schools, many of them state subsidized and many of them Catholic, comprise about 15% of primary and 20% of secondary education.

All work and no play
During holidays the majority of French high school children take with them the bestselling *Cahier de Vacances*. Around four million copies of the book, containing texts and exercises to study, are sold each year. By mid-August, the country becomes a frenzy of preparation for *la rentrée:* parents snap up books, pencil cases and everything needed for the new term, and the Sunday papers even print stress relief hints for students gearing up to sit *le bac.*

Crème de la crème

The *grandes écoles* trace their roots to the end of the *Ancien Régime* and the engineering-based École Nationale des Ponts et Chaussées established in 1747. Elite students follow a two year post-*bac* course simply to prepare for a *grande école* entry exam. If they pass, a further three years of study usually follows. Today the *grandes écoles* consume some 30% of the overall university budget yet educate a mere 4% of the nation's students. The leading *grandes écoles*, École Polytechnique (often referred to as *l'X*) and École Nationale d'Administration (ENA), wield huge influence. Former Presidents Valéry Giscard d'Estaing, Jacques Chirac and numerous Prime Ministers all attended the ENA.

16-6-1945

1. Identity:
the foundations of
French culture   2. Literature
and philosophy   3. Art, architecture
and design   4. Performing arts   5. Arbiters of style:
cinema, photography
and fashion   6. Media and
communications   7. Consuming culture:
food and drink   **8. Living culture: the
state of the nation**

Away days

The French enjoy and jealously guard their free time – and with a minimum of five weeks' paid holiday a year, they have plenty to protect. The majority of French workers take annual leave during August when much of the country closes down for a month and millions take to the roads. There are ten national holidays in France, on which many businesses close for the day or even longer. With hordes of people heading off for a break, national holidays will often clash with well-timed strike action organized by the service unions.

Five state holidays

New Year's Day *(Jour d l'an)* 1st January
France picks itself up from the previous night's revelry to give the children presents and sit down for a big family meal.

Labour Day *(Fête du travail)* 1st May
Trade Unions dust off their banners while friends and families recall more ancient customs by giving each other lilies of the valley.

Victory Day *(Fête de la victoire)* 8th May
The cessation of war in Europe in 1945 is commemorated with street parties and fetes.

Bastille Day *(Fête nationale)* 14th July
Brace yourself and lock up the animals – France goes firework mad to celebrate the storming of the Bastille.

Armistice Day *(L'armistice)* 11th November
The President lays a wreath at the Arc de Triomphe while children nationwide raise money by selling blue cornflower stickers.

Local colour: regional festivals

State holidays are observed nationwide, but each region also celebrates its own annual festivals where distinctive local traditions are kept alive. Some festivals may be rooted in religion or historical events while others, to the foreign observer, border on the truly eccentric. All, however, are celebrated with passionate exuberance.

Making the bridge

When a public holiday falls on a Tuesday or a Thursday many workers will *faire le pont,* taking the Monday or Friday off to stretch out the weekend.

Party people: Saint's Days

Most French people have their own Saint's Day, that blessed time when a canonized namesake appears on the calendar and ushers in a day of potential gift receiving. Many towns also have a patron saint, guaranteeing another annual knees up for all concerned.

Get your goat The Brotherhood of Goat Meat Eaters meet on the first Sunday in September in Bellegarde-en-Marche, Limousin, to welcome new members. The locals are passionate about their goats, celebrating the hollow-horned, cud-chewing mammals with a colourful costumed parade.

Fowl Play In Saint Sever, Aquitaine, the Chicken Festival is an annual celebration of domesticated fowl. Each November a market and medieval party fill the town's streets while the hapless chickens are roasted to a local recipe.

A load of bull Not for the faint-hearted, during the summer months many towns in southern France both fight and run with their bulls. Béziers, Arles and Nîmes are three places where feats of derring-do can involve being trampled by bulls in narrow streets or more gory pursuits in the local arena. The animal rights lobby have cried foul for years.

Frenchie says relax

While French weekends haven't always been cherished (DIY, gardening and the like traditionally dominated), today workers are finding more time to relax. Of course, they're happy to spend out of work hours on the everyday pleasures of life, not least buying, preparing and eating food (although café and bistro time have both fallen significantly). Beyond this, cultural pursuits prove enduringly popular. Recent years have seen a boom in theatre, art gallery and museum attendance, although cinema remains the most popular cultural pastime by some margin. Government initiatives like the *Journées du Patrimoine*, two September days when most historic buildings and museums open for free or at a reduced rate, have helped stir public interest. The French have also begun to ditch a historical mistrust of group activities, signing up for clubs in droves to enjoy everything from photography to amateur dramatics and table football (at which, incidentally, they lead the world).

Les Grandes Vacances: the French on holiday

When the annual summer escape begins, only around one in ten French people choose to stray abroad. On home soil the most popular destinations are, as you might expect, the Riviera and the Rhône-Alpes regions. The French aren't as big on hotels or gîtes as foreign visitors. Instead, holidaymakers are more likely to spend time under canvas, visiting relatives out in the sticks or ensconced in a second home (of which the French middle classes are phenomenally fond). However, younger holidaymakers are increasingly drawn to long haul destinations, where activity-led breaks are eclipsing the traditional beach-based retreat.

In the Club

Club Méditerranée or *Le Club* began offering a hedonistic, intrinsically French escape for the middle classes back in the 1950s. People stayed in Polynesian-style huts in purpose-built resorts around the Med. All-inclusive breaks with the low pressure option of joining in the organized activities, from cabaret to snorkelling, reflected *Le Club's* philosophy. Guests enjoyed a certain anonymity engendered by the resorts' distance from everyday life. The concept proved hugely popular and *Le Club* duly opened its doors to foreign holidaymakers, accruing over 100 destinations worldwide. Today the organization is trying to adapt in the face of diminishing popularity.

Armchair athletes
Televised sporting events are hugely popular in France, with the highest audience figures recorded for international football, rugby union, basketball and tennis.

Let's get physical: joining in

The French are passionate about sport in all its forms. While around 14 million are members of a sporting federation, or a club that gains local government support, even more regularly play sport without belonging to any organization. The fitness revolution has slowly enveloped the country and increasing numbers are sloping off to the gym. Outdoor pursuits like horse riding, skiing, cycling, water sports and hiking are all popular. The *Grande Randonnée* network of long distance footpaths plots a course through some of the country's finest scenery. But perhaps the most uniquely French of participation sports is *boules*, also known as *pétanque*. Regional variations abound, but essentially the men throwing metal balls about on the gravel patch in the middle of town are trying to get as close to the *cochonnet* (jack) as possible.

"FOOTBALL IS A FANTASTIC AND INTELLIGENT GAME WHICH TEACHES US HOW TO LIVE TOGETHER, HOW TO SHARE WHEN YOU ARE BETTER THAN OTHERS. FOOTBALL IS AN EXTRAORDINARY EDUCATION FOR LIFE."
Michel Platini, French footballing legend and President of UEFA

On the ball: popular spectator sports

Football is the national sport. A high point came in 1998 when *les bleus*, as hosts, won the World Cup, beating Brazil 3-0 in the final. The two-goal hero of the hour (indeed the decade) Zinedine Zidane, captained France to the World Cup Final eight years later. Alas, Zidane's swan song went memorably awry: reacting to comments from Italy's Marco Materazzi he poleaxed the player with a head butt. The subsequent red card signalled Zidane's – and eventually the team's – ignoble departure from the competition. Domestically, the French game suffers from a lack of crowds and cash. Top players like Zidane, Thierry Henry and Patrick Vieira have all made their fortunes playing for richer, foreign sides. Le Championnat de France de Football harbours two professional national leagues, each stocked with 20 clubs. Paris Saint-Germain, Lille, Bordeaux, Auxerre, Olympique de Marseille and Monaco are usually among the top finishers. The annual *Coupe de France* pits these giants against amateur minnows from around the country. In 2000, amateur side Calais famously made it to the cup final.

Rugby union also occupies the national imagination, although the majority of clubs are concentrated in the south-west. The likes of Toulouse, Biarritz and Clermont provide the backbone of the national side that competes annually for *le Tournoi de six nations*. France is celebrated for its creative, elegant approach to the game; they're also renowned for poor discipline when it doesn't quite go to plan. The top professional league in France is comprised of 14 clubs, the winner of which emerges via end of season play-offs.

Tennis has been a staple of the French sporting diet for decades. The annual French Open on the clay courts of the Roland Garros Stadium (named after a First World War fighter pilot) in early summer sits among the four Grand Slam tournaments of world tennis. However, considering the game's popularity at grass roots level, France has endured a lengthy lean period on the international stage. Yannick Noah was the last Frenchman to win a Grand Slam tournament, back in 1983. Amélie Mauresmo, ladies' champion at Wimbledon and the Australian Open in 2006, is finally putting French tennis back in the spotlight.

The varying course, alternately clockwise and anticlockwise, covers around 2,500 miles annually.

Roadside spectators number around 15 million. 189 riders take part, split into 21 teams of nine.

The Tour is made up of 21 stages, the final leg ending on the Champs-Elysées in mid July.

American Lance Armstrong has won the Tour a record seven times: the last victory came in 2005.

Wheels of steel

Tough and gruelling, the world's greatest cycle race, Le Tour de France, has always demanded the utmost from competitors. Since its inception in 1903, the race has been marked by incredible feats of endurance alongside tales of scandal. Early race accounts talk of poisoned riders, nails left in the road and riders expected to cycle through the night. Accusations of doping have dogged the Tour for decades, with early riders using alcohol and ether to dull physical pain. In 1998, the race was labelled the 'Tour of Shame' as police raids, arrests for possession of testosterone and growth hormones, and sit-down strikes by riders made world headlines. Then, in 2006, Tour winner Floyd Landis tested positive for a banned substance. Cycling only lags behind football as the French participation sport of choice and, when it comes to the Tour, many enthusiasts will complete the stages early in the day, ahead of the main *peloton*.

Bernie the badger

Bernard Hinault is the greatest cyclist France has ever produced. Nicknamed 'The Badger' on account of his tenacity, Hinault was an all-rounder whose climbing and sprinting skills took him to five Tour de France victories in the late 1970s and early 80s.

The Tour's famous *maillot jaune* was introduced in 1919. Now highly coveted, the first rider to be offered the yellow jersey refused it as being too conspicuous to opponents.

Bloodsport for all

Hunting remains a popular, relatively classless pursuit in France. The country has approximately 1.5 million licensed hunters engaged in hunting on horseback, on foot, and shooting with dogs. Hunting is seen as a social event, as evidenced by the estimated 30,000 followers who regularly attend hunts across the country. A million people also participate in the 25 hunt-organized game fai held each summer.

Three French legends

Suzanne Lenglen was the first celebrity of tennis. In the early 1920s her athleticism and, at the time, revealing outfits, earned her a huge following and the nickname 'The Divine'. She won 28 Grand Slam titles, including six at Wimbledon, allegedly taking sips of brandy between sets. She set up a successful tennis school after retirement, yet died tragically young of leukaemia in 1938. In 1997, a court at the Roland Garros Stadium was named in her memory.

Toulouse-born **Jean Pierre-Rives** captained the French rugby union side 34 times. Famed for his flowing playing style and blond locks, he was elected France's Player of the Year in 1977, 1979 and 1981. Under his captaincy, the team even beat the All Blacks on their own antipodean turf. Today he creates sculpture from scrap metal.

The son of Algerian immigrants, former footballer **Zinedine Zidane** grew up in the tough streets of Marseilles. His on-field elegance thrilled fans during periods playing for Cannes, Bordeaux, Juventus and Real Madrid. He retired following the 2006 World Cup final and his sending off: President Chirac promptly hailed Zidane a hero, while philosopher François Sureau wrote that his actions had, "given us back our beautiful reputation for insolence." Despite being an icon for a generation of *beurs*, the shy Zidane rarely speaks out on the racial tensions in modern France.